Accounting and Business
Valuation Methods

Accounting and Business Valuation Methods

Malcolm K. Howard

AMSTERDAM • BOSTON • HEIDELBERG • LONDON
NEW YORK • OXFORD • PARIS • SAN DIEGO
SAN FRANCISCO • SINGAPORE • SYDNEY • TOKYO

CIMA Publishing is an imprint of Elsevier

CIMA Publishing is an imprint of Elsevier
Linacre House, Jordan Hill, Oxford OX2 8DP, UK
30 Corporate Drive, Suite 400, Burlington, MA 01803, USA

First edition 2008

British Library Cataloguing in Publication Data
A catalogue record for this book is available from the British Library

978 0 7506 8468 2

For information on all CIMA publications
visit our website at books.elsevier.com

Typeset by Integra Software Services Pvt. Ltd, Pondicherry, India
www.integra-india.com

Printed and bound by CPI Group (UK) Ltd, Croydon, CR0 4YY

Transferred to Digital Print 2012

Contents

List of Figures

Acknowledgements

The author would like to thank the following individuals:

Michael Glover for suggesting this book should be written in the first place and for his editing of the HgCapital Trust plc case study.

Dr Dermot Golden, Paddy Power plc's Head of Risk, for the help in writing that company's case study.

His son, Philip Howard, a mathematics graduate from Pembroke College, Oxford, for providing and explaining the Black-Scholes formula.

Geoffrey Pickerill, a lawyer specialising in mergers and acquisitions, for his valuable advice.

The author would also like to thank the following organisations:

The British Venture Capital Association for granting permission to reproduce their Code of Conduct and extracts from their 'International Private Equity And Venture Capital Valuation Guidelines'.

Oxford University Press for granting permission to reproduce extracts from '3i – Fifty Years Investing in Industry'.

In addition, the author would like to thank the directors of the following companies for granting permission to reproduce their company's accounts:

HgCapital Trust plc
Morrison (Wm) Supermarkets plc
Paddy Power plc
Topps Tiles plc
UNITE Group plc

Introduction: How to interpret IFRS Accounts

This book explains the methods used in accounting and business valuations by using the fictional story of a new start-up business, from original concept to eventual acquisition. Enamoured with entrepreneurial spirit, a business woman buys her family's secret salad dressing recipe from her brother and sets up a business. Chapter 1 illustrates double entry bookkeeping and how to prepare a Trial Balance, Profit and Loss Account and Balance Sheet and also discusses the working capital cycle, asset management and how to negotiate with banks. At the forefront of this chapter is how the combination of inexperience and insufficient funds can lead to near disaster, which is clearly illustrated via the fictional story.

Chapter 2 shows how to produce a 5-year plan and discusses capital structures and the importance of getting gearing right. The fictional business woman, Amanda, raises equity through a wealthy business angel who operates as if he were a venture capital firm. This chapter discusses the basic tools of analysis to enable Amanda to assess her business and which ratios are of utmost importance in certain circumstances. Finally, Amanda is made aware that controlling cash is a key requirement in any business and why the Cash Flow Statement is probably the most important statement in a set of accounts. The reader learns the possible exit strategies for a small business in this position.

Chapter 3 covers financial reporting and the International Financial Reporting Standards (IFRS) used by quoted companies that replaced UK GAAP (generally accepted accounting principles). We see that the Profit and Loss Account is replaced by an Income Statement and that the Balance Sheet and Cash Flow Statement use different terminology and have a different format than before. We discuss the essential changes from UK GAAP to IFRS being the move away from historical cost accounting to fair value accounting and how the new system is less prudent than the old.

In Chapter 4, Amanda receives a telephone call that leads to the sale of her business and a new company is set up by her acquirer. She becomes a director of the new company: after all taxes are paid she has over £1 million in the bank and considers building an external portfolio. This chapter illustrates how IFRS accounts might be interpreted and how such evaluations can sometimes give the assessor a small advantage in the market place. Different methods used to value companies are illustrated. Four case studies featuring real events and real company accounts illustrate the points made in this chapter.

Accounting students are often faced with a series of bland exercises, none of which relates to each other; accordingly, to many the subject is uninteresting. But accounts often tell an interesting story, in numbers rather than in words. The fictional story of Amanda was chosen to illustrate this, but in addition it is designed to help readers with entrepreneurial spirit to understand the financial challenges they will face when they start a business and how they might make profitable investments after they have been successful.

Telling the story

Chapter 1 explains that accounts tell a story, but in numbers rather than words. The story in this chapter is about Amanda and how, armed with an inherited secret recipe, she started a business selling salad dressing. She had a traumatic time in her first year nearly losing her business, but was determined to learn from her mistakes to put herself on the road to recovery. This chapter describes the process from the first transaction through to producing a Profit and Loss Account and Balance Sheet and the steps that need to be taken to have a financially sound business.

The topics covered are the following:

- Basic principles of accounting
- Primary and secondary books of account
- Accounting conventions
- Double entry bookkeeping
- How to account for value added tax (VAT)
- How to reconcile accounts with externally provided information
- How to prepare and examine the Trial Balance
- How to prepare the Profit and Loss Account and Balance Sheet
- Post year-end entries
- The working capital cycle
- How to negotiate with banks
- Asset management

Basic principles of accounting

Accounting has been around for thousands of years and yet, perhaps like an elephant, it is easier to recognise than to define, but a useful (and much quoted) assessment of what it is has been defined by the American Accounting Association:

... the process of identifying, measuring and communicating economic information to permit informed *judgements* and decisions by the users of the information

(*Source*: Accounting Manual, originally devised by Alex Noble for the School of Management for the Service Sector, University of Surrey.)

The word 'judgements' is shown in italics for, as this book discusses, this is a key word and its significance needs to be taken on board straight away.

There are many potential users of published accounts, including shareholders and potential investors, bankers and other lenders, suppliers, customers, competitors and those responsible for collecting taxes.

Accounts can be prepared for a sole trader, partnership or limited company. Limited companies fall into two categories: private limited companies, where the shares are owned by the owners of the business and not available to the general public, and public limited companies (plc's), where the shares are available to the general public and can be bought on a recognised stock exchange. In the case of published accounts for a limited company (private or plc), the accounts will relate to the company and such company will be a separate entity from its shareholders, directors and employees.

To prepare accounts, accountants keep several primary books of account:

> *The cash book* – records entries that match the company's bank accounts.
> *The petty cash book* – records petty cash held outside the cash book.
> *The purchase ledger* – records buying transactions and creditor balances.
> *The sales ledger* – records sales transactions and debtor balances.
> *Stock records* – records details of each stock item, showing the stock balance at any given time.
> *The plant (or fixed asset) register* – records asset purchases and disposals together with the appropriate depreciation rates and charges.

A summary of the entries made in the primary books of account will be posted to the secondary book of account – the nominal ledger. Accounting is based on the principle of double entry, where for every transaction there is a debit (relating to what has come in) and a credit (relating to what has gone out). For example, if an authorised employee of a company bought goods for resale (stock) costing £100, the entry in the company's books would be debit 'stock' for £100 and the credit entry would be credit 'cash' with £100 if cash was paid (cash in this context means cash or any transaction involving a bank, such as a cheque) or credit 'creditors' with £100 if the goods were not paid for at the time they were bought. Sometimes a transaction requires two debits and two credits. This happens when one transaction triggers another. For example, suppose the stock purchased for £100 was sold for £160 to someone who agreed to pay 30 days later. In this case, the transaction would be debit 'debtors' with £160 and credit 'sales' with £160. But if the stock has been sold, then it must be taken out of stock, so there need to be a second entry, which would be debit 'cost of sales' £100 and credit 'stock' £100.

From this example, it can be seen that 'cash received' is always a debit, while 'cash paid' is always a credit. Students often say that this cannot be correct as if they have cash in the bank, it is always shown as a credit. Well the answer is that accounting is all about opposites. If you have cash in the bank, it will be a debit in your books, but a credit in the bank's books because as far as the bank is concerned, they owe you money and therefore they see you as a creditor.

Knowing that a credit balance on your bank statement means you have cash in the bank leads to another misconception that credits must be good and debits must be bad. The truth is that debits are neither good nor bad, likewise credits. If you have a debit balance, then the account must either be an expense or an asset, while a credit balance must be either income or liabilities.

Before the entries are complete for any accounting period, the accountant must ensure that a number of accounting conventions, or rules, have been followed:

The matching concept states that sales must be matched with the total cost of achieving those sales in a given period. This gives rise to *accruals* and *prepayments*. An accrual arises when goods or services have been received and the cost of such goods or services has not been recorded in the books. For example, stock might be received on the last day of the accounting period, and counted in stock, but the invoice from the supplier of that stock might not arrive until well into the new accounting period. A prepayment is the opposite, where a charge has been made in advance of the service being purchased. For example, a company might negotiate a rent for a period of 2 years and has to pay up front. Assuming that the company's year end finished at the end of the first year of rent, then one-half of the amount paid would be treated as a prepayment.

The prudence concept states that assets in the Balance Sheet must not be overstated and liabilities in the Balance Sheet must not be understated. This means, in particular, that all assets should be reviewed before the entries are finalised. Current assets (stocks, debtors and cash) should be reviewed to ensure their valuation could be justified while fixed assets must be appropriately depreciated (tangible assets) or amortised (intangible) assets. However, it will be appreciated that such reviews will always be a matter of judgement.

Historical cost convention (UK Generally Accepted Accounting Practice) (GAAP) states that costs are recorded in the books at their actual (historical) cost. For example, a businessman buys a car privately for £7000, but believes the fair value of such car, based on the car guides in his possession, is £10 000. The debit and credit would be recorded as £7000. However, where an asset, such as land, has increased in value over time, then it is a standard practice to show the correct value of the asset in the books. For example, a land was purchased in 1980 for £50 000, but in 2006 it has a valuation of £750 000. Over this time, the asset would have been debited with £700 000 and a capital reserve of an equal amount would have been created.

Fair Value Accounting (International Financial Reporting Standard) (IFRS). With effect from 2005, public companies' published accounts must be prepared using international standards. The main difference between UK GAAP and IFRS is that the latter accounts are prepared not on an historical cost basis, but rather on a 'fair value' basis. What this means is that the Profit and Loss Account must be charged with the 'fair value' of any contracted position, even where the actual transaction will take place in the future and might not even take place at all.

Under IFRS, the Balance Sheet must reflect the 'fair value' of the assets and liabilities at the Balance Sheet date. As an example, a company buys assets costing £10 000 and believes that these assets will be in use for 5 years. At the end of the second year, the directors believe that the assets in question could be sold for £7000. Under UK GAAP, the assets would be valued at £6000 at the end of the second year (£10 000 multiplied by 60%), while under IFRS, it would be shown in the Balance Sheet with a value of £7000. To achieve this, the cumulative depreciation charge of £4000 would be reduced to £3000.

It can be seen that under IFRS, those reading published accounts will be ever more reliant upon the judgements made by the directors of the company being reviewed. The implications of this and the significant differences between the two systems will be discussed in following chapters.

Accounts tell a story and should be read like a book; sometimes a mystery it has to be said, but nevertheless a book. Accounts are sometimes cryptic and difficult to understand, but what the reader is trying to do is to deduce the story. Reading accounts can be likened to solving a code or completing a jigsaw puzzle, but get the storyline right and it can be very rewarding. In a set of published accounts there are plenty of clues for as well as the main body of the accounts there are attached notes and many individual reports. To the uninitiated, some of the jargons will look like a secret code, but one of the purposes of this book is to help the reader decipher such code.

To do this, we will first start with a story and show how this story builds up into a full set of accounts. This story is all about Amanda and how she became a sole trader with near fatal results, but was determined to learn from the mistakes she had made and put herself on the road to recovery.

Case study – Amanda

Amanda inherited £50 000 and her brother inherited £20 000, plus their family's secret recipe for salad dressing, a formula developed a few generations earlier. The brother was not interested in this recipe, but Amanda saw that it had the potential to generate a successful business.

Starting a new business and taking risks associated with being self-employed seemed daunting. However, Amanda recalled a lecture on Entrepreneurship; the lecturer had said that the opportunity to start your own business does not often happen and you might wonder for the rest of your life what might have been if you lacked courage at the very time it was needed.

Amanda approached her brother about buying the recipe but he was reluctant to sell. It might be very valuable, he suggested, although he had no idea of how he could make money out of it. Eventually, she persuaded him to sell for £40 000. She put the remaining £10 000 into her newly opened business account.

The amount of £10 000 was an insufficient capital to allow Amanda to set up a factory, especially as she expected it would be some time before she received her first order. Nevertheless, Amanda started to develop a plan to start producing her product.

Her first step was to produce a sample batch in her jam pan and fill into old bottles that had been sterilised. These samples cost £2000 to produce, which she paid out of her business account. Amanda approached supermarket buyers with samples of the dressing. She found them very accommodating, and four companies agreed to give her a trial order paying 50 pence per bottle, or £50 per case, each case containing 100 bottles.

With this success, she started to put together a business plan, the starting point being her forecasted sales for the first year. She wanted to make sure that her bank manager had read and understood her plan and was willing to back it on its merits. She felt that she had achieved this when the bank agreed to lend her £250 000 and accept a fixed and floating charge on the business's assets as security, conditional upon debtors being insured. The premium for this turned out to be £200 plus 2% of 'debtor' value, inclusive of all taxes. The 'debtor' value was defined as 'sales value plus VAT', but as Amanda was going to sell a product that was counted as food and was, therefore, zero rated, 'debtor value' was the same as 'sales value'. The premium was paid in full before the year end.

The next step was to carry out some basic research to find out how much it would cost to set up a small factory to manufacture the product. This took several weeks making telephone calls, receiving e-mails and quotations, but at the end of this process, Amanda realised that £250 000 simply was not enough money. So she found a food manufacturer that was willing to produce her salad dressing whilst ensuring that her intellectual property was safe. Zehin Foods plc agreed to manufacture the salad dressing in accordance with the formula supplied to them for 40 pence per bottle, or £40 per case. However, in recognition of the product development costs associated with scaling up from Amanda's formula, it was agreed that she would pay a one-off charge of £12 000 (plus VAT at the standard rate) and would agree to order a minimum of 12 000 cases per year from Zehin Foods plc, for a minimum of 5 years. If in any year during this period she failed to order the minimum quantity, she had to pay the manufacturer an additional £10 000.

Amanda's solicitor told her that she must register for VAT, which she did. He also drew up the contract between Amanda and Zehin Foods plc for which he charged £5000, plus VAT at the standard rate of 17.5%.

On 1 January 2004, Amanda placed an order for 12 000 cases of salad dressing at £40 per case, the product to be delivered at the rate of 1000 per month. Credit terms were agreed at strictly 30 days and at the year end, only one delivery costing £40 000 was still to be paid.

In the year ended 31 December 2004, sales had been made to the customers shown, as follows:

	ABZ Ltd	CDZ Ltd	EFZ Ltd	GHZ plc
Cases	3600	1400	1500	3300
	180 000	70 000	75 000	165 000

Payments made by these companies during the year had been:

£	150 000	35 000	60 000	132 000

Amanda needed to control the selling and supply operation, so she rented an office for £20 000 and bought fixtures and fittings for this at a cost of £5875, inclusive of VAT at the standard rate. She also bought a van for £17 625 (of which £2625 was VAT) and rented a warehouse at a cost of £12 000. In Amanda's case, there was no VAT on rented items. She had paid in full for all these items by the year end.

The cost of delivering 9800 cases of salad dressing was £16 000 (plus VAT at the standard rate), which included all costs associated with running the van. The other expenditures that had been paid in full had been £600 for stationery (plus VAT at the standard rate), £1500 for insurances, £9000 wages and £1000 for national insurance. Insurances, wages and national insurance were not subject to VAT.

As she had registered for VAT, this meant that although she had no output VAT, she had input VAT, which was recoverable from Revenue and Customs. However, Amanda did not opt to go onto monthly VAT and submitted returns on a quarterly basis. During the year she received a cheque for £7000 from Revenue and Customs, being the amount of VAT she had paid in the first 9 months.

Fixtures and fittings were expected to last for 4 years and would be depreciated using the straight line method. The van was expected to last for 3 years and would be depreciated using the reducing balance method. The office and warehouse rent paid covered 2 years and ended on 31 December 2005. £1800 wages and £200 national insurance had been incurred, but remained unpaid on 31 December 2004.

Just before her year end, Amanda telephoned her accountant to ask how much he would charge for preparing her accounts and for calculating her tax liabilities. He told her that the amount he would have to charge would be dependent on the time it took, but his best guess was that his charges would amount to £1200. Not being registered for VAT, this would be the final figure.

At the end of January 2005, Amanda received a telephone call from CDZ Ltd. They said that they had received several complaints from their customers about the product and due to the volume of such complaints they had taken her product off the shelves. They were returning 200 cases and wanted to receive full credit. In addition, they said that it would cost £500 to return these cases and wanted reimbursing for this also.

When these cases were returned, Amanda took a sample of 100 bottles and tasted them. She believed that there was nothing wrong with them and believed she could sell the remaining 199 cases to cost cutter stores for £41 per case. It would cost her £398 to deliver these 199 cases. This story now has to be converted into a set of accounts, comprising a Profit and Loss Account and a Balance Sheet, but before this we need to understand VAT.

Value added tax

VAT replaced purchase tax and was designed to cover services and goods. It was called 'value added tax' as it was (and is) simply a tax on added value with only the end user (the person getting the benefit of the cumulative added value) actually paying any tax.

If you are in business with an annual turnover of £61 000 or more (with effect from 1 April 2006), you must register as a taxable person, although you can apply to be exempt if all your supplies are zero rated (*Source*: Revenue and Customs website). If you do not have a business with an annual turnover of £61 000, for example, if you are an employee in someone else's business, then you are exempt from VAT.

This notion of being 'exempt' is rather curious. The Concise Oxford dictionary defines 'exempt' as 'free from an obligation or liability, etc. imposed on others, especially from payment of tax'. In the case of VAT, being 'exempt' means the opposite of this, as it means being exempt from accounting for VAT and having dealings with Revenue and Customs with regard to VAT. However, the only people who actually pay VAT are those classified as 'exempt'.

Goods and services supplied by business fall into four categories:

(1) Those that are subjected to VAT at the standard rate of 17.5%.
(2) Those that are subjected to VAT at the lower rate of 5%.
(3) Those that are zero rated.
(4) Those that are exempted.

If you are registered for VAT and your goods and services are chargeable at the standard rate, then you charge your customer VAT at the standard rate (output tax) and recover VAT on your purchases (input tax).

Wherever there is a chain, it works out as follows:

'A' makes a particular part and charges 'B' £40.
'B' continues to work on the part to refine it and sells it to 'C' for £120.
'C' takes the refined part, makes further adjustments and sells it to 'D', the end user and exempt person, for £200.

With VAT added:

> A charges B £40 + VAT £7 = £47.00 in total.
> B charges £120 + VAT of £21 = £141 in total.
> C charges £200 + VAT of £35 = £235 in total.

A pays £7 to Revenue and Customs, but as B has paid this, it has cost A nothing. B pays £14 to Revenue and Customs, being £21 charged to C, less £7 paid to A. Again this has cost B nothing. C pays £14 to Revenue and Customs, £35 being charged to D, less £21 paid to B. Like A and B, C has paid nothing.

What has happened is D has paid £35 as VAT, which cannot be recovered, but this money has been paid over to Revenue and Customs by A, B and C.

The entry for VAT in the books is straightforward. In the case of B, assuming A offered credit and C was being allowed credit, the entries would be:

Purchases	....	Debit	£40
VAT	....	Debit	£7
Creditors	....	Credit	£47

Sales		Credit	£120
VAT		Credit	£21
Debtors		Debit	£141

Whether goods and services are to be charged at the standard rate, reduced rate or zero rate is not always easy to ascertain. For example, food is normally zero rated, provided it is of a kind used for human consumption. A food is deemed fit for human consumption if:

> the average person, knowing what it is and how it is used, would consider it to be food or drink; and it is fit for human consumption.

However, dietary supplements, food additives and similar products, although edible, are not generally regarded as food and would not be zero rated, but products like flour, although not eaten by themselves, are generally recognised food ingredients and would be zero rated.

With regard to ingredients and additives used in home cooking and baking, prepared cake, sauce, soup and other mixes, vegetable oil, corn oil and olive oil are all zero rated, while mixes for ice cream and similar frozen products, linseed oil and essential oils are standard rated.

You can zero rate chocolate couverture, chips, leaves, scrolls, etc, for the purpose of cake decorations, but chocolate buttons must be standard rated as these are regarded as confectionery.

(*Source of information with regard to VAT classification of food (as above)*: HMRC Reference Notice 701/14 (May 2002) taken from HM Revenue and Customs website.)

What this demonstrates is that with regard to VAT it is never safe to assume anything and that any person registered for VAT should consult the Revenue and Customs helpline (number available from their website) if they are in any doubt as to how VAT should be charged on any of their products or services.

An important aspect of this tax for such VAT registered businesses is the 'tax point'. This is the point at which the VAT output must be put through the books. The tax point is deemed to be the *earlier* of the date at which the sales invoice is issued or payment for the goods or service is received. In the latter case, a sales invoice will be raised to reflect the payment received. This rule can create a problem for businesses with poor credit control as it can mean that VAT is due to be paid to Revenue and Customs before the equivalent amount has been received from the debtor.

Revenue and Customs recognises this problem and if a business has an annual turnover of not more than £660 000 (excluding VAT) then it may opt to account for VAT on a cash basis. This means that the tax point is determined by the dates cash is received and paid, not by invoice dates. Obviously, this option is not advisable for those businesses with good credit control, especially if they tend to take extended credit from their suppliers. Businesses opting to pay VAT on a cash accounting basis can continue to do so until their annual turnover reaches £825 000 (excluding VAT).

(*Source*: Revenue and Customs website. Figures shown are as at the midpoint of the 2006/7 tax year.)

There are other options available to small businesses, full details of which are available from Revenue and Customs.

Amanda's transactions

From the above storyline, we can list Amanda's transactions in her first year:

(1) Received £50 000 inheritance, paid £40 000 for secret salad dressing formula and banked £10 000.
(2) Produced samples costing £2000, paying cash.
(3) Borrows £250 000 from bank.
(4) Pays debtor insurance costing £10 000.
(5) Pays setting up costs of £12 000, plus VAT of £2100 (multiply £12 000 by 0.175 to calculate VAT of £2100).
(6) Pays legal costs of £5000, plus VAT of £875.
(7) Purchases 12 000 cases of salad dressing costing £480 000 and pays supplier of salad dressing £440 000.
(8) Sells 9800 cases of salad dressing on credit for £490 000 and receives £377 000 from debtors.
(9) Pays office rent of £20 000.
(10) Buys fixtures and fittings costing £5000, plus VAT of £875 (divide £5875 by 1.175 to arrive at a cost excluding VAT), paying cash.
(11) Buys van for £15 000, plus VAT of £2625, paying cash.
(12) Rents warehouse for £12 000, paying cash.
(13) Incurs delivery costs of £16 000, plus VAT of £2800, paying cash
(14) Incurs stationery costs of £600, plus VAT of £105, paying cash.
(15) Pays general insurances of £1500.
(16) Pays wages of £9000.
(17) Pays national insurance of £1000.
(18) She received £7000 from Revenue and Customs.

We now have to complete a double entry to reflect all of these transactions. These are shown in Figure 1.1, being transactions numbered 1 to 18. Having completed the double entry for each transaction, the next step for Amanda is to reconcile her nominal ledger with her primary books of account. Of course, these days both the primary books and nominal ledger are computerised; nevertheless, they must still be reconciled.

Capital					
Number	Debit	£	Number	Credit	£
			1		50,000

Cash at bank					
Number	Debit	£	Number	Credit	£
1		50,000	1		40,000
3		250,000	2		2,000
8		377,000	4		10,000
18		7,000	5		14,100
			6		5,875
			7		440,000
			9		20,000
			10		5,875
			11		17,625
			12		12,000
			13		18,800
			14		705
			15		1,500
			16		9,000
			17		1,000
			19		85,300
			Balance		220
		684,000			684,000
Balance b/d		220			

Figure 1.1 Case study – Amanda – transactions (double entry)

Goodwill (intangible asset)					
Number	Debit	£	Number	Credit	£
1		40,000	21		15,000
			Balance		25,000
		40,000			40,000
Balance b/d		25,000			

Samples					
Number	Debit	£	Number	Credit	£
2		2,000			

Loan					
Number	Debit	£	Number	Credit	£
19		50,000	3		250,000
Balance		200,000			
		250,000			250,000
			Balance b/d		200,000

Debtor insurance					
Number	Debit	£	Number	Credit	£
4		10,000			

Setting-up costs					
Number	Debit	£	Number	Credit	£
5		12,000			

Figure 1.1 (*Continued*)

15

VAT					
Number	Debit	£	Number	Credit	£
5		2,100	18		7,000
6		875			
10		875			
11		2,625			
13		2,800			
14		105			
			Balance		2,380
		9,380			9,380
Balance b/d		2,380			

Legal costs					
Number	Debit	£	Number	Credit	£
6		5,000			

Stock					
Number	Debit	£	Number	Credit	£
7		480,000	8		392,000
20		8,000	20		40
			20		199
			Balance		95,761
		488,000			488,000
Balance b/d		95,761			

Trade creditors					
Number	Debit	£	Number	Credit	£
7		440,000	7		480,000
Balance		40,000			
		480,000			488,000
			Balance b/d		40,000

Figure 1.1 (*Continued*)

Sales					
Number	Debit	£	Number	Credit	£
20		10,000	8		490,000
Balance		480,000			
		490,000			490,000
			Balance b/d		480,000

Trade debtors					
Number	Debit	£	Number	Credit	£
8		490,000	8		377,000
			20		10,500
			Balance		102,500
		490,000			490,000
Balance b/d		102,500			

Cost of sales					
Number	Debit	£	Number	Credit	£
8		392,000	20		8,000
			Balance		384,000
		392,000			392,000
Balance b/d		384,000			

Rent (office)					
Number	Debit	£	Number	Credit	£
9		20,000	24		10,000
			Balance		10,000
		20,000			20,000
Balance b/d		10,000			

Figure 1.1 (*Continued*)

Fixtures and fittings					
Number	Debit	£	Number	Credit	£
10		5,000	22		1,250
			Balance		3,750
		5,000			5,000
Balance b/d		3,750			

Van					
Number	Debit	£	Number	Credit	£
11		15,000	22		5,000
			Balance		10,000
		15,000			15,000
Balance b/d		10,000			

Warehouse Rent					
Number	Debit	£	Number	Credit	£
12		12,000	24		6,000
			Balance		6,000
		12,000			12,000
Balance b/d		6,000			

Delivery costs					
Number	Debit	£	Number	Credit	£
13		16,000			
20		500	Balance		16,500
		16,500			16,500
Balance b/d		16,500			

Figure 1.1 (*Continued*)

Stationery

Number	Debit	£	Number	Credit	£
14		600			

General insurances

Number	Debit	£	Number	Credit	£
15		1,500			

Wages

Number	Debit	£	Number	Credit	£
16		9,000			
23		1,800			
			Balance		10,800
		10,800			10,800
Balance b/d		10,800			

National insurance

Number	Debit	£	Number	Credit	£
17		1,000			
23		200			
			Balance		1,200
		1,200			1,200
Balance b/d		1,200			

Interest

Number	Debit	£	Number	Credit	£
19		20,000			

Figure 1.1 (*Continued*)

19

Bank charges					
Number	Debit	£	Number	Credit	£
19		15,300			

Stock losses					
Number	Debit	£	Number	Credit	£
20		40			
20		199			
				Balance	239
		239			239
Balance b/d		239			

Goodwill impairment					
Number	Debit	£	Number	Credit	£
21		15,000			

Depreciation					
Number	Debit	£	Number	Credit	£
22		1,250			
22		5,000			
				Balance	6,250
		6,250			6,250
Balance b/d		6,250			

Figure 1.1 (*Continued*)

Accruals					
Number	Debit	£	Number	Credit	£
			23		2,000
			23		1,200
Balance		3,200			
		3,200			3,200
			Balance b/d		3,200

Prepayments					
Number	Debit	£	Number	Credit	£
24		16,000			

Accounting and audit expenses					
Number	Debit	£	Number	Credit	£
23		1,200			

Figure 1.1 (*Continued*)

Amanda's reconciliations

The first reconciliation that Amanda attempted was to reconcile her cash book with the bank statement she had received. The bank had debited her account with £85 300, made up of:

(1) First repayment of loan, £50 000
(2) Interest on loan, £20 000
(3) Bank charges of £15 300, including £600 penalty charges for overdrawing without authorisation.

Amanda was surprised by this, but she put the above through her books, as transaction number 19, and decided to see her accountant to see what could be done. Her next reconciliation was reconciling the purchase ledger with suppliers' statements, and these were found to be in order. However, reconciling the sales ledger was much more difficult. Her age debt list (simply a list of debtors analysed by age, showing not overdue, 30 days overdue, 60 days overdue, etc.) showed that her credit control procedures were not good enough and while her debtor insurance would ensure that she got paid in the end, her insurance did not cover her for returned goods. She had to deal with the returned goods from CDZ Limited and felt that, in order to maintain goodwill, she had to reimburse that company with £500 it cost to return the goods to her. Of course, she had to make a 'judgement' as to the value of the goods returned. She believed that she could sell 199 cases to cost cutter stores for £41 per case, but if these stores found out that they were buying returns rejected by other companies, they might not want to deal. If this happened, then eventually the goods would have to be written off.

The entries required to account for this returns are:

(1) Credit CDZ Limited £10 500 (sales ledger)
(2) Debit sales £10 000 and debit 'delivery costs' £500
(3) Debit stock £8000 and credit cost of sales £8000
(4) Credit stock £40 and debit stock losses £40 for the case written off
(5) Credit stock for £199 and debit stock losses £199, for the reduction in value of returned stock

Based on the prudence concept, stock is valued at the lower of cost and net realisable value, where net realisable value is defined as the selling price less the cost of getting the goods to the customer. In this case, it will cost £398 to deliver 199 cases, which is equal to £2 per case. If the selling price is going to be £41 per case and it will cost £2 per case to get them to the cost cutter stores, then the net realisable value is £39 per case. As this is lower than the cost of £40 per case, this stock has to be written down to £39 per case. In Amanda's case, all her purchases are at the same price, but usually prices change over time. In such cases, stock is usually charged to cost of sales on a first in first out (FIFO) basis.

These entries are shown as transaction 20 in Figure 1.1. After these adjustments, stock is valued at £95 761 and this figure is reconciled to the actual stock counted:

	£
2200 cases at £40 per case	88 000
199 cases at £39 per case	7761
	95 761

Now Amanda must note that while she is committed to buying 12 000 cases per year, in her first year she has sold only 9600 cases. It could be argued that a contingency reserve should be created to allow for the fact that Amanda *may* in the future have to make a £10 000 penalty payment to Zehin Foods plc. She chose not to; but, again, this is a matter of judgement that can materially affect her declared profit.

The final reconciliation is to do with assets. Firstly, Amanda wanted to make sure that the goodwill in her Balance Sheet reflected what the secret recipe was really worth, given the experience of her first year of trading. She had paid £40 000 for it, but concluded that £25 000 was a more reasonable valuation and reduced goodwill in the Balance Sheet to this figure. This reduction in value is called 'impairment' and is shown as transaction 21 in Figure 1.1.

Secondly, the fixed assets have to be depreciated. Most assets are depreciated using the straight line method. Straight line means that the net cost of the asset is depreciated at the same rate over the life of the asset. Suppose an asset was bought for £30 000 and at the end of 6 years it was estimated that it would be sold for £6000, then the net cost of the asset would be £24 000 and the annual depreciation charge would be £4000.

Another method of depreciation is by using the reducing balance method. This method calculates the depreciation over the expected life of the asset, but on the basis of its written-down value, not original cost. Also, the asset's estimated residual value is ignored. Assets such as cars and vans are usually depreciated this way as they depreciate more in their earlier years than in the later years, although to compensate the cost of repairs increases over time. Suppose a car was bought for £30 000 and it was estimated that it would sell for £10 000 at the end of 4 years, then by using the reducing balance method, depreciation would be calculated as follows:

	£
Asset at cost	30 000
Depreciation in year 1	7500
Written-down value	22 500
Depreciation in year 2	5625
Written-down value	16 875
Depreciation in year 3	4219
Written-down value	12 656
Depreciation in year 4	3164
Written-down value (at the end of year 4)	9492

Depreciation for Amanda's fixtures and fittings and van is shown as transaction 22 in Figure 1.1.

Now the assets have been reconciled, the only other matter is to deal with the matching concept and this means dealing with accruals and prepayments, so that in timing terms the sales and the costs associated with those sales match. The entries for accruals and prepayments are:

Accruals – debit the appropriate expense and credit accruals.

Prepayments – debit prepayments and credit the appropriate expense.

The entries for Amanda's accruals are shown as transaction 23 in Figure 1.1 and the entries for Amanda's prepayments are shown as transaction 24 in Figure 1.1. Once these entries are completed, each account is 'balanced off', so that only the net balance is showing. This is shown in Figure 1.1. Each of these balances is then listed in the form of a Trial Balance, as shown in Figure 1.2.

The Trial Balance

The purpose of a Trial Balance is to make sure that the accounts are in balance and this means that the sum of the debits must equal the sum of the credits. Assuming they do, the next step is to review each of the accounts. Starting with the debit side, the question is: Is what is being looked at something the business owns? If the answer is yes, then the next question is: Is what is being looked at something the business will own for 12 months or more? If the answer is yes again, you are looking at a fixed asset, if no, you are looking at a current asset. If the asset is a fixed asset, the next question is: Can this asset be seen and touched? If the answer is yes, it is a tangible asset and if the answer is no, it is an intangible asset. Both current assets and fixed assets appear in the Balance Sheet.

If the answer to the first question is no, what was being looked at was not something the business owns, then the item is an expense and appears in the Profit and Loss Account. In this case, the next question is: Was this expense incurred in the ordinary course of business to get the business's product or service to the point it was available to customers? If the answer to this question is yes, then the expense appears in the top half of the Profit and Loss Account and is shown before 'gross profit'. If the answer to this second question is no, then the third question is: Was this expense incurred in the ordinary course of business and is it a type of expense that is likely to be repeated? If the answer to this third question is yes, then the expense will be shown in the bottom half

Trial Balance at December 31 2004

	Debit (£)	Credit (£)
Capital		50,000
Cash at bank	220	
Goodwill	25,000	
Samples	2,000	
Loan		200,000
Debtor insurance	10,000	
Setting-up costs	12,000	
VAT	2,380	
Legal costs	5,000	
Stock	95,761	
Trade creditors		40,000
Sales		480,000
Trade debtors	102,500	
Cost of sales	384,000	
Rent (office)	10,000	
Fixtures and fittings	3,750	
Van	10,000	
Warehouse rent	6,000	
Delivery costs	16,500	
Stationery	600	
General insurances	1,500	
Wages	10,800	
National insurance	1,200	
Interest	20,000	
Bank charges	15,300	
Stock losses	239	
Goodwill impairment	15,000	
Depreciation	6,250	
Accruals		3,200
Prepayments	16,000	
Accounting and audit expenses	1,200	
	773,200	773,200

Figure 1.2   Case study – Amanda – Trial Balance

of the Profit and Loss Account and is shown before 'operating profit'. If the answer to this third question is no, then it will be an extraordinary expense that is shown below the 'operating profit' line.

To demonstrate this, we can go down the Trial Balance (Figure 1.2).

Cash at bank. Is it something owned? Yes. Will it be owned for a year or more? No. Therefore, 'cash at bank' is a current asset.

Goodwill. Is it something owned? Yes. Will it be owned for a year or more? Yes again, it must be a fixed asset. Can Amanda see and touch this asset? The answer to this is no, so goodwill must be an intangible fixed asset. Goodwill is simply the difference between what has been paid for an asset and the tangible value of that asset based on its book value. In addition to goodwill, other intangible assets might be patents, brands and intellectual property rights.

Samples. Is it something owned? No, then it must be an expense. Did Amanda need to make these samples to demonstrate that the product could be manufactured to the secret formula? If yes, then the expense would appear in the Profit and Loss Account before the 'gross profit' line. However, if the samples were made to entice customers to buy the product, they would be a selling expense and would appear below the 'gross profit' line. So we are back to this word 'judgement' again! What were the samples *really* made for?

Debtor insurance. Is it something owned? No, then it must be an expense. Why did Amanda take out debtor insurance? Because taking out such insurance was a condition for getting the loan. Therefore, debtor insurance could be regarded as a finance cost and would come below the 'gross profit' line.

Setting up costs. Is it something owned? No, then again it must be an expense. Why were these costs incurred? The answer was that this expense related to the costs Zehin Foods plc would incur in scaling up from Amanda's jam pan recipe. Here again, some judgement is required. Some would argue that as these setting up costs related to a one-off cost that covered contracts over a 5-year period, they should be capitalised, treated as a fixed asset, and written off over 5 years. Amanda took the prudent view and charged this expense to the Profit and Loss Account, but treated it as an extraordinary item that comes below 'operating profit'.

VAT. Is it something owned? Yes. Will it be owned for a year or more? No, then VAT must be a current asset. It must be noted here that in the vast majority of cases, VAT is a current liability, representing the amount owed by the business to Revenue and Customs. It is only a debtor here because food is zero rated, which means that Amanda does not charge VAT on sales, but VAT is charged on many of the goods and services she buys. In this case, Revenue and Customs is a debtor and the amount in the Trial Balance represents the amount of VAT that Amanda has paid, but not yet recovered at her year end.

Legal costs. Is it something owned? No, then it must be an expense. What type of expense is it? This is an administrative expense, so it would appear below the 'gross profit' line.

Stock. Is it something owned? Yes, as stocks are the goods we are holding with a view to sell later on. Will stock be owned for a year or more? Hopefully not and if it were, it would have to be written off. Accordingly, stock is a current asset.

Trade debtors. Is it something owned? Yes, as debtors are people or companies who owe us money and we certainly expect these debtors to pay us within a year. Trade debtors are classified as current assets.

Cost of sales. Is it something owned? No, because 'cost of sales' is the direct cost associated with the sales Amanda has made in the period. Cost of sales is always the first item in the Profit and Loss Account after sales.

Rent (office). Is it something owned? No, then it must be an expense. Amanda does not own her office, but pays the owner to be able to use it.

Fixtures and fittings. Is it something owned? Yes. Will it be owned for a year or more? Yes. Can fixtures and fittings be seen and touched? Yes, then they must be a tangible fixed asset. What has happened is that Amanda has rented an unfurnished office and has had to furnish it. She could take her fixtures and fittings with her if she moves to another office.

Van. Owned for over a year, can see and touch, so a tangible fixed asset.

Warehouse rent. Like 'office rent', but this time the rented space is a store for Amanda's finished products. Because this expense is incurred before the goods are delivered to customers, it would come above the 'gross profit' line in the Profit and Loss Account.

Delivery costs. These are the costs associated with delivering the goods to customers and would come under the heading of 'distribution' that fall below the 'gross profit' line.

Stationery. Paper, envelopes, etc. might be something that Amanda owns at the year end, but the value would be so immaterial that the full cost would be expensed and being an administrative expense would come below the 'gross profit' line.

General insurances. This is another administrative expense.

Wages. Here it is related to the warehouse manager who organised the transport and is, therefore, an expense that comes above the 'gross profit' line.

National Insurance. It is the employer's contribution of this tax, relating to wages paid and accordingly falls into the same category. Employers deduct income tax and national insurance from their employees and each month they have to pay the sum of the amount they have deducted, plus their contribution, to Revenue and Customs. It is the employer's contribution that appears in the Profit and Loss Account.

Interest. It is the amount paid to a lender, to compensate the lender for the money he has loaned the business. In the Profit and Loss Account, interest is charged after all other expenses, including extraordinary items, with the exception of tax. But as Amanda is a sole trader, we are not accounting for tax in the example shown.

Bank charges. It is the amount that the bank has charged for providing banking services and is treated as an ordinary administrative expense.

Stock losses. It is the amount that has been lost because stock has gone missing or lost value for whatever reason. It is usually charged above the 'gross profit' line.

Goodwill impairment. It is the amount that goodwill has had to be written down, because its valuation cannot be justified based on the predicted future earnings. Given 'goodwill impairment' is often an unexpected event that does not regularly happen, it is treated as an extraordinary item in the Profit and Loss Account.

Depreciation. It is a book entry having no impact on cash, which indicates how much the assets have been written down in the financial year. Depreciation on assets to do with production would be charged above the 'gross profit' line, while all other depreciation would be regarded as a distribution or administrative expense and would be charged below the line.

Prepayments are payments made in advance and are regarded as debtors and are accordingly classified as current assets.

Accounting and audit expenses are yet another administrative expense coming below the 'gross profit' line.

If an item is on the credit side of a Profit and Account, then the question is: is the item something the business owes? If the answer is yes, it is a liability and will appear in the Balance Sheet. If the answer is no, then it will be income generating and will appear in the Profit and Loss Account. We can now go down the Trial Balance on the credit side.

Capital. Is this something the business owes? Yes, capital is what the business owes to the owner of the business. Remember that although a sole trader as a person and his or her own business are treated as the same entity, the books of the business will not record any transactions that are for personal use. A sole trader is not paid a wage or a salary, but rather is taxed on the profits his or her business makes, but will still get the personal and other allowances given to salaried or waged employees based on their personal circumstances. However, a sole trader has unlimited liability, which means that if the business cannot meet all its debts, then the sole trader will have to sell personal assets to make good. Will the business owe capital to the owner of the business for a year or more? Well, the owner of the business will certainly hope to stay in business for a year or more, so capital is a fixed liability.

Loan. This is the amount that the business owes to the bank and as the intention is to pay it off over 5 years, it is another fixed liability.

Trade creditors. Is it something the business owes? Yes, so it must be a liability. Will the business still owe what will appear in the Balance Sheet in a year's time? No, because creditors are people the business owes money to and they will certainly expect to be paid within 12 months. Therefore, creditors are classified as current liabilities.

Sales. Is it something the business owes? No, so sales must be income generating and therefore will appear in the Profit and Loss Account.

Accruals. They relate to goods and services received by the Balance Sheet date, but not put through the books as a permanent entry at the Balance Sheet date. Accruals are regarded as creditors and are therefore classified as current liabilities.

So, now we have classified each item in the Trial Balance as either going to the Profit and Loss Account or Balance Sheet; we can prepare these two statements.

The Profit and Loss Account

The Profit and Loss Account is simply a statement showing sales or income over a set period, together with the costs associated with such sales or income over the same period. Where sales or income exceed costs, a profit has been made and where costs exceed sales or income a loss had been incurred. Sales relate to goods, while income (fees charged by an accountant or a solicitor, for example) relates to services.

With the exception of certain businesses such as banks, insurance companies and investment trusts (dealt with in chapter five), the Profit and Loss Account is usually produced in the standard format:

	Manufacturer	Retailer	Service Provider
	Sales	Sales	Income
Less:	direct production costs	Purchases	Direct cost (time spent at cost)
=	Gross margin	Gross margin	Gross margin
Less:	Indirect production costs	Product modifications	--------
=	Gross profit	Gross profit	Gross profit
Less:	Distribution costs	Distribution costs	
	Administration costs	Administration costs	Administration costs
=	Profit before exceptional items	(as manufacturer)	(as manufacturer)
Less:	exceptional items (if any)	(as manufacturer)	(as manufacturer)
=	Operating profit	Operating profit	Operating profit
Less:	Interest	Interest	Interest
=	Net profit	Net profit	Net profit

In the case of a sole trader, the net profit will be added to the capital, which will be reduced by the sole trader's drawings. The sole trader's tax will be paid out of his or her drawings. For a partnership, each partner has a capital account and a current account and all adjustments are made to the current account. If there is no partnership agreement, then profits will be shared as determined by the Partnership Acts of 1890 and 1909.

Suppose there were three partners in the ABC Partnership, A, B and C, and they put in capital of £20 000, £40 000 and £60 000, respectively. A worked full time in the business, B worked part-time and C was a sleeping partner.

A 'sleeping partner' is one who puts capital into a business, but does not work in it. Under the partnership agreement they have signed, profits/losses are to be shared on the following basis and in the following order:

(1) The partners shall receive 'notional' interest at the rate of 10%.
(2) A shall receive a 'notional' salary of £40 000 and B shall receive a 'notional' salary of £25 000.
(3) Any remaining profits will be shared equally.
(4) In the event a loss is made, 'notional' interest will be paid, but 'notional' salaries will not be paid and remaining losses will be shared equally.

The word 'notional' means that it is not real in the sense that it is only being used as a mechanism to divide up the profits. If the partnership does not make a profit, then there is no share out. If the interest is 'real' rather than notional, then each partner would receive interest in full even if the partnership made a loss.

Based on the partnership agreement, we can work out the share of the profits if (say) the partnership made a profit of £89 000, £9000 and £44 500, respectively, or a loss of (£21 000):

	A (£)	B (£)	C (£)	Total (£)
Profit				89 000
Notional interest	2000	4000	6000	(12 000)
				77 000
Notional salaries	40 000	25 000	Nil	65 000
				12 000
Profit share	4000	4000	4000	12 000
	46 000	33 000	10 000	89 000

	A (£)	B (£)	C (£)	Total (£)
Profit				9000
Notional interest	1500	3000	4500	(9000)
	1500	3000	4500	9000

	A (£)	B (£)	C (£)	Total (£)
Profit				44 500
Notional interest	2000	4000	6000	(12 000)
				32 500
Notional salaries	20 000	12 500	Nil	(32 500)
	22 000	16 500	6000	44 500

	A (£)	B (£)	C (£)	Total (£)
Loss				(21 000)
Notional interest	2000	4000	6000	(12 000)
				(33 000)
Share of losses	(11 000)	(11 000)	(11 000)	33 000
	(9000)	(7000)	(5000)	(21 000)

Partners, like sole traders, have unlimited liability. This means that if the partnership makes a loss, each partner must make good their share of the loss out of their own personal assets. Each partner is also responsible for paying their own income tax. If the partnership pays a particular partner's income tax, then it counts as drawings and comes out of their current account.

Partnerships work on the basis that each partner is jointly and severally liable to meet the partnership's liabilities. Suppose, for example, the ABC Partnership had liabilities of £21 000, which equated to the loss of £21 000 they made in the year, and B was declared bankrupt. He was, therefore, unable to make good his loss of £7000. In such a case, this loss would be allocated to A and C in proportion to their own liabilities. So A would have to find an additional £4500 and C's share would be £2500.

However, it is possible, in certain circumstances, to form limited partnerships where each partner has a limited liability. Such partnerships are governed by the Limited Liability Partnership Act 2000.

In the case of a partnership, the Profit and Loss Account would be completed by reducing the net profit down to nil, as shown below:

Manufacturer	Retailer	Service Provider
Net profit	Net profit	Net profit
Less: transfer to the Partner's current account	(as manufacturer)	(as manufacturer)
Nil	Nil	Nil

In the case of a limited company, 'net profit' would be replaced by 'profit before tax' and the Profit and Loss Account would carry on as below:

	Manufacturer	Retailer	Service Provider
	Profit before tax	Profit before tax	Profit before tax
Less:	Corporation tax	Corporation tax	Corporation tax
=	Earnings	Earnings	Earnings
Less:	(proposed) dividends	(proposed) dividends	(proposed) dividends
=	Retained earnings	Retained earnings	Retained earnings

The Profit and Loss Account for Amanda is shown in Figure 1.3.

Amanda Profit & Loss Account for 12 months ended December 31 2004

	£	£
Sales		480,000
Less: cost of sales		384,000
Gross margin		96,000
Warehouse rent	6,000	
Wages	10,800	
National insurance	1,200	
Stock losses	239	18,239
Gross profit		77,761
Samples	2,000	
Debtor insurances	10,000	
Legal costs	5,000	
Rent (office)	10,000	
Delivery costs	16,500	
Stationery	600	
General insurances	1,500	
Bank charges	15,300	
Depreciation	6,250	
Accounting and audit expenses	1,200	68,350
Profit before exceptional items and interest		9,411
Setting up costs	12,000	
Goodwill impairment	15,000	27,000
Loss before interest		(17,589)
Interest		20,000
Net loss		(37,589)

Figure 1.3   Case study – Amanda Profit and Loss Account

The Balance Sheet

The Balance Sheet is a statement showing the assets and liabilities that a business has *on a set day only*. The Balance Sheet could look completely different on the day before the set date or on a day after the set date.

Before the introduction of UK GAAP, the Balance Sheet was prepared horizontally with assets on the right and liabilities on the left. For Amanda, this is shown as Figure 1.4(a).

The problem with Balance Sheets prepared this way is that they were very confusing and could easily be used to fool the numerically challenged. A common trick, when selling a business at that time, was to suggest that the business was worth its asset value. A finance specialist given the job of selling Amanda's business might suggest that a selling price of £250 000 was an absolute unbeatable bargain, given that the business had assets of £293 200, as certified by an auditor. Of course, this finance specialist would not tell the unsuspecting buyer that Amanda's Profit and Loss Account was on the debit (asset) side; this meant that she had made cumulative losses. The Profit and Loss Account should always be on the credit (liability) side of the Balance Sheet, as this is where it will be found if a profit has been made. It is a liability as it indicates what the business owes to its owner. In order to present the Balance Sheet in a more meaningful way, it was revised to look as in Figure 1.4(b).

Intangible assets are shown net of amortisation to date, or impairment as is currently the case, and tangible assets are shown net of depreciation. The sum of intangible assets and tangible assets are 'net fixed assets', but will often be shown in accounts in the abbreviated form as 'fixed assets'. Next comes current asset, and from current assets, current liabilities are deducted. The difference between current assets and current liabilities is known as 'working capital'. This is shown in accounts as 'net current assets', where current assets

Amanda   Balance Sheet as at December 31 2004

Liabilities	£	Assets	£
Capital	50,000	Intangible assets	25,000
Long term loans	200,000	Tangible assets	13,750
Creditors and accruals	43,200	Stock	95,761
		Dobtorε and prepaymemts	118,500
		Other debtors	2,380
		Cash at bank	220
		Profit and Loss Account	37,589
Total liabilities	293,200	Total assets	293,200

Figure 1.4(a)   Case study – Amanda – Balance Sheet (prior to UK GAAP)

Amanda   Balance Sheet at December 31 2004

	£	£
Intangible assets		25,000
Tangible assets		13,750
		38,750
Stock	95,761	
Debtors and Prepayments	118,500	
VAT	2,380	
Cash at bank	220	
Total current assets	216,861	
Creditors and accruals	43,200	
Net current assets	———	173,661
Total assets less current liabilities		212,411
Less: long term liabilities – loan		200,000
Total net assets		12,411
Capital		50,000
Less: loss In year		(37,589)
Closing capital		12,411

Figure 1.4(b) Case study – Amanda – Balance Sheet

are higher than current liabilities, and as 'net current liabilities', where current liabilities are higher than current assets. Working capital is added to net fixed assets to give 'total assets less current liabilities' and this represents the total capital employed in the business. Long-term liabilities, such as long-term loans, are deducted from total capital employed to give 'net assets', and this 'net assets' figure is the true (assuming the accounts are accurate) asset value of the business. As can be seen from Figure 1.4(b), the true asset value of Amanda's business at 31 December 2004 is £12 411, and this is a long way from the £293 200 as it would have been shown in the old format.

The bottom block of a Balance Sheet will be different for a sole trader, partnership and Limited Company. Take three scenarios.

Sole trader

A sole trader starts with a capital of £120 000 and in the first year makes a net profit of £89 000. In the year he takes £50 000 out of the business and the business pays his tax bill of £28 000. The bottom block of the sole trader's Balance Sheet at the end of his first year would be:

	£
Net assets	131 000
Capital	131 000

Capital would be calculated:	£
Opening capital	120 000
Add: net profit	89 000
	209 000
Less: Drawings	78 000
	131 000

Partnership

A, B and C start a partnership, bringing in a capital of £20 000, £40 000 and £60 000, respectively. The partnership makes a profit of £89 000, and the profit is divided up as shown in the example on previous pages. In the first year of trading, A has received £30 000 and B has received £20 000 from the partnership. Also, the partnership had paid a tax bill of £13 000 for A, £7000 for B and £8000 for C.

Now the Balance Sheet would look like:

	£
Net Assets	131 000

Capital Accounts	£
A	20 000
B	40 000
C	60 000
	120 000

Current Accounts

A	3000
B	6000
C	2000
	11 000

Total Partnership capital 131 000

The partners' current accounts would be calculated as follows:

£

Current account – A

Opening Balance	0
Add: share of profits	46 000
	46 000
Less: Drawings	43 000
	3000

Current account – B

Opening Balance	0
Add: share of profits	33 000
	33 000
Less: Drawings	27 000
	6000

Current account – C

Opening Balance	0
Add: share of profits	10 000
	10 000
Less: Drawings	8000
	2000

Limited company

If A, B and C had decided to set up a limited company, rather than a partner-ship, then they would have to divide up the net profit after tax, called 'earnings' in proportion to the capital they put in. However, those being employed in the company as well as providing capital would be paid a salary and they would be taxed on the amount of their salary and not on the profits the com-pany made. However, in addition to the personal tax borne by the sharehold-ers, the company would pay corporation tax on profits after the deduction of salaries.

Had A, B and C formed a company, with a view to achieving a similar share of the profits that they would have received had they been in a partnership, then they might have structured the company as below:

Issued share capital – 120 000 ordinary shares of 25 pence, purchased for £1 each.

A buys 20 000 ordinary shares, B buys 40 000 ordinary shares and C buys 60 000 ordinary shares.

A is to be paid a salary of £27 000 per annum and B is to be paid an annual salary of £17 000.

Now the bottom part of the Profit and Loss Account might read:

ABC Limited – Profit and Loss Account for the year ended ....

	£	£
Profit before salaries, national insurance and pension costs		89 000
Less:		
Salaries	44 000	
National insurance and pension costs	6729	50 729
Profit before tax		38 271
Corporation tax		7271
Earnings		31 000
Dividends		20 000
Retained Earnings		11 000

ABC Limited – Balance Sheet at...

	£
Net assets	<u>131 000</u>

	£
Share capital: 120 000 Ordinary shares of 25 pence	30 000
Share premium account	90 000
Profit and Loss Account	<u>11 000</u>
Equity shareholders' funds	<u>131 000</u>

The Balance Sheet for limited companies will be dealt with more fully in later chapters, but with regard to the above Balance Sheet:

(1) The share premium account shows the difference between what shares were sold for and their par value. A share's par value is the value shown on the share certificate.
(2) Share capital and share premium are capital reserves, while the Profit and Loss Account is a revenue reserve.
(3) Dividends can only be paid out of revenue reserves.
(4) The word 'equity' means ordinary shares, as against preference shares.

Now that Amanda's Profit and Loss Account and Balance Sheet for the year ended 31 December 2004 are complete, her nominal ledger would be adjusted in preparation for the new financial year. Firstly, all items in the Trial Balance that were designated to be Profit and Loss Account items would be written down to zero and replaced by one line reading 'Profit and Loss Account'. This is shown in Figure 1.5. Secondly, entries would be made in the nominal ledger to reverse all the reversible entries from the previous year. This is shown in Figure 1.6.

Trial Balance at December 31 2004

	Debit (£)	Credit (£)
Capital		50,000
Cash at bank	220	
Goodwill	25,000	
Samples	0	
Loan		200,000
Debtor insurance	0	
Setting-up costs	0	
VAT	2,380	
Legal costs	0	
Stock	95,761	
Trade creditors		40,000
Sales		0
Trade debtors	102,500	
Cost of sales	0	
Rent (office)	0	
Fixtures and fittings	3,750	
Van	10,000	
Warehouse rent	0	
Delivery costs	0	
Stationery	0	
General insurances	0	
Wages	0	
National insurance	0	
Interest	0	
Bank charges	0	
Stock losses	0	
Goodwill impairment	0	
Depreciation	0	
Accruals		3,200
Prepayments	16,000	
Accounting and audit expenses	0	
Profit and Loss Account	37,589	
	293,200	293,200

Figure 1.5 Case study – Amanda – Trial Balance (after completion of 2004 accounts)

Reversing double entries after year end close

Accurals					
Number	Debit	£	Number	Credit	£
			Opening balance		3,200
23R		2,000			
23R		1,200			

Prepayments					
Number	Debit	£	Number	Credit	£
Opening balance		16,000			
			24R		16,000

Wages					
Number	Debit	£	Number	Credit	£
			23R		1,800

National insurance					
Number	Debit	£	Number	Credit	£
			23R		200

Accounting and audit expenses					
Number	Debit	£	Number	Credit	£
			23R		1,200

Rent (office)					
Number	Debit	£	Number	Credit	£
24R		10,000			

Warehouse Rent					
Number	Debit	£	Number	Credit	£
24R		6,000			

Figure 1.6 Case study – Amanda – reversible entries

Case study – Amanda

Her accountant came straight to the point. Her accounts were awful. Sales volumes were not high enough to justify her contract with Zehin Foods plc and her gross margin percentage at 20% was too low. Then, she had 91 days of stock at her year end and could not control this by reducing her orders as she was committed to buying minimum quantities from her supplier. Debtor days stood at 78 days and while there was not a bad debt risk because her debtors were insured, this indicated a complete lack of control.

Why, the accountant asked, were the debtors insured anyway when her sales were to large supermarkets that were very unlikely to go bust? Amanda explained that debtor insurance was a condition for getting the bank loan, but this did not satisfy her accountant. Why were her bank charges, being over 3% of turnover, so high? Amanda's accountant believed that she could have negotiated with the bank for a better deal.

It was explained to her that the accounts demonstrated that her business was being run badly, to the effect that she had lost £37 589 of her original £50 000 capital, leaving her with only £12 411. The accountant explained that if she had difficulty selling any of her stock, the bank might get nervous and demand their money back. That would put her out of business; the only saving grace being that as they would have to write off some of their debt, they would not rush into such action.

The accountant suggested that Amanda needed to understand the meaning of the working capital cycle, so that she could work out how much cash she needed to run her business, to negotiate with her banker to get a fair deal and finally to understand and implement the concept of asset management. Otherwise, her business was going to end up like a lot of start-ups – dead within 3 years.

The working capital cycle

Current assets appear in the Balance Sheet in the order of least liquidity, stock, debtors and then cash. Current liabilities aro deducted from current assets to arrive at working capital, and from these two figures, the current ratio, being simply current assets divided by current liabilities, can be calculated.

If the current ratio is greater than 1, it means the business has sufficient cash to meet its short-term liabilities, while a current ratio of less than 1 means, in theory at least, that the business will require the support of the banks to meet such short-term liabilities.

In the real world, the current ratio will differ by industry and by different businesses within a particular industry. It will, therefore, be a matter of judgement as to what will be reasonable for a particular business. For Amanda's business, she might conclude for her plan that she should always have one month's stock, creditors will always give her 30 days credit and she will have to give her customers 60 days credit. If she did not start with any cash and her plan suggested that she would need £7000 per month for expenses (paid as incurred), then at the end of her first three months, her working capital would be:

	£
Stock	40 000
Debtors	100 000
Current assets	140 000
Creditors	40 000
Bank overdraft	91 000
Current liabilities	131 000
Current ratio	1.069

On this basis, she might conclude that she needed £100 000 to finance her working capital, in which case her working capital would be:

	£
Stock	40 000
Debtors	100 000
Cash	9000
Current assets	149 000
Creditors	40 000
Current liabilities	40 000
Current ratio	3.725

On top of calculating the cash needed to finance working capital, it is also necessary to compute the amount that will be spent on fixed assets. In Amanda's case, she needed £60 000 for fixed assets; add this to her £100 000 working capital requirement and she would need to have borrowed £160 000. But she had net borrowings of £200 000 at her year end and yet only managed to have

£220 in her bank account. The reason for this difference was that Amanda did not do as well as she might have expected. What this tells us is that when it comes to funding, businesses need a contingency. It also tells Amanda that lack of knowledge of the working capital cycle (raw materials and work-in-progress if a manufacturer, purchases if not, to stock, then debtors, then cash) was not the cause for her problems.

Of course, many companies can get away with a working capital ratio of less than 1. These are usually in service industries where there is little or no stock and being effectively cash businesses, debtors overall amount to only a few days. Therefore, they can expand by investing the cash generated in their business and although in theory a current ratio of less than 1 means they cannot meet their liabilities, they will be able to do so when they fall due under the terms they are able to negotiate.

Negotiating with banks

Individuals and small businesses tend to bank with one institution and stay there. The bank chosen might be the one used by parents, or it might be because of perceived convenience, such as having a branch at a university campus. It never occurs to individuals that they may be getting a poor deal or that banks are in business to make a profit. Banks are very clever in that they market their products in a way that creates the illusion that they are doing their customers a favour, whereas they are unveiling their latest money-making schemes.

Examples of such money-making schemes are almost endless, but the type of marketing to look out for is as the following: The large print might suggest that a high rate of interest would be paid on the account, while the small print would tell you about an annual fee. Put the two together and the net result might be a low rate of interest. The account might offer benefits such as discounts on selected products, but the small print will not acknowledge that customers could negotiate many discounts for themselves. The general rule is that if something is advertised in large print in the shop window, there are likely to be catches. What is advertised will almost certainly be truthful, but the good news will be in the large print, while the bad will be found in the 'conditions'.

Banks do sometimes come up with very reasonable offers, but these are often found by reading leaflets; it is unlikely that such a gem would be advertised in large print, nor are bank staff likely to push such a product. Getting a good deal out of banks takes much research, patience and tenacity.

Researching the bank issue with students reveals some awful cases of what amounts to finance abuse. One foreign student had parents who were well able to support their offspring but they did not want their money to be frittered away; so they discussed with the student how much financial support was needed and it was made clear that the parents would not be best pleased if more than this amount was spent.

The parents transferred the money on the first day of each month, but the bank took up to 10 days to clear the funds. Because of the bank's negligence, the student was forced to go overdrawn, which resulted in a 'no authorisation' penalty. The student visited the bank to agree an overdraft limit, but this was exceeded when the bank charged interest, which triggered further charges for 'exceeding credit limit'. Within a few months, the account was £250 overdrawn, all of which were interest and penalties. The student did not know how to get out of this downward spiral.

The student was advised to consult the local Yellow Pages and to list on one side of A4 all the banks operating in the area and armed with this make an appointment to see the bank manager. The strategy was to point out to the manager the competition this bank faced, to complain that the overdraft had only been incurred because of the bank's negligence and to make it clear that their customer had suffered hurt because of it. The advice was to insist that the account be credited with all the charges and interest and a further amount be credited as compensation for the suffering. Failure to agree this, the bank manager was advised, would result in the account being moved elsewhere and fellow students at the university being made aware of the treatment that had been received. In addition, the bank's claim to recover their money would be rigorously defended if the case went to the court. Faced with this, the bank credited the account with all charges and credited a further £100 as compensation.

The point is that overdrawn accounts can always be closed. If the amount owed to the bank is legitimate, then the strategy is to open an account elsewhere, take out a loan to clear the original debt and move on. If the overdraft has come about because of unreasonable charges (as in the example), then the strategy is to simply move on and leave the overdraft unpaid. In such cases, it is important to pay in full all legitimate charges and write to the bank pointing out why payment is not being made for the remainder.

It must be remembered that banks sometimes make excessive profits because their customers are lethargic, and if individuals are to get a fair deal, then they must be prepared to move from one bank to another. People not being prepared to act because 'it isn't worth the hassle of moving for £25' forget that £25 becomes £35 and so on. Banks adopt what can be described as the 'children' strategy' in that they will ratchet up the charges slowly and surely to find out how much they can get away with. If the bank knows you will not put up with any unnecessary charges, there will be a marker put on your account to make sure it does not happen. It should be the objective of every account holder to have such a marker put on their account.

Now whereas sensible individuals ensure that they have bank accounts that incur no bank charges or fees and receive interest on credit balances, for the business customer it is never that easy. Many believe there is nothing they can do, but it is never the case that nothing can be done.

Like the individual customer, business customers believe that they are in a very vulnerable position if they owe their bank money, but they can also clear any monies due by agreeing a loan with another bank. For many though, it is simply a case of not being bothered. Small business owners seem prepared to spend weeks and weeks chasing potential customers, but they will not reserve a week to visit all the banks in the area. It is a simple matter of preparing a basic business plan and then visiting each bank in turn. Give them a copy of the business plan, explain the business and ask the bank for the best deal that can be offered in the circumstances. Explain that you are looking for a long-term relationship, but you want a good deal and are prepared to visit every bank to see who is prepared to offer it.

To open a business account, it is important that negotiations are confined to large branches in which there are managers of sufficient seniority to be able to make decisions. Otherwise, it will be like the 'Little Britain' sketch in which 'the computer says no'.

There are three important rules to consider when negotiating a business account, but they are only relevant in full if the business is a limited company, rather than a sole trader or partnership. Remember, sole traders and partnerships (but not certain 'limited partnerships') have unlimited liability and have no protection if the business fails:

- Never give personal guarantees.
- Have the bank's 'on demand' clause eliminated.
- Agree in advance what the bank can charge for and what those charges will be.

Never give personal guarantees

The bank will often ask that you give them a guarantee that if the business fails, you will make good from your personal finances. This should always be refused because there is no point in having limited liability (your loss in a limited company is limited to the amount you paid for your shares) and then giving it away. Instead, agree that the bank can have a fixed and floating charge over the assets of the company.

Have the bank's 'on demand' clause eliminated

The bank's standard 'on demand' clause is exactly what it says. The bank can demand its money back 'on demand' and without notice at any time of its choosing. So the business might have one bad month, the bank manager gets nervous and the bank calls its money in. For obvious reasons, the business cannot pay up immediately, so the bank has the business wound up. Admittedly, this is not very likely but it is certainly possible.

The answer is to insist that the 'on demand' clause is deleted. Instead there would be a clause inserted, which stated that the bank would give the business 'three months' notice, if it wanted to recover its money. This notice period would allow the directors of the company sufficient time to negotiate alternative facilities.

Of course, there might be legitimate reasons why the bank should be entitled to ask for its money back, on demand, for example, if the owner of the business was acting fraudulently. The answer, in discussion with the bank, is to agree 'bank covenants'. A covenant is something you agree with the bank that you will do. Examples of covenants might be the following:

- I agree to run my account honestly and advise the bank immediately if I believe I may have financial problems ahead.
- I will ensure that interest cover never falls below 1.25, on a cumulative basis.
- I will ensure that I never make a loss for three consecutive months.

The deal would be that if you were in breach of any covenant, the bank would have the right to revert to their 'on demand' clause. In reality, a breach of a bank covenant must be considered to be a serious matter that would always require negotiations to immediately commence.

Eliminating the 'on demand' clause does mean that there is one less thing to worry about, but the real benefit is that it focuses the mind. Having agreed covenants with the bank, one objective of the owners of a business must be to review the performance of their company against such covenants. For example, if a covenant stated that there would never be three consecutive months making a loss, the combination of making a loss for two consecutive months and the covenant would focus the mind to ensure that the third month was in profit.

Agree the charging structure

A key part of any negotiation with a bank is what they can charge you for and how much they can charge you for what. Failure to negotiate and agreeing a charging structure will result in you signing the bank's standard contract, which although going to several pages of small print will amount to: 'we can charge you what we want, when we want, for whatever reason we choose.'

The business section of the press is littered with horror stories related to banks, probably the most famous being the 'golf jolly'. A company, as part of its marketing effort, organised a golf day. Recipients were invited to participate in a round of golf, where generous prizes were on offer including one for winning, one for 'a hole in one', one for the best putting round, etc. After the round, dinner was served with plenty of drinks, all provided free by the company. To maintain good relations with its bank, the name of the bank manager was added to the invitation list. He accepted the invitation and had a great time. You can imagine, therefore, the fury inside the company when they received an invoice from the bank for their 'manager's time' and, to add insult to injury, were told that their account had been debited accordingly.

The bank might propose that the amount charged is based on a fixed charge per quarter, or a charge per transaction or a combination of the two. It could be even more complicated with debits carrying a higher charge than credits, for example. The method of charging might be appropriate in the circumstances, but again might not be.

A charity was organised to provide a service, with the objective of utilising all the income it received to get to as many people as possible. One bank offered a set monthly fee to run the account, while another wanted to charge 90 pence per transaction, with the first seven transactions in any 1 month free. The problem was that although it was a very small charity, its £10 annual subscription per member tended to arrive in the same month, so the bank would be effectively taking just under 9% commission on each £10 cheque. Clearly, the fixed monthly fee was the better deal in this case, but it was bettered by a third bank who offered free banking for charities.

So the strategy must be to visit all the large branches of the banks in the area and ask for the best deal each will give you. Then, taking into account the circumstances of your own business, work out what each bank is likely to charge over a full year. Pick out the top three and arrange another appointment with each, at which you ask if they can tweak their quotation.

When the bank is selected, ask the bank to draw up a contract setting out what has been agreed. It is recommended that when the contract arrives, it is checked over by the company's solicitor to make sure that it matches the expectations. Now, all this has taken time and money, but at the end of the day, it is likely to be considered as an investment with a relatively quick payback.

Asset management

When 'asset management' is referred to, all it means is the process by which the managers of a company seek to protect the company's assets and ensure that the company makes the best use of its capital. What this entails is examining every asset:

Intangible assets

The objective is to examine every intangible asset to ensure their valuation in the Balance Sheet is reasonable. It does not matter whether the intangible assets is brands, research and development or goodwill, the test is the same. This test is whether or not the intangible asset is capable of generating future income streams commensurate with its value. Clearly, this decision will be a matter of judgement and will be discussed fully in later chapters.

Fixed assets

The first thing to do is to find every asset shown in the Plant Register to make sure they really exist. It is not uncommon for a manager to scrap an asset and then fail to tell the accountant what has happened. The first the accountant hears of it is when it cannot be found. The asset should be removed from the books of account and a figure showing 'loss on disposal of asset' will equal the written-down value of the asset at the time it was discovered it no longer existed.

The second test is to make sure the asset is still being used. If not, it should be sold, if possible, scrapped, if not. What tends to happen occasionally is that assets are found in a dusty state and enquiries reveal 'we haven't used that old thing for years and its replacement is getting close to its sell-by date.' In this case, the depreciation should be increased so that cumulative depreciation equals the total cost of the asset, giving a written-down value of zero. When the asset is disposed of, the total cost of the asset and the total depreciation to date will be taken out of the Balance Sheet, although the figure for 'net fixed assets' would remain unchanged.

Assuming the asset is being used, an assessment of its likely life needs to be made on a regular basis to ensure that the depreciation being charged fairly reflects reality.

Current assets – stock

Of all assets, stock is the most difficult to control, for it has the nasty habit of going missing. Retailers, in particular, suffer from what they call 'shrinkage' as stock gets stolen by both customers and employees, despite security measures such as tags and cameras. It seems rather sad that as an additional security measure, the store manager will sometimes position a member of staff outside changing rooms so that they can see what customers are taking in. From an accounting point of view, it is important that the latest technology is used to ascertain stock, on a real-time basis. As the goods going through the tills are scanned, stock records should be automatically updated. Regular stock checks should then be carried out to see if the physical stock count matches the book stock.

For manufacturing businesses, stock can also be a problem. In this case, where stock goes missing the problem is more likely to be faulty record keeping rather than pilferage, but theft cannot be ruled out. Businesses can no longer afford not to keep detailed stock records, as the old method of recording purchases only means that there is no control over stock. Using this method, all purchases are coded to 'purchases' and at the end of each month, the stock is physically counted. Using this method:

Opening stock plus purchases, less closing stock = cost of sales.

The problem is that in this case 'cost of sales' = actual cost of sales + stock losses, and there is no way of knowing how these two figures might be split. Accordingly, even manufacturing businesses should record every stock item. So, the entries would be:

Debit 'raw materials' credit 'creditors' (or 'cash'); then
Debit 'work-in-progress' (with raw material used), credit 'raw materials'; then
Debit 'work-in-progress' (with labour used), credit 'production labour'; then
Debit 'finished stock (with finished products), credit 'work-in-progress'; finally
Debit 'cost of sales' (cost of goods sent out to customers), credit 'stock'

As can be seen from the above, it is quite an exercise to track movements between raw materials, work-in-progress, finished goods and cost of sales and then have spot physical counts in all these areas. However, the only alternative to this is to risk huge stock losses and worse, not even know what the stock losses amount to.

Current assets – debtors

The first thing to ascertain is whether a particular customer is likely to pay for the goods and services received. Assuming there is nothing wrong with the goods and services supplied and therefore no dispute, there are two reasons why debtors do not pay up. The first is that they are trying to extend their credit as far as possible, the remedy for which is initiating effective credit control procedures. The second and far more serious reason is that they cannot pay due to lack of funds. Companies must, therefore, vet their potential customers before they offer credit terms.

Companies often vet potential customers by asking for references from the firm's suppliers and also asking for a bank reference, but both these vetting methods are fraught with danger. Many companies have the strategy of ascertaining their three most important suppliers. They make sure that these three suppliers are paid on time, even if all their other suppliers are made to wait. It does not take a genius to work out which three suppliers will be given for reference purposes.

The problem with bank references is that the bank has a duty to its customers as well as an obligation to tell the truth. Accordingly, the reference is usually coded and unless the code is known, it can be difficult to ascertain what it is all about. The following examples might help.

What the bank reference says	What the bank means
Undoubted	Absolutely no problem here and should your customer default, we will make good any losses
'A' should prove good for the amount of your enquiry	Well, it is up to you to take the risk; we can see no reason why A would default, but you never know
'B' should prove good for the amount of your enquiry, even though it is larger than the usual enquiry	You should realise you are taking one hell of a risk, something we would not do
'C' should prove good for the amount of your enquiry. There is a charge in favour of the bank	You must realise that you are taking a big risk here. We have got everything covered this end and if C goes belly up, you will be at the end of the queue.

So, unless the bank reference says 'undoubted' the only way to make an effective judgement is to review the potential customer's accounts. This is discussed in Chapter 4.

Having offered your customer credit, the objective is to ensure that the credit terms are met. This is achieved by regularly checking the age-debt list and chasing overdue debtors through telephone and e-mail. If gentle reminders fail to get payment, the next step is to advise the customer that credit is suspended and that further orders will be considered on a 'cash with order' basis only. If that fails to achieve the objective, then debt collection agencies and the courts can be used as a last resort.

The problem about using debt collection agencies and the courts is that you will incur costs that will not be recoverable if the debtor cannot pay as against wilfully refuses to pay. As lawyers will tell you: 'It is pointless suing a man of straw.' So again a review of the customer's accounts is recommended before committing to additional costs.

Current assets – cash

Companies never go out of business because their profit and loss account indicates they have made a loss, rather it is running out of cash without the necessary facilities in place that causes disaster to strike. Indeed, very profitable companies expanding rapidly have run out of cash and gone out of business, a phenomenon known as 'overtrading'. So managing cash is one of the most important controls a company should have in place.

On a regular basis, the company's cash book should be reconciled to the bank statement, but it is vital that a company knows what is going to happen to its cash balance in the future. So to do this, companies prepare cash budgets, as shown in the following example.

On 31 December 2006, Reliable Retail Limited's Balance Sheet was as below:

	£'000
Fixed assets at cost	2400
Depreciation to date	960
Net fixed assets	1440
Stocks	160
Debtors	1128
Cash at bank	407
Current assets	1695
Trade creditors	188
Creditors – VAT	126
Current liabilities	314
Net current assets	1381
Total assets less current liabilities	2821
Less: long term loans	0
Total net assets	2821
Share capital	2000
Retained earnings	821
Shareholders' funds	2821

For the first six months of 2007, the planned purchases were (excluding VAT):

	Jan	Feb	March	April	May	June
Purchases (£'000)	200	280	240	320	400	360

Purchases made in any one month were expected to be in stock at the end of that month and sold the following month. The selling price to the customer was calculated by taking the cost price (excluding VAT) and multiplying by 300% as an add-on. To this cost price + 300% of cost price, there was then added a further 17.5% to cover VAT. Because of the high prices, customers pay by credit card and Reliable Retail receive payment for their sales two months after they were made (January sales would be paid in March, etc,). They pay for services (subject to VAT) and wages in the month they were incurred, but purchases of goods are paid for in the month following receipt (January purchases paid in February, etc.).

In May, Reliable Retail planned a major refurbishment costing £800 000, plus VAT of £140 000, which they would pay at the end of that month. The amounts owed by debtors at the Balance Sheet date of 31 December 2006 were expected to be paid in two equal instalments in January and February, while outstanding creditors at 31 December 2006 would be paid in January. VAT was always paid quarterly in arrears (VAT for January, February and March was paid in April, etc.).

The budget for Reliable Retail for the first six months of 2007 was as below:

(£'000)	Jan	Feb	March	April	May	June	Half-year
Sales	640	800	1120	960	1280	1600	6400
Cost of sales	160	200	280	240	320	400	1600
Gross profit	480	600	840	720	960	1200	4800
Services	200	200	200	200	200	200	1200
Wages	250	250	250	250	250	250	1500
Depreciation	40	40	40	40	40	40	240
Net profit (loss)	(10)	110	350	230	470	710	1860

Reliable Retail had not negotiated overdraft facilities with its bankers, but the lender had agreed to provide a loan to cover working capital requirements and the planned refurbishment. A loan of up to £1 million was agreed to be drawn down in one lump sum that had to be in whole £100 000 units and taken in time to prevent the company from being overdrawn.

The objective, therefore, is to prepare a cash budget for the first six months of June with a view to calculating the amount of loan required and when it would be required. Looking at the above Profit and Loss Account, it might seem that Reliable Retail would not need a loan to finance its refurbishment as it is starting the year (2007) with £407 000 in the bank and is planning to make a profit of £1 860 000 in the first six months of 2007. Note that corporation tax can be ignored for this exercise.

So, guess now to see how much should be borrowed and when. List the months and take in all possible borrowing from £nil to £1 million, and the odds of getting both the month and the amount right by sticking a pin in (i.e. a random selection) are 65/1.

The first step in calculating the cash budget is to work out debtors, creditors and VAT.

	Jan	Feb	March	April	May	June	Half-year
(£'000)							
Sales	640	800	1120	960	1280	1600	6400
VAT on sales	112	140	196	168	224	280	1120
Debtors	752	940	1316	1128	1504	1880	7520
Purchases	200	280	240	320	400	360	1800
VAT on purchases	35	49	42	56	70	63	315
Creditors	235	329	282	376	470	423	2115
Services/other	200	200	200	200	1000	200	2000
VAT on services	35	35	35	35	175	35	350
Payments for services	235	235	235	235	1175	235	2350
Output VAT	112	140	196	168	224	280	1120
Input VAT	70	84	77	91	245	98	665
Due to Revenue and Customs	42	56	119	77	(21)	182	455

Armed with this information, we can now compute the cash budget

(£'000)	Jan	Feb	March	April	May	June	Half-year
Opening cash	407	172	16	(46)	(90)	(575)	407
Receipts from debtors	564	564	752	940	1316	1128	5264
Payments (goods)	188	235	329	282	376	470	1880
Payments (services)	235	235	235	235	235	235	1410
Payments (wages)	250	250	250	250	250	250	1500
Refurbishment					940		940
Payments – (VAT)	126			217			343
Closing cash	172	16	(46)	(90)	(575)	(402)	(402)

This cash budget may come as quite a surprise, for despite starting with a healthy bank balance and generated a high level of profitability, we need our loan as early as March and given the highest computed overdraft is £575 000, we will need to borrow £600 000. So the correct answer is March and £600 000. Of course, what causes the cash problem and therefore the requirement for funds is the working capital cycle. In this case, it takes 3 months to convert purchases into cash. Given the loan requirement, the final cash budget would look:

Reliable Retail Limited – Cash Budget for the first half of 2007

(£'000)	Jan	Feb	March	April	May	June	Half-year
Opening cash	407	172	16	554	510	25	407
Receipts from debtors	564	564	752	940	1316	1128	5264
Loan from bank			600				600
Payments (goods)	188	235	329	282	376	470	1880
Payments (services)	235	235	235	235	235	235	1410
Payments (wages)	250	250	250	250	250	250	1500
Refurbishment					940		940
Payments – (VAT)	126			217			343
Closing cash	172	16	554	510	25	198	198

Now that a cash budget has been prepared, the final step in the process is to prepare the forecast Balance Sheet at 30 June 2007. We know from our cash budget what remains outstanding at this date and given that we have the Profit and Loss Account, we can complete our Balance Sheet, as shown below:

Reliable Retail Limited	Balance Sheet	Actual 31/12/06	Budget 30/7/07
		£'000	£'000
Fixed assets at cost		2400	3200
Depreciation to date		960	1200
Net fixed assets		1440	2000
Stocks		160	360
Debtors		1128	3384
Cash at bank		407	198
Current assets		1695	3942
Trade creditors		188	423
Creditors – VAT		126	238
Current liabilities		314	661
Net current assets		1381	3281
Total assets less current liabilities		2821	5281
Less: long-term loans		0	600
Total net assets		2821	4681
Share capital		2000	2000
Retained earnings		821	2681
Shareholders' funds		2821	4681

Regarding the computation of the Cash Budget for the 6 months ended 30 June 2007 and the Budget Balance Sheet at that date, the following should be noted:

- Depreciation in the Profit and Loss Account is only a book entry (debit depreciation in the Profit and Loss Account and credit cumulative depreciation in the Balance Sheet) and therefore has no impact on cash. Accordingly, depreciation never appears in a cash budget.
- Retained earning in the Balance Sheet is the cumulative retained earnings since the business started.

Current liabilities – creditors

On ethical grounds, creditors should be paid as they fall due, but for many businesses this is not always possible due to cash flow problems. In such cases, any delay-paying trade creditors should be kept to a minimum, as undue delay will result in loss of reputation and suppliers demanding cash with order.

It is simply not worthwhile delaying paying Revenue and Customs as this organisation is not renowned for having a sense of humour in such cases. Pretending that the problem will go away is really the worst option to take. Revenue and Customs may be sympathetic if they are kept fully informed about temporary inability to pay, but they will show absolutely no mercy if they believe they are being strung along. Hence comes the need for good cash management that ensures that funds are always available when they are really needed.

Amanda's meetings

Amanda wanted to find out how she could review her accounts so that she could judge for herself how well she was doing or not as the case may be. She contacted her accountant who told her various ratios, which in Amanda's view were difficult to remember. She asked him how he remembered all these ratios; the accountant told her that he used an acronym – Pam Sir.

P stood for 'Performance';
AM stood for Asset Management;
S stood for Structure; and
IR stood for Investor Ratios.

Once you know what you are assessing, he had told her that it was relatively easy to remember the ratios themselves.

To get a second opinion as to how she should proceed with her business, she arranged to meet a friend. The friend worked at a firm of solicitors and suggested that she meet a specialist in mergers and acquisitions who also ran an investment club, financed by several business angels. This specialist also dealt with several venture capital companies.

Discussion Questions

An employee at a hairdressing salon was banking some cheques and casually mentioned to the bank manager that starting a business one day was an ambition. The bank manager said that as the employee had been a long-standing customer it was likely the bank would be willing to help realise such an ambition. The hairdresser took this to mean that it was possible to go overdrawn, not realising that formal arrangements had to be entered into.

A friend offered help to get the hairdresser started by setting up a limited company. The hairdresser used life savings to buy 51% of the company and the friend subscribed for the remaining 49%. Overall, 25 000 ordinary shares with a par value of 25 pence were issued for £1 each. The cost of setting up the company was £1250 (debited to 'share premium account').

On 1 April 2007, the new hairdressing company bought a business for £32 060. For this money, it took over a shop lease covering the period 1 April 2007 to 31 March 2009, valued at £20 000, fixtures and fittings valued at £9000 and 100 bottles of shampoo valued at £60.

The hairdresser felt confident about the future because many of the customers said that they would transfer their custom to the new business. Wanting to live the life associated with being a Managing Director, rather than a mere employee, the new business owner went out and bought a BMW car for £33 000 and managed to dissuade the garage about the necessity of a bankers' draft, paid by cheque.

The next step was to arrange a credit account with a supplier of toiletries, and an order was placed for 300 bottles of shampoo at a cost of £270, payable on 30 days credit. The shampoo was duly delivered. Having placed this order, the telephone rang; it was the bank manager who was minded to bounce the £33 000 cheque for the car on the grounds of 'insufficient funds' but would delay such action if the hairdresser came to the bank straight away.

The hairdresser apologised and asked the bank manager to take into consideration of the fact that it was thought that an overdraft had been agreed. The bank manager agreed to lend £24 000, repayable quarterly over 4 years at an interest rate of 8% per annum, calculated on the opening balance at the beginning of each quarter. Interest would be debited to the account at the end of each quarter. On the matter of the £33 000 cheque, it would be cleared provided it was agreed that an overdraft interest of £536 and a bank charge of £100, being an unauthorised overdraft charge, was accepted, both amounts being chargeable at the end of the first quarter. The hairdresser realised that this was the only option and agreed.

Back at the salon, the hairdresser ordered and received toiletries for use in the salon, costing £1300, on credit. In the first quarter, business was brisk; customers paid a total of £31 100 for haircuts and in addition bought 330 bottles of shampoo for £660. In both cases, the hairdresser received cash.

Before the quarter end, the company had paid an electricity bill of £150, covering the quarter ended 30 June 2007, and had paid wages totalling £10 000. The company also paid creditors £1215. On 30 June 2007, stock was physically counted and valued at £200. At the end of her first quarter, the company owed £400 in wages and £164 for telephone charges.

The owners of the business believed that goodwill should be amortised over 5 years, fixtures and fittings would last 5 years, but the car should be depreciated over 3 years.

The requirement of this question:

(1) Prepare all the journal entries for the 'Hairdressing company' for the first quarter ended 30 June 2007, ensuring that the entries take account of amortisation, depreciation, accruals and prepayments.
(2) For the 'Hairdressing Company', prepare the Profit and Loss Account for the 3 months ended 30 June 2007 and a Balance Sheet at that date.

Capital structure and basic tools of analysis

In chapter 2, Amanda's lawyer introduces her to a financial adviser. Together they produce a 5-year financial plan that is put to a business angel who agrees to fund Amanda's business. This chapter illustrates how small companies raise capital and how their capital structure changes as they grow. The chapter concludes by going through the basic tools of analysis that calculate ratios to try to read between the lines of a company's published accounts.

The topics covered are the following:

- Venture capital (private equity)
- The Enterprise Investment Scheme (EIS)
- Venture Capital Trusts (VCTs)
- The Alternative Investment Market (AIM)
- Capital structures
- Gearing
- The weighted cost of capital
- The financial planning process
- Deal structures
- The Cash Flow Statement
- Exit strategies
- Basic tools of analysis – ratio analysis
- The importance of cash and key ratios

Case study – Amanda's lawyer introduces her to a financial adviser

Amanda's lawyer explained that he was a corporate lawyer specialised in mergers and acquisitions, over the years he had met hundreds of entrepreneurs and that most problems were surmountable.

Amanda told her lawyer about her family's secret recipe for salad dressing and how her first year had been a disaster nearly wiping out her capital. She had carried out a self-assessment and concluded that not being able to manufacture her salad dressing had led to unacceptably low margins, but what made matters worse was her inability to chase debtors or control any of her assets effectively. She concluded that she needed to invest in a small factory and employ a part-time accountant, but could not see how she could do this given her current financial position. Amanda also admitted that she had a contract that tied her into buying in her salad dressing for 5 years.

The lawyer assured her that money itself should never a problem; although the equity gap still existed, really good businesses with a committed management team could usually get the funding they required. What was needed was an investor with experience in the food industry whose contacts would enable the business to go forward. Amanda was concerned that such an investor would badly dilute her equity, but her lawyer assured her that a capital structure could be put in place that would give her the incentive to be able to keep a reasonable slice of the business. He would look for a suitable investor, but in the meantime she would need to produce a 5-year plan.

This plan would need to have an executive summary, a brief history of the business and a schedule showing the management team, their strengths and the gaps in expertise that needed to be plugged. Next the plan should include details of the products the company would produce, the markets being served, an analysis of the competition and what strategy the management had to beat the competition. The plan should also show risks, rewards, objectives and milestones. In addition, there should be a detailed finance plan.

Amanda's lawyer told her that he would introduce her to an accountancy firm whose chosen adviser would show her how to construct a 5-year plan. Fees would be constructed so that only a nominal charge would be made, reflecting basic costs, if things did not work out. However, the opposite side of the coin was that in addition to the standard fee, a 'success' fee would be charged on completion of any deal. In such a case, fees would be paid by the company out of the proceeds of the share issue.

Capital structures – venture capital (private equity)

How companies are structured financially is often debated by academics. Some argue that the capital structure of the company is determined by the 'pecking order', while others argue that there is an optimum structure. Those favouring the 'pecking order' theory suggest that companies will first use profits to grow their business, then debt and lastly equity. The optimum structure theorists argue that it is possible to calculate a debt to equity balance that will maximise shareholder value.

However, reality is often different from the theory. Most businesses in the United Kingdom are small- to medium-sized enterprises (SMEs) often owned by families. Many of such SMEs are run on the basis that the objective is to provide their owners with sufficient profit to enable them to maintain their preferred lifestyle. Growing the business is not on the agenda as the owners will simply not allow their equity holding to be diluted. Expansion is, therefore, limited to that that can be generated from profits and an acceptable level of debt. An acceptable level of debt will be dependent on the personal view of each owner but the maximum amount of debt will be determined by the level of security each business is willing or capable of offering their banker.

So for SMEs, the pecking order theory has to apply. Such companies cannot determine their gearing ratio (the comparison of debt to equity) as how much capital they have is determined by how much capital they can get their hands on. Once the owners of a business have found out how much debt they can have, they have to make a decision – do I aim to grow the company and settle for equity dilution, or do I retain total control of the business and accept limited growth? Many small business owners opt for the latter and this is given as one of the main reasons why businesses fail to achieve their growth potential in the United Kingdom.

Even where equity dilution is accepted, it can be difficult for small businesses to attract equity capital. What happens is that as businesses grow they need capital investment on top of higher levels of working capital and cannot offer sufficient security to meet their escalating needs. In addition, the SME will not have grown big enough to attract capital on the equity markets. Also, the cost of raising money on equity markets, together with the additional costs of meeting the required compliance requested by those markets, means that below a certain level, such a course of action would not be viable. This was first discovered in the United Kingdom by the Committee on Finance and Industry, set up by MacDonald's Labour government in 1929 and chaired by Lord Macmillan. This phenomenon became known as the MacMillan Gap or the Equity Gap.

Nothing much was done to alleviate the Equity Gap until 1945 when the incoming Labour government set up the Industrial and Commercial Finance Corporation (ICFC), a state-owned organisation. The setting up of this organisation that eventually became 3i Group plc is described fully in Coopey and Clarke (1995).

In this book, they describe the early problems found by ICFC:

> In many cases the central problem was that firms could not provide an established profit record, so good judgement on the part of the investor was crucial. In addition, the kind of expansion involved often entailed a high element of risk, since it meant investing in new, and often unproven products and markets. The risk was all the more acute because money would be tied up over a long period. Yet another drawback was that there was little or no secondary market for any equity which ICFC might take.

What this meant, of course, was that a new paradigm had to be developed to assess young and growing companies, operating in entrepreneurial markets with no financial track record. ICFC was (due its size and capital structure) effectively the start of what is known today as venture capital, or private equity, although there had been a few privately owned venture capital houses set up before Second World War.

Despite the progress made by ICFC and others to provide capital for innovative small companies, by the late 1960s, it was obvious that many had difficulty in raising the capital needed. A government enquiry was set up and in 1971 the Bolton Report concluded that the equity gap still existed. The problems were the same; the bankers were unwilling to take risks, the cost of raising equity on the capital markets was prohibitive and financial institutions were wary of SMEs.

In the early 1970s, the incoming Labour government took the view that as the concept of free markets was not working, they had to improve the deteriorating economic position through state intervention. So the National Enterprise Board (NEB) was set up to provide venture capital to innovative SMEs, especially those set up in areas of deprivation, and to fund state takeover of larger failing businesses. Unfortunately, it was the latter that fell under media spotlight, portraying the Labour government of being akin to the then USSR, thereby putting it on the back foot. This and the 'winter of discontent' in the late 1970s led to the Conservatives winning the 1979 general election with Margaret Thatcher becoming Prime Minister.

In her first term, Margaret Thatcher set out to do away with state intervention and encourage enterprise, based on free markets. So the NEB was sold off piecemeal and what was left was split into two and privatised, with Grosvenor Venture Managers taking over the business in the south of the United Kingdom and Northern Venture Managers doing likewise in the north.

ICFC had undertaken many name changes since its formation and in the early 1990s the business was known as 3i (three i's, with iii standing for investors in industry), but it was still state-owned. Privatising the business had proved difficult over the years, as investors were unsure about investing in what was seen as a risky option. However, the government took the plunge in June 1994, pricing the shares at 272 pence, a price that seemed a fair valuation given that the net asset value of the business at 31 March 2004, the year end, had been 315 pence. The first day of dealings had been fixed for 18 July 1994 and soon the price of 3i plc's shares moved above 300 pence, allowing the company to join the FTSE 100 on 19 September 1994 (Coopey et al.).

As ICFC had originally discovered, the big disadvantage for those offering venture capital was that there was no secondary market, so the investments could be realised only through a trade sale or flotation on the main stock exchange. To alleviate these problems, the Conservative government helped to set up the Unlisted Securities Market (USM) and the Business Start-up Scheme (BSS). Under BSS, high-rate tax payers could reduce their income tax liability, but the restrictions placed upon it to avoid mere tax avoidance made the scheme virtually unworkable. Accordingly, it was replaced by the Business Expansion Scheme (BES) where both income tax relief and capital gains tax relief were available.

This government action spurred on the venture capital industry and it led to the formation of the British Venture Capital Association in 1983. This organisation has hundreds of members who over the last 20 years or so have invested over £60 billion to help start-up, expand and buyout over 25 000 companies (BVCA directory 2004/5). In addition, there is also an European Venture Capital Association with members providing equity and other capital in the United Kingdom and rest of Europe.

Over the last 20 years, the tax incentives available to those investing in venture capital, or private equity, and the capital markets have changed. The BES has been replaced by the EIS and VCTs, while the USM closed down to be replaced by the AIM.

The Enterprise Investment Scheme

The EIS was set up to encourage individuals to invest in small, higher-risk unquoted trading companies and applies to both start-up and established companies. The scheme offers investors a stream of tax incentives if they subscribe to new ordinary shares in such companies. The shares must not carry any preferential rights to dividends or to the company's assets on winding up, and they must not carry any rights to be redeemed.

Only shares issued by companies carrying out a qualifying trade or carrying out research and development or oil exploration leading to a qualifying trade will qualify for relief. Most trades qualify, but the following trades do not:

- Dealing in land, in commodities or futures in shares, securities or other financial instruments
- Financial activities such as banking, money-lending, insurance, debt-factoring and hire purchase factoring
- Dealing in goods other than in the ordinary trade of retail or wholesale distribution
- Leasing or letting assets on hire, except in the case of certain ship-chartering activities
- Receiving royalties or licence fees, except in the case of the exploitation of an intangible asset created by the company or its group
- Providing legal or accountancy services
- Property development
- Farming and market gardening
- Holding, managing or occupying woodlands, or other forestry activities or timber production
- Operating or managing hotels, guest houses or hostels in which the company carrying on the trade has an interest or which it occupies under licence or any other form of agreement
- Operating or managing nursing homes or residential care homes in which the company carrying on the trade has an interest or which it occupies
- Providing services to another company in certain circumstances where the other company's trade consists, to a substantial extent, of excluded activities.

(*Source*: Revenue and Customs Website (2006/2007).)

Subject to the investment being made in a qualifying company issuing qualifying shares, then income relief at the rate of 20% will be given on investments from £500 to £400,000 in any tax year. This is the relief for 2006/7, but may be varied each year.

Investments can be made in single companies and also through managed Enterprise Investment Trusts, in which case the minimum investment rule of £500 does not apply. In addition to income tax relief, it may be possible to benefit from 'capital gains relief' on the EIS investment, 'capital gains tax deferral relief' on other investments, together with other tax benefits.

All these tax relief sound good, so what is the catch? Well, the catch is that there is no tax relief of any description if the investor is connected with the company. You are deemed to be connected to such company if you are a director, partner or employee of the company or are entitled to receive any money from the company apart from goods or services provided on a genuine commercial basis. If, as an individual, you supplied secretarial, managerial or other 'outsourcing' services, you would be deemed to be connected. You are also deemed to be connected if you hold more than 30% of the equity of the company or can effectively influence the way the company is run by virtue of voting power, assets held or loans given.

However, there is one exception to the above rules and these are those that are applied to 'business angels'. A business angel is defined by Revenue and Customs (EIS Income tax relief, capital gains tax exemption and loss relief, chapter 3) as 'an individual who provides managerial, financial or entrepreneurial advice to small companies.'

To qualify as a business angel, the individual must not have been connected to the company prior to the investment made or been involved in carrying on the trade, and subsequently has become a director who receives or is enti-tled to receive remuneration. Such a person may make further investments within 3 years of the original investment. This means that apart from a recog-nised business angel all investors who are entitled to tax relief are 'betting blind'.

One objective of this book is to look at things from the perspective of the ordinary investor. In this context, an 'investor' is defined as a person who has an interest in a particular company either through buying ordinary shares in it or by being an employee in the company or by providing goods or services for the company. For each type of investor, the ultimate risk is the same. The shareholder risks losing his investment, the employee risks losing his job and consequently his earnings, while the supplier risks losing money through not being paid for goods and services provided.

In respect of the EIS a potential investor may receive a prospectus. Such a prospectus will be written by experts and will be very cleverly worded. All the information that are needed to make an informed decision will be there; it will likely be accurate but not usually in a format that will be easily understandable.

For example, the prospectus might say:

> The company is forecasted profitable for 2009 and is rated at 11 times estimated 2010 earnings PBIT (profit before interest and tax). We consider the valuation as attractive based on the forecasted growth.

We now have to read between the lines. The expression 'forecasted profitable' means that at the date of the prospectus, the company was not profitable. The 11 times earnings may seem attractive because in our mind we have the word 'earnings' and the fact that some quoted companies in the sector are trading at 27 times earnings. But the word 'earnings' means profits available to ordinary shareholders, that is, profits after interest and tax, but before dividends.

Obviously, the example prospectus does not give a clue as to what the interest and tax might be, so the only assumption that can be made is that it will be consistent with the like for like ratio for the quoted company. If you then examine the accounts of a quoted company (for example), you might find that the price/earnings (P/E) ratio, if it were based on 'earnings PBIT' rather than on 'earnings', falls to 11.5, very similar to our 'attractive' valuation. But, the quoted company is both profitable and quoted whereas the company in the prospectus is not profitable and its shares will be illiquid. So we must apply appropriate discounts of 40% for not being profitable and 25% for being illiquid. These discount percentages are, of course, based on 'judgement' and other percentages might be equally valid. The point, though, is that some discounting must be applied to take account of the additional risks being taken on.

Now by applying a discount of 40% and 25% to the 11.5 times valuation of the quoted company, assuming that the information in the prospectus is accurate, we can have a rating of 5.2 earnings. We are asked to pay 11 times earnings, but if we discount this for the 20% tax relief we will be getting, then we are being asked to subscribe at 8.8 times, for something realistically valued at 5.2 times. The conclusion is that the proposed investment is not such a good idea when analysed properly.

Anyone reading an EIS prospectus should trawl it carefully to see how the shares in the company have been issued. What sometimes happens is that shares are originally offered to the directors and sponsors at £1 per share, then is split one thousand times to become shares of 0.1 pence. Outside investors are invited to subscribe for the shares at 1.5 pence; what looks like a bargain is anything but. It must be remembered that there is nothing illegal or dishonest in this, as the information will be accurately supplied in the prospectus. It is simply a case of 'caveat emptor', let the buyer beware.

Another ruse that can be used in raising capital for EIS companies is that the directors are to be paid a 'success fee'. Again the exact details will be shown in the prospectus and the effect needs to be calculated. In one prospectus where the directors paid the same price for their shares as the general public, their proposed success fee had a dramatic impact. If they were successful, they would receive a compound return of 153% over 5 years, while ordinary investors after tax relief would receive a compound return of a staggering 6.8% over the same period.

The message is that investors considering investing in the EIS need to tread very carefully. Each prospectus needs to be examined in great detail, for in addition to the risk of losing the value of the investment, there is another trap lurking. It is at least arguable that if an investment is made that turns out to be extremely imprudent, then Revenue and Customs might reject the concept of tax relief, because one of the conditions of allowing relief is that 'the subscription is made for bone fide commercial reasons and not for tax avoidance purposes'. This leads to the first of the investment rules, but before we do, we need to define 'rules' in this context.

Investment rules

When it comes to investments, there is no rule that can guarantee that by following it the correct decision will be made. It will always be a matter of judgement. What the rule will indicate is the likely outcome. In other words, by following the rule, your chance of success should be better than random, but there are no guarantees. For example, I might have written:

> *Rule*: No reader of this book will win the jackpot on the National Lottery within twelve months of buying it.

This rule should be on safe ground because if every reader of this book bought a lottery ticket twice a week, then there would have to be 140 000 copies of the book sold before it was likely that we had a jackpot winner. But, of course, it is possible that the first person to buy the book could win the jackpot with the first lottery ticket bought after such a purchase. Such an outcome would be extremely unlikely, but possible.

Investment rule 1. Never make an investment where the sole reason for making such an investment is to obtain tax relief.

Investment rule 2. Never invest in Enterprise Investment Scheme companies or trusts unless you are skilled in reading prospectuses or unless you are making the investment on the advice of a professional financial adviser you are convinced you can trust.

Venture capital trusts

Like the EIS scheme, VCTs were set up to encourage investors to supply finance for small unquoted higher-risk trading companies. VCT's were introduced on 6 April 1995 and have to be quoted on the London Stock Exchange to qualify for their tax status. They can invest in companies carrying on the same trades approved for the EIS scheme, provided they are independent companies with gross assets of not more than £7 million immediately before the VCT makes the investment. This £7 million limit took effect from 6 April 2006 (before this the limit was £15 million) and of course can change from time to time. The maximum investment a VCT can make in any one company is £1 million, provided that a single investment does not represent more than 15% (by value) of its investments.

At least 70% (by value) of a VCT's investments must be in qualifying investments, as defined above, and at least 30% (by value) of its qualifying holdings must be in ordinary shares with no preferential rights. Unlike the EIS scheme, investments do not have to be in new ordinary shares, but investments are limited to unquoted companies. However, shares that are bought and sold solely on AIM or on Ofex (owned and operated by PLUS Market Group plc) count as unquoted companies.

Provided that a VCT qualifies as such as determined by Revenue and Customs, an investor is given an income tax relief of 30% (from 6 April 2006, and, as always, subject to change) on investments of up to £200 000 in any one tax year. However, income tax relief is available only on new issues of VCT's shares and is not available for the existing shares that are traded on the London Stock Exchange. If, however, shares are sold within 5 years of their purchase, then Revenue and Customs can withdraw all or part of the tax relief previously allowed. The amount withdrawn is calculated as 30% of the amount received for the shares, provided the amount withdrawn does not exceed the amount allowed in the first place. Note that this paragraph applies only to VCT shares bought on or after 6 April 2006; VCT shares bought prior to this are subject to different rates and/or rules. There is no income tax due on dividends paid by VCTs.

In addition to income tax relief, there is no capital gains tax due on gains made on VCT's ordinary shares irrespective of whether they were new shares or second-hand shares bought on a stock exchange.

A big drawback of VCTs was that the trust had to meet the 70% and 30% rule defined above within 3 years of issuing its shares. This meant that the trust managers were forced to make investments that they would not have made out of choice simply to maintain VCT status. Such investments by their very nature were more likely to fail, so that some investors saw the value of the VCT investment fall below the amount they paid, even after taking account of all the tax savings available to them.

However, this will change from 6 April 2007, as cash held by VCTs will count as an investment for the purpose of meeting the 70% and 30% rules. VCTs have the advantage that investments are spread over more companies than would be the case for EIS, but nevertheless investing in them must be considered a high risk.

> *Investment rule 3.* Invest only in a VCT where your research indicates that the fund manager operating that VCT is worthy of support. Never select a VCT at random simply to get tax relief.

The Alternative Investment Market

The AIM was set up in 1995 to enable trading in new, small and growing companies. Where private equity providers had invested in what turned out to be a successful company, AIM offered a means whereby they could realise their investment. Investing on AIM carries far more risk than investing on the main stock exchange. There are several reasons for this, including:

- AIM is less regulated than the main stock exchange
- Companies quoted on this exchange will be relatively small
- The stock will be relatively illiquid, so that there will be a significantly wider spread.

The spread is the difference between the price at which you can buy a share (the 'ask' price) and the price at which you can sell a share (the 'bid' price). At the end of 2006, a random selection of 10 shares quoted on the FTSE 100 gave a spread range between 0.04% and 0.19%, with an average spread of 0.08%, whereas a random selection of 10 shares quoted on AIM gave a spread in the range of 6.67%–40.00%, with an average spread of 16.28%. By and large, the spread is inversely proportional to the price of the share. This means that, on average, a share quoted on AIM has to gain in excess of 16.5% before the investor moves into profit. There are tax incentives for investing on AIM, but given the risks involved, investment rule number 1 has to be remembered.

Capital structures

Companies can raise capital to finance their business from several sources; equity capital can be provided by institutions, such as pension funds, and private investors, while debt can be provided by banks, other institutions and private individuals.

A particular company's cost of capital will be dependent upon the perceived risk as judged by the market. Both the investors buying equity and the banks and others providing debt will require a higher return if they perceive that the company they are being asked to supply capital for is considered risky.

However, a company's cost of equity capital is not the same as the investors' overall expected return buying into that company. Likewise, the company's cost of debt capital will not be the same as the expected return of the banks lending the debt. In both cases, the difference will amount to the cost of 'risk'. Not all of the investors' investments will meet the expected return and banks will expect that some of their lending will not be recoverable. The only time the cost of capital is equal to investors' expected return is when risk-free government bonds are purchased.

This concept is the same as the principle of insurance. Insurers assess risk and calculate premiums accordingly. For example, they might charge an eighteen-year old £2400 to cover a particular car fully comprehensive, but charge a 54-year old only £800 for the same level of cover on the same car in the same geographical area. The cost of cover for the two individuals is vastly different, but the insurance company would expect to make the same return on both, the difference being they would forecast that the 18-year old was more likely to make a claim.

A company's cost of equity capital will be equal to investors' expected return only where 'expected return' is defined as 'the return required for the investor to make the investment'. 'Overall expected return' can be defined as 'the net return the investor expects to make after accounting for the poor investments in the portfolio.'

Equity – ordinary shares

A private equity provider will expect a compound return ranging from 30% to invest in management buyouts and established but unquoted businesses to 100% for start-ups. For companies quoted on main stock exchanges, the cost of capital for an individual company is said to be dependent upon its beta, as determined by the capital asset pricing model (CAPM). This model was developed by William F. Sharp and was described in his 1964 paper 'Capital asset prices: a theory of market equilibrium under condition of risk', *Journal of Finance* (September 1964). Mr. Sharp won the Nobel Prize in Economics for his development of the CAPM.

The CAPM states that the expected return from a security is

> The risk free rate + (expected return of the market portfolio − risk free rate) × beta.

The beta is a calculation of how a particular share would be expected to move in line with the market as a whole. If a particular company's share price was expected to move in line with the market as a whole, it would have a beta of 1, while if a ±10% movement in the market would result in the share price moving ±20%, then the beta would be 2.

So, if we assume that the risk free rate is 4.70% and the expected return on the market portfolio was 14.00%, then the expected return for shares with a beta of 0.8, 1.0 and 1.5, respectively, would be:

$$4.70\% + (14.00\% - 4.70\%) \times 0.8 = 12.14\%$$
$$4.70\% + (14.00\% - 4.70\%) \times 1.0 = 14.00\%$$
$$4.70\% + (14.00\% - 4.70\%) \times 1.5 = 18.65\%$$

The CAPM is calculated using various economic assumptions, some of which can be considered dubious from a practical point of view. These assumptions form the basis of what is known as the 'efficient market hypothesis' and include the following:

- Investors are rational, are risk averse and will assess securities on the basis of the expected return and standard deviation or variance of return.
- The market is perfect (shares go on a 'random walk') and there are no transaction costs.
- Investors will diversify away unique risk, so only market risk needs to be considered.

In his book *Where Genius Failed – The Rise and Fall of Long Term Capital Management* (Harper Collins, 2001), Roger Lowenstein describes how belief in the efficient market hypothesis led the managers of a fund with the name 'Long Term Capital Asset Management' to lose $3.6 billion. He quotes a senior US official and a US economist:

> Lawrence Summers, at the time a US Treasury Secretary, is quoted as saying, "the efficient market hypothesis is the most remarkable error in the history of economic theory" (p. 74).

> Robert J. Schiller, an American economist, agreed and dared to suggest that "markets were too volatile to fit the model of perfect markets" (p. 75).

For some academics, the thought that the efficient market hypothesis is not valid is simply too much to bear. Lowenstein describes 'how Eugene Fama, Scholes's thesis adviser, devoted the rest of his career to justifying the efficient market hypothesis' (p. 74) even though his own research into stock prices suggested otherwise (p. 71).

Many academics do, however, recognise the importance of human behaviour with regard to investment decisions and are trying to develop models that take account of this. However, they are currently outnumbered by the traditionalists, who argue that mixing finance with human behaviour is effectively mixing different disciplines. These academics argue, with valid reasoning, that models developed using invalid assumptions are better than having no model at all. A model that will give the correct answer 80% of the time must be better than being in the position where everything is unknown. Otherwise, they question: how can progress be ever made?

Such reasoning is, of course, perfectly sensible as long as it is appreciated that, with regard to projecting the future in respect of making investments in stocks and shares or other forms of gambling in markets buying and selling financial products, mathematical models are fallible. Occasionally they must give the wrong answer, and any investor having absolute faith that they will always give the right answer in the long term, like Long Term Capital Management, will risk losing everything. However, in perfect or near perfect markets, mathematical models will enable the gambler using such models to have a winning advantage.

In gambling terms, a perfect market is one where human nature cannot have an impact on the result, such as a spin of a coin, a roll of the dice, the spin of a wheel or a game of cards. In all these games, the gambler will win in the long term where the odds received on bets are greater than the true odds (i.e. the true probability) of an event happening and will lose in the long term where the odds, expressed as a probability, are lower than the true probability of an event happening. The simplest example is the spin of a coin where the probability of heads and tails coming up on any spin is 0.5. If a gambler was offered 6/4 against the chance of a head coming up on the next spin and in every subsequent spin thereafter, then in the long term he would be guaranteed to win. In this case, if the stake was £10, then the expected value (EV) would be:

EV = (Benefit of winning × probability of winning) − (Cost of losing
$\quad$ × probability of losing)
EV = (£15 × 0.5) − (£10 × 0.5) = £7.50 − £5.00 = £2.50

If there were to be 1000 spins of the coin, the expected winnings would be 1000 × £2.50 = £2500. This could be represented as:

500 winning bets, winning £15 = £7500, less 500 losing bets, losing £5000 = £2500.

Now, the EV simply suggests what is likely to happen, as heads could come up more than 500 times in 1000 spins and, of course, could come up less than 500 times. What is known is that the more times the coin is spun, the greater likelihood that the cumulative result will get closer to the probability.

In any game of cards where the full pack is used, the player who can remember the cards already played and therefore is able to calculate with a fair degree of accuracy the probability of which cards are about to come up will have a distinct advantage of playing against a player not having that ability. This is why some people can make a living playing cards on internet websites, while the majority of players will lose.

An example of a market that is as near to perfect as it is possible to get is the horserace betting market. The form of each horse, the rider and the trainer are known before the start of each race and can be ascertained very quickly by a click of a mouse at the appropriate website. In addition to this, as the market progresses, 'insider' knowledge, being up to date information known only to the connections of a particular horse, may become freely available. What can happen is that as horses are backed, their odds contract, while the odds are pushed out for those not being backed. In other words, by the off of the race, the market has reflected what is perceived to be the probability of each horse winning. Now, bookmakers make a profit by offering odds that are slightly worse than the true probabilities and accordingly, in the long term, they can expect to win.

The cornerstone of modern financial economic theory is that markets are perfect, but it is a simple matter to prove that imperfections in the market make this supposition unrealistic. For a start, the information available to the market place is very complex and is open to different interpretations. The notion that at any one time the market has priced in the information available to it about a particular share and that accordingly that share will go on a 'random walk', meaning that it is impossible to tell whether it should go up or down, is stretching the imagination. Is it really realistic to imagine that as a piece of information (such as a new set of accounts, or profit warning) hits the market, 'the market' assimilates it in an instant to arrive at a new 'correct' market price?

What happens is that as a piece of information comes in, the market will react, but not necessarily in a rational way. Chapter 4 will give actual examples where advantage could have been taken because 'the market' reacted to the headlines and had not fully studied the detail. The following example illustrates the point: If interest rates suddenly go up to 2%, the market will panic and downgrade everything, including companies sitting with millions in the bank who would likely benefit. Clearly, in this example, the market would correct the anomaly relatively quickly, nevertheless the quick witted would have had an opportunity.

In a perfect market, all players have identical information at the same time and can act upon it accordingly, but to suggest that this can happen in financial markets is again not realistic. An objective of this book is to show that by analysing published accounts, private investors can gain an advantage against the market as a whole. The reason for this is that in the same way that a small company can be more entrepreneurial than a large conglomerate company, private investors have the advantage of speed over fund managers who are often constrained by rules laid down by their employer.

But the real problem is that the financial information is not clear-cut. Even if it was believed that all investors have the same information available to them and act upon such information in unison, it will be open to interpretation, and with investors having different opinions, it all comes down to judgement. We know that some investors will be rational and risk averse, but we also know that others will act irrationally and take risks. But there is a further problem; what will be rational and risk averse to one investor might seem irrational and risky to another. When accounting for human nature, the wisest view to take with regard to the future is that anything can happen. Even where the market is in general agreement, it is not possible to forecast which event will force it into the panic mode with the effect that investors simply follow the crowd rather than act rationally.

What this means is that neither mathematic models based on economic financial theory nor an analysis of financial accounts can provide guaranteed results, but it is argued that the latter by trying to predict the better companies in the market as a whole has the advantage (if the analysis is correct) of *really* eliminating specific risk. Diversification does not, as it is said, '*diversify away* specific risk', rather it ensures that bad companies are mixed with good companies to achieve the market mean.

Nevertheless, the CAPM illustrates, correctly, that the expected return will increase as the perceived risks increases. However the 'expected return' should not be confused with the 'overall expected return'. It must be remembered that the return an investor can expect is the 'overall expected return' and NOT the 'expected return'.

The 'overall expected return' = 'Percentage of successful investments × expected return

The following table illustrates:

	Percentage of successful investments	Expected return	Overall expected return
Government bonds	100	4.7	4.7
Quoted companies	96	14.0	9.4
Unquoted investments (private equity)	80	40.0	12.0

Now, even the 'overall expected return' will not be accurate in the sense that actual is very unlikely to equal budget or forecast. Certainly, it is unlikely that for any given security, the expected return as calculated by the CAPM will equal the actual.

The CAPM is dependent upon the accuracy of the beta calculation for each stock, but how accurate this can be is debatable. The beta for each share is calculated by comparing its stock price with the market average over a significant length of time, but how much a share has moved because of the market and how much it has moved due to unique events within the company seem difficult to deduce. If it is assumed that the beta has to be correct and that any difference in total movement in a share price and that calculated due to the market is movement due to 'unique events', then the CAPM is a self-fulfilling prophesy.

For example (see Chapter 4 – The Experiment), Chaucer Holdings plc was selected as one of the four companies to be backed against a portfolio of 16 companies. On December 2006, this company's beta was quoted as 0.33, so (given the expected return of the market portfolio for FTSE Smallcap stocks is 17.5%) the expected return would be: $4.7\% + (17.5\% - 4.7\%) \times 0.33 = 8.92\%$.

The share started at 60 pence in 2006 and ended the year at 100 pence, and assuming dividends cover transaction costs, the actual return for the year was 66.67%. Of course, it could have gone the other way, the point being that when one is trying to predict the future, any formula you use requires a sprinkling of judgement.

Ordinary shares (new issues) are usually sold by companies at a different price than that shown on the share certificate. The price shown on the share certificate will be the 'par value' and the difference between this price and the actual selling price will be credited to the 'share premium account'. In the EIS example, with regard to the shares sold to the public, 0.1 pence would go to 'share capital' and 1.4 pence would go to 'share premium'. The cost of a share issue is usually debited to the share premium account.

Say, for example, a company issues 1 million ordinary shares of 10 pence for 75 pence and the cost of issuing the shares is £45 000, then the entries would be:

Debit 'cash received' £705 000 (£750 000 less £45 000)
Credit 'share capital' £100 000 (1 million shares at 10 pence)
Credit 'share premium' £605.000 (1 million shares at 65 pence = £650 000 less £45 000).

The cost of capital for ordinary shares of quoted companies will usually be in the range of 10%–25%, the actual rate being dependent upon the size of the company and its credit rating.

Preference shares

Preference shares are simply shares that take preference over ordinary shares. Preference shares are issued with a fixed coupon. For example, a company issuing 8% £1 preference shares would pay a dividend of 8 pence on every share each year, provided the company made sufficient profit to do so. If the company had to pass this dividend (not pay it), then the directors of the company would not be allowed to pay any dividend on the ordinary shares. No dividend can be declared on ordinary shares until the preference shareholders have been paid. Likewise, if the company had to be wound up, ordinary shareholders would not be entitled to receive a penny until the preference shareholders had been paid in full.

Cumulative preference shares

A company might have had a bad year and have been unable to pay the dividend due on its preference shares, and then follows a brilliant year allowing it to pay not only the preference dividend but also a bumper dividend on the ordinary shares. Not surprisingly, under such circumstances, preference shareholders are likely to feel miffed; so to avoid such a scenario, companies issue cumulative preference shares. This means that the preference shareholders must receive ALL the dividends due to them before ordinary shareholders could be paid. So, if a shareholder holding 6% £1 cumulative preference shares had not received a dividend for 2 years, in the third year he would have to receive a dividend of 18 pence per share, before an ordinary dividend could be declared.

Preference shares can also be varied to carry various entitlements or conditions:

9% Cumulative Redeemable Convertible preference shares:

- Shares are preference shares that carry a 9% fixed dividend.
- If the dividend is not paid in any year, the shareholder is entitled to be paid a double dividend in the following year, etc.
- Subject to the conditions set down at the time of issue, the company can redeem (buyback) the shares.
- The company can convert the preference shares into ordinary shares or debt, as determined by the conditions set at the time of the issue.

Debentures

Debentures are loan notes issued by companies that are secured against the assets of the business, usually in the form of a fixed and floating charge over all the assets. A debenture will usually be issued for a fixed term, with a coupon showing the fixed interest rate per annum. The interest rate payable will usually be a few percentage points over the base rates.

Bonds

Bonds are loan notes that are unsecured. In other words, the bond holder would be an ordinary creditor, rather than a preferential creditor if the company were wound up. Where companies have a good credit rating, the bonds are deemed to be investment-rated bonds, whereas companies have a poor credit rating, the bonds are known as junk bonds. Investment-rated bonds will pay interest at an annual percentage rate in single figures, while to attract investors to take risks, the annual interest rate for junk bonds will often be in double figures.

Loans

Debentures and bonds will be issued to individuals, whereas loans usually refer to money lent by banks. Banks will usually lend money this way if they are preference creditors by having a fixed and floating charge against the company's assets. The interest rate charged will vary from one-quarter of 1% above the bank base rate for large blue chip companies to four percentage points above the risk-free rate for smaller, riskier companies; so if the risk-free rate were 5%, a small company might have to pay 9% per annum for a loan. The objective for the owners of such businesses is to persuade the bank that they are not that risky as to be placed in this high-risk category. The loans are usually repaid over a fixed period in instalments, with instalments due every quarter, half-year or year, as determined by the agreement.

Bank overdraft

In addition to loans, bank will sometimes allow a firm's current account to be overdrawn. Bank overdrafts are not usually secured, so carry a much higher interest rate than for loans. This rate will be determined by negotiation.

Hire purchase

Companies that cannot offer sufficient security to be given a loan, or are deemed to be too risky for the banks to take on, often have to resort to hire purchase to acquire new assets. In this case, the lender having paid for the asset will be its legal owner and will 'hire' it to the company. There will be a clause in the agreement that when the company has repaid the principal in full, together with the cumulative interest, the company can purchase the asset for a nominal (very small) amount. The interest rate charged under hire purchase agreements is usually much higher than that charged for loans.

Debtor discounting/factoring

For companies unable to secure a bank overdraft and therefore unable to fund working capital, an alternative form of funding is debtor discounting or factoring. This is a very expensive option in that the lender buys the company's debtors at a heavily discounted rate. The discount demanded will take into account a very high interest rate, together with an amount to insure against bad debts. Companies can negotiate a slightly lower rate of discount if they take on bad debts themselves. Under such arrangements, the lender will pay the company for the invoice as it is issued, but will then demand repayment, plus interest, if they are unable to recover the money from the company's debtor after a set period of time.

Gearing

Gearing is simply the relationship between debt and equity, with debt being every source of capital, apart from ordinary shares, which is equity. The point about 'gearing' is that the higher it is (the percentage of debt compared to the percentage of equity) the higher is the risk. If a company had no gearing because all of its capital came from equity, then, provided losses in any one year did not force it to borrow, such losses would not, in themselves, be a concern. The company would not pay a dividend on the ordinary shares, but as there is no compulsion to do so, there is no problem.

On the other hand, if a company's capital largely came from debt, then the same losses would mean that the company would be unable to pay the interest on the debt and the company's creditors could, at their discretion, wind the company up. Of course, this extreme example is unlikely because a company in this position would be unable to obtain such a level of debt in the first place.

For large established companies that can acquire debt without a problem, one key decision that must be made is the level of gearing to be aimed at. In other words, what percentage of equity and what percentage of debt the company should aim at.

If a company required £1 million of capital and acquired this through having £400 000 of equity and £600 000 of debt, then gearing would be calculated as follows:

> The 'gearing percentage' (traditionally a UK measure) would be 60% (£600 000 of debt divided by total capital of £1 million).
>
> 'Debt to equity percentage' (traditionally a US measure) would be 150% (£600 000 of debt divided by equity of £400 000).

A company is said to be low geared if its gearing percentage is less than 50% or its debt to equity percentage is less than 100%, while a company is said to be high geared if its gearing percentage is greater than 50% or its debt to equity percentage is greater than 100%. Of course, gearing is all about getting the balance right between debt and equity and the optimum level will differ from company to company.

The weighted cost of capital

In theory, a company's cost of capital will be determined by its gearing or debt to equity percentage. Suppose, for example, the company (as above) had calculated that its cost of equity was 15% and its cost of debt was 7%, then its weighted cost of capital would be 10.2%, calculated:

$$
\begin{array}{ll}
£400\,000 \text{ at } 15\% = & £60\,000 \\
\underline{£600\,000 \text{ at } 7\%} \ = & \underline{£42\,000} \\
£1\,000\,000 & = \underline{£102\,000} = \underline{10.2\%}
\end{array}
$$

Now, given that debt costs less than equity, it must follow that a high geared company will have lower cost of capital than a low geared company, and this fact can impact investors' decision-making processes.

According to financial theory, a company should take on a project where the expected return from the project is greater than that of the company's cost of capital. This means that a high geared company might find a project with a low return acceptable, while a low geared company would need a higher return. The implication of this is that when an investor is reviewing a particular company with a view to making an investment, the investor must consider the risk relative to:

- that associated with the gearing percentage for the company being reviewed; and
- that associated with the project itself.

The main issue to be considered here is whether or not an individual company's cost of capital is the correct benchmark to be used, given the varying levels of risk associated with different levels of gearing, or whether the cost of capital to be used when assessing a project should be based on a fixed gearing percentage. In the latter case, risk would be assessed on the project itself as it would be assumed that all companies had the same gearing risk. In other words, the latter calculation would take away the benefit of having a lower cost of capital for being high geared on the grounds that being high geared carries a higher risk overall.

Case Study – Amanda's meeting her solicitor and his recommended financial adviser

Amanda was sat in her solicitor's office. Also present was the financial adviser from the firm of Accountants. The solicitor explained that many individuals and companies providing private equity had grown in financial stature in the 1980s and 1990s, and this had resulted in many private equity firms chasing larger deals. Accordingly, there had been fewer firms chasing smaller deals, but at least some of the slack had been taken up by successful entrepreneurs, turned business angels. It is to these business angels that he will turn to in order to get finance for Amanda's fledgling business.

Amanda was advised that when her business plan was complete, her solicitor would negotiate on her behalf with a business angel for equity and with a banker for debt. He would be accompanied by her financial adviser throughout these negotiations, but it had to be this way as both the business angel and the banker had to agree with the arrangements before the legal contracts could be drawn up. The financial adviser assured Amanda that no final decision would be taken without her approval.

Once these negotiations were complete, Amanda's solicitor would form a company, the new legal entity for the business, in which Amanda would be a director. He would arrange for the new legal entity, xxxyz Limited, to buy the assets from Amanda's business as a sole trader and would prepare all the legal documentation to account for these transactions. Finally, with agreement between her and her business angel, he would draw up her service agreement, or contract of employment.

The first part of the process for generating capital was to produce a business plan. The financial adviser explained that the finance section of this plan often meant that a plan Profit and Loss Account, plan Balance Sheet, and plan Cash Flow Statement had to be produced showing 5 years forward. The first year was shown by month or by quarter, thereafter years 2–5 would be shown by year.

The financial planning process

The first part of the financial planning process is to assess the amount of capital that is required to meet the objectives of the business. Firstly, the total amount of capital is computed; secondly, how much debt can be arranged is calculated, given the security the company can offer. The balance is the amount of equity that would be required.

The first step is to calculate sales (or turnover) and the costs associated with this turnover. The second step is to work out how much capital expenditure is needed and when it would be required.

The plan figures for sales would be broken down into sales by product, sales by customer, etc. Next, costs would be assessed in detail, listing items such as raw materials, salaries and wages, electricity, repairs, delivery costs, business rates, legal and accountancy costs, etc. Then, planned capital expenditure would be detailed and depreciation rates for each class of asset would be agreed. Figure 2.1 shows the base workings for Amanda's 5-year plan.

The following lines are where numbers have been inserted following deliberations as discussed in the above two paragraphs:

Line 10: Turnover – zero rated
Line 11: Turnover – standard rated
Line 16: Wages
Line 22: Cost of sales – existing products
Line 23: Cost of sales – new products

	E			G	H	I	J	L	M	M	O	P

Amanda — **Five Year Plan** — Base estimates for Earnings Statement and Balance Sheet

Line Number	Prior Year £		Qu 1 £	Qu 2 £	Qu 3 £	Qu 4 £	Year 1 £	Year 2 £	Year 3 £	Year 4 £	Year 5 £
		Calculation of VAT									
10	480,000	Turnover – zero rate	150,000	180,000	200,000	240,000	770,000	924,000	1,200,000	1,200,000	1,200,000
11	0	– standard rated			60,000	170,000	230,000	826,000	1,250,000	2,500,000	4,000,000
12	480,000	Total turnover	150,000	180,000	260,000	410,000	1,000,000	1,750,000	2,450,000	3,700,000	5,200,000
14	416,800	Purchases – zero rate	122,000	146,000	122,000	146,000	536,000	592,120	766,000	766,000	766,000
15	47,300	– standard rated	10,600	21,200	92,800	134,880	259,480	591,660	942,760	1,862,760	2,812,760
16	12,000	Wages	6,900	6,900	12,000	14,980	40,780	134,980	170,000	250,000	450,000
17	21,489	Depreciation and other non-VAT	1,145	1,146	17,396	17,397	37,084	68,472	67,731	165,988	165,658
18	497,589	Total costs	140,645	175,246	244,196	313,257	873,344	1,387,232	1,946,491	3,044,748	4,194,418
20	(17,589)	Profit/(loss) before interest	9,355	4,754	15,804	96,743	126,656	362,768	503,509	655,252	1,005,582
22	384,000	Cost of sales – existing	120,000	144,000	120,000	144,000	528,000	582,120	756,000	756,000	756,000
23	0	– new products			27,000	76,500	103,500	413,000	600,000	1,250,000	2,000,000
24	384,000		120,000	144,000	147,000	220,500	631,500	995,120	1,356,000	2,006,000	2,756,000
26	12,000	Cost of sales – wages	3,000	3,000	8,000	8,000	22,000	75,000	100,000	170,000	250,000
27	6,000	Cost of sales – rent	1,500	1,500	9,000	9,000	21,000	36,000	36,000	60,000	60,000
28	239	Cost of sales – other	0	4,000	4,000	4,000	12,000	0	0	0	0
29	18,239		4,500	8,500	21,000	21,000	55,000	111,000	136,000	230,000	310,000
31	402,239	Total 'cost of sales'	124,500	152,500	168,000	241,500	686,500	1,106,120	1,492,000	2,236,000	3,066,000
33	18,500	Distribution costs	5,000	7,200	13,000	20,500	45,700	87,500	200,000	364,000	532,000
34	43,600	Administration costs	10,000	14,400	20,800	33,860	79,060	125,140	186,760	278,760	430,760
35	6,250	Depreciation	1,145	1,146	17,396	17,397	37,084	68,472	67,731	165,988	165,658
37	68,350	Total distrbution & administration	16,145	22,746	51,196	71,757	161,844	281,112	454,491	808,748	1,128,418
40	9,411	Operating profit/(loss)	9,355	4,754	40,804	96,743	151,656	362,768	503,509	655,252	1,005,582
42	27,000	Exceptional items	0	0	25,000	0	25,000	0	0	0	0
44	(17,589)	Profit/(loss) before interes	9,355	4,754	15,804	96,743	126,656	362,768	503,509	655,252	1,005,582
46		Capital expenditure			650,000		650,000			1,000,000	
48	5,000	Van – depreciation (3 yr reducing balance)	833	833	834	834	3,334	2,222	1,481	988	658
49	1,250	Fix. & Fittings – depr. (4 year straight line)	312	313	312	313	1,250	1,250	1,250	0	0
50	0	New assets – depr. (10 year straight line)			16,250	16,250	32,500	65,000	65,000	165,000	165,000
52		Output VAT	0	0	10,500	29,750	40,250	144,550	218,750	437,500	700,000
53		Input VAT – purchases (exenses)	1,855	3,710	16,240	23,604	45,409	103,541	164,983	325,983	492,233
54		Input VAT (Capital expenditure)	0	0	113,750	0	113,750	0	0	175,000	0
56		Due to (from) Customs & Revenue	(1,855)	(3,710)	(119,490)	6,146	(118,909)	41,009	53,767	(63,483)	207,767

Figure 2.1   Case study – Amanda – 5-year plan – base estimates

Line 26: Cost of sales – wages

Line 27: Cost of sales – rent

Line 28: Cost of sales – other

Line 33: Distribution costs

Line 34: Administration costs

Line 42: Exceptional items – the figure of £25 000 is the estimated cost for buying out the 5-year purchasing contract with Zehin Foods plc.

Line 46: Capital expenditure

Line 48: Depreciation on the van, calculated as 33.33% per annum on a reducing balance basis

Line 49: Depreciation on fixtures and fittings, calculated as 25% per annum on a straight line basis

Line 50: Depreciation on the new assets, calculated as 10% per annum on a straight line basis

Other rows in Figure 2.1, are calculated using a formula, as below:

With regard to all the formula shown, the following applies:

An 'asterisk' means 'multiply', so $* = \times =$ multiply.

A 'forward slash' means 'divide', so $/ = \div =$ divide.

A 'dot' means 'add together' the full range, i.e. sum(J11.J13) would mean $J11 + J12 + J13$.

Where a cell has to be equal to another, the $=$ symbol is used. For example, Line 131 in column G must equal line 142 in column G, the script would say:

Line 131:

Column G $=$ G142.

In this case, the formula that would go into cell G131 would be: $=$ G142.

With regard to the above line numbers, an amount has been inserted in every column, except column L. In every case, column L can be calculated as the sum of columns G through J. So, for example:

L10 $=$ sum(G10.J10)

L11 $=$ sum(G11.J11)

With regard to lines that are computed by formulae, rather than by inserting a number, column L can be calculated by using either the formula above or any of the formulae below.

Line 12: On each column it is the sum of line 10 and line 11, so:

Column G $=$ G10 + G11 and column H $=$ H10 + h11, etc.

Line 14: For each of the four quarters, $=$ column on line 22 + £2000 (estimating quarterly zero-rated supplies other than food to be £2000) and from year 2 $=$ column on line 22 + £10 000, so:

Column G $=$ G22 + £2000.

Column H $=$ H22 + £2000

Column I $=$ I22 + £2000

Column J $=$ J22 + £2000

Column L $=$ sum(G14.J14)

Column M $=$ M22 + £10 000

Column N $=$ N22 + £10 000, etc.

Line 15: Each column is calculated by using the same formula, so:
  Column $G = G18 - sum(G14 + G16 + G17)$
  Column $H = H18 - sum(H14 + H16 + H17)$, etc.
Line 17: Each column is calculated by taking the sum of lines 48–50, so:
  Column $G = sum(G48.G50)$
  Column $H = sum(H48.H50)$, etc.
Line 18: Each column is calculated by using the same formula, so:
  Column $G = G12 - G44$
  Column $H = H12 - H44$, etc.
Line 20: Each column is calculated by using the same formula, so:
  Column $G = G12 - G18$
  Column $H = H12 - H18$, etc.
Line 24: Each column is calculated using the same formula, so:
  Column $G = G22 + G23$
  Column $H = H22 + H23$, etc.
Line 29: Each column is calculated using the same formula, so:
  Column $G = sum(G26.G28)$
  Column $H = sum(H26.H28)$, etc.
Line 31: Each column is calculated using the same formula, so:
  Column $G = G24 + G29$
  Column $H = H24 + H29$, etc.
Line 35: Each column is calculated using the same formula, so:
  Column $G = G17$
  Column $H = H17$, etc.
Line 37: Each column is calculated using the same formula, so:
  Column $G = sum(G33.G35)$
  Column $H = sum(H33.H35)$
Line 40: Each column is calculated using the same formula, so:
  Column $G = G12 - sum(G31 + G37)$
  Column $H = H12 - sum(H31 + H37)$
Line 44: Each column is calculated using the same formula, so:
  Column $G = G40 - G42$
  Column $H = H40 - H42$, etc.
Line 52: Each column is calculated using the same formula, so:
  Column $G = + round((G11 * 0.175), 0)$
  Column $H = + round((H11 * 0.175), 0)$
  Column $I = + round((I11 * 0.175), 0)$
  etc.

Line 53: Each column is calculated using the same formula, so:

Column G = +round((G15 ∗ 0.175),0)

Column H = +round((H15 ∗ 0.175),0)

Column I = +round((I15 ∗ 0.175),0)

etc.

Line 54: Each column is calculated using the same formula, so:

Column G = +round((G46 ∗ 0.175),0)

Column H = +round((H46 ∗ 0.175),0)

Column I = +round((I46 ∗ 0.175),0)

etc.

Line 56: Each column is calculated using the same formula, so:

Column G = G52 − sum(G53+G54)

Column H = H52 − sum(H53+H54)

Column I = I52 − sum(I53+I54)

etc.

Having completed the above workings, with the exception of inserting the figure for 'intangible assets' into the Balance Sheet and inserting stock, debtor and creditor days into the spreadsheet, the 5-year plan for the Earnings Statement and Balance Sheet can be completed totally by using formulae.

Figure 2.2 shows the 5-year plan Earnings Statement. The formulae for Figure 2.2 are shown below. Throughout the 5-year plan Earnings Statement, each column is calculated using the same formula:

Line 68: = G12, H12, etc.

Line 70: = G31, H31, etc.

Line 72: = G68 − G70, H68 − H70, etc.

Line 74: = G33, H33, etc.

Line 75: = G34 + G35, H34 + H35, etc.

Line 77: = G72 − sum(G74+G75), H72 − sum(H74+H75)

Line 79: = G42, H42, etc.

Line 81: = G77 − G79, H77 − H79, etc.

Line 83: = G161, H161, etc.

Line 85: = G81 − G83, H81 − H83, etc.

Line 87: = G85 ∗ 0.25, H85 ∗ 0.25, etc.

E											

Amanda Five Year Plan Earnings Statement (Prior to equity investment)

Line Number		G	H	I	J		L	M	N	O	P
		Qu 1 £	Qu 2 £	Qu 3 £	Qu 4 £		Year 1 £	Year 2 £	Year 3 £	Year 4 £	Year 5 £
68	Turnover	150,000	180,000	260,000	410,000		1,000,000	1,750,000	2,450,000	3,700,000	5,200,000
70	Cost of sales	124,500	152,500	168,000	241,500		686,500	1,106,120	1,492,000	2,236,000	3,066,000
72	Gross profit	25,500	27,500	92,000	168,500		313,500	643,880	958,000	1,464,000	2,134,000
74	Distribution	5,000	7,200	13,000	20,500		45,700	87,500	200,000	364,000	532,000
75	Administration	11,145	15,546	38,196	51,257		116,144	193,612	254,491	444,748	596,418
77	Operating profit before Exceptional item	9,355	4,754	40,804	96,743		151,656	362,768	503,509	655,252	1,005,582
79	Exceptional items	0	0	25,000	0		25,000	0	0	0	0
81	Operating profit after Exceptional item	9,355	4,754	15,804	96,743		126,656	362,768	503,509	655,252	1,005,582
83	Interest	2,330	1,782	2,075	11,924		18,111	53,508	51,311	55,748	117,830
85	Profit/(loss) before tax	7,025	2,972	13,729	84,819		108,545	309,260	452,198	599,504	887,752
87	Corporation tax	1,756	743	3,432	21,205		27,136	77,315	113,050	149,876	221,938
89	Earnings	5,269	2,229	10,297	63,614		81,409	231,945	339,149	449,628	665,814
91	Preference dividend										
93	Earnings available to equity holders	5,269	2,229	10,297	63,614		81,409	231,945	339,149	449,628	665,814

Figure 2.2 Case study – Amanda – 5-year plan – Earnings Statement (prior to equity investment)

95

Corporation tax has been calculated by charging the small company with the rate of 25% against net profit, or profit before tax. This will be inaccurate for a number of reasons, including the following:

(1) In later years, the full tax rate of 30% (note that this rate can change from one year to the next) would apply.
(2) Depreciation is not allowed for corporation tax purposes. Instead capital allowances at the rate of 25% per annum on a reducing balance basis are usually allowed, although this rate can be higher in certain circumstances.
(3) Certain expenditure, such as entertainment, is not allowed for corporation tax purposes.

The point is that to compute corporation tax accurately, it is necessary to carry out what can be complex computations. All we are doing here is preparing a 5-year plan with the idea of providing potential lenders with an overview of the business so that they can make a decision whether or not to become involved with the company.

Any potential lender reading this plan would realise that if profitability were better than forecast, then the actual cash available to the company would be different from that shown.

Line 89: = G85 − G87, H85 − H87, etc.
Line 91: Will be zero in all columns, but this will change later when the investment structure has been worked out (see Figure 2.5).
Line 93: = G89 − G91, H89 − H91, etc.

Figure 2.3 shows the 5-year plan Balance Sheet. The formulae for Figure 2.3 are shown below:

Column E is taken from Amanda's actual result as shown in Chapter 1. Where totals appear between two lines, the formula for column E is the same as that for every other column.
Line 106: The figure in each column is £25 000 and this is the valuation of the salad dressing recipe. In practice, the value of this intangible asset would be assessed every year.
Line 108:
Column G = E108 + G46
Column H = G108 + H46
Column I = H108 + I46
Column J = I108 + J46

Amanda

Five Year Plan Balance Sheet (prior to equity investment)

Line Number	Days		Prior Year £	Qu 1 £	Qu 2 £	Qu 3 £	Qu 4 £	Year 1 £	Year 2 £	Year 3 £	Year 4 £	Year 5 £
			(E)	(G)	(H)	(I)	(J)	(L)	(M)	(N)	(O)	(P)
106		Intangible Assets	25,000	25,000	25,000	25,000	25,000	25,000	25,000	25,000	25,000	25,000
108		Tangible assets	20,000	20,000	20,000	670,000	670,000	670,000	670,000	670,000	1,670,000	1,670,000
109		Depreciation to date	6,250	7,395	8,541	25,937	43,334	43,334	111,806	179,537	345,525	511,183
110		Net tangible assets	13,750	12,605	11,459	644,063	626,666	626,666	558,194	490,463	1,324,475	1,158,817
112		Total net fixed assets	38,750	37,605	36,459	669,063	651,666	651,666	583,194	515,463	1,349,475	1,183,817
114	20	Stock	95,761	33,425	36,822	52,932	60,609	60,609	81,753	122,521	168,000	193,200
115	60	Debtors	118,500	98,630	118,356	177,863	289,151	289,151	311,433	438,699	680,137	969,863
116		Cash at bank	220	(33,610)	(71,706)	(846,610)	(188,296)	(188,296)	206,201	502,870	30,851	1,563,023
117		Total current assets	214,481	98,445	83,472	(615,815)	161,464	161,464	599,387	1,064,090	878,988	2,726,086
119	30	Creditors	43,200	44,204	56,190	75,958	100,104	100,104	105,807	154,006	242,856	334,602
120		VAT	(2,380)	(1,855)	(3,710)	(119,490)	6,146	6,146	10,252	13,442	27,879	51,942
121		Corporation tax	0	1,756	2,499	5,932	27,136	27,136	77,315	113,050	149,876	221,938
		Dividends	0	0	0	0	0	0	0	0	0	0
123		Total current liabilities	40,820	44,105	54,979	(37,601)	133,386	133,386	193,374	280,498	420,611	608,482
125		Net current assets/(liabilities)	173,661	54,339	28,493	(573,214)	28,078	28,078	406,013	783,593	458,377	2,117,604
128		Total assets less current liabilities	212,411	91,944	64,952	93,849	679,744	679,744	989,207	1,299,056	1,807,852	3,301,421
130		Less: long term loans	200,000	124,265	95,043	113,643	635,924	635,924	713,442	684,143	743,311	1,571,066
131		Total net assets	12,411	(32,320)	(30,091)	(19,795)	43,820	43,820	275,765	614,913	1,064,541	1,730,355
134		Share capital	50,000									
135		Share premium account										
137		Capital reserves										
138		Retained earnings	(37,589)	(32,320)	(30,091)	(19,795)	43,820	43,820	275,765	614,913	1,064,541	1,730,355
139		Total net capital	12,411	(32,320)	(30,091)	(19,795)	43,820	43,820	275,765	614,913	1,064,541	1,730,355
141		Preference shares	0									
142		Total equity	12,411	(32,320)	(30,091)	(19,795)	43,820	43,820	275,765	614,913	1,064,541	1,730,355

Figure 2.3 Case study – Amanda – 5-year plan – Balance Sheet (prior to equity investment)

    Column L = J108
    Column M = J108 + M46
    Column N = M108 + N46
    Column O = N108 + O46
    Column P = O108 + P46

Line 109:

    Column G = E109 + G35
    Column H = G109 + H35
    Column I = H109 + I35
    Column J = I109 + J35
    Column L = J109
    Column M = L109 + M35
    Column N = M109 + N35
    Column O = N109 + O35
    Column P = O109 + P35

Line 110: G = G108 − G109, H = H108 − H109, etc.

Line 112: G = G106 + G110, H = H106 + H110, etc.

Line 114: The '20' in column D represents the number of stock days it is envisaged the company will have at any one time.

    Column G = round(((((1/365) * (H70 * 4)) * D114),0)
    Column H = round(((((1/365) * (I70 * 4)) * D114),0)
    Column I = round(((((1/365) * (J70 * 4)) * D114),0)
    Column J = round(((((1/365) * (M70 * 1)) * D114),0)
    Column L = J114
    Column M = round(((((1/365) * (N70 * 1)) * D114),0)
    Column N = round(((((1/365) * (O70 * 1)) * D114),0)
    Column O = round(((((1/365) * (P70 * 1)) * D114),0)
    Column P = O114 * 1.15

Stock days are calculated on estimated future cost of sales, rather than on historical cost of sales, as the concept is to assess how much stock is needed to meet future demand. For this reason, it is impossible to calculate the stock for year 5. Accordingly, the figure in the plan is simply the best guess.

Line 115: The '60' in column D represents the number of debtor days it is envisaged the company will have at any one time.

    Column G = round(((((1/365) * ((G12 + G52) * 4)) * D115),0)
    Column H = round(((((1/365) * ((H12 + H52) * 4)) * D115),0)

Column I = round(((((1/365) * ((I12 + I52) * 4)) * D115),0)
Column J = round(((((1/365) * ((J12 + J52) * 4)) * D115),0)
Column L = J115
Column M = round(((((1/365) * ((M12 + M52) * 1)) * D115),0)
Column N = round(((((1/365) * ((N12 + N52) * 1)) * D115),0)
Column O = round(((((1/365) * ((O12 + O52) * 1)) * D115),0)
Column P = round(((((1/365) * ((P12 + P52) * 1)) * D115),0)

Line 116:
Column G = G117 − sum(G114 + G115)
Column H = H117 − sum(H114 + H115)
etc.

Line 117:
Column G = G123 + G125
Column H = H123 + H125
etc.

Line 119: The '30' in column D represents the number of creditor days it is envisaged the company will have at any one time.
Column G = round(((((1/365) * ((G14 + G15 + G53) * 4)) * D119),0)
Column H = round(((((1/365) * ((H14 + H15 + H53) * 4)) * D119),0)
Column I = round(((((1/365) * ((I14 + I15 + I53) * 4)) * D119),0)
Column J = round(((((1/365) * ((J14 + J15 + J53) * 4)) * D119),0)
Column L = J119
Column M = round(((((1/365) * ((M14 + M15 + M53) * 1)) * D119),0)
Column N = round(((((1/365) * ((N14 + N15 + N53) * 1)) * D119),0)
Column O = round(((((1/365) * ((O14 + O15 + O53) * 1)) * D119),0)
Column P = round(((((1.365) * ((P14 + P15 + P53) * 1)) * D119),0)

Line 120: It is assumed in this plan that VAT is paid (or rebated) quarterly in arrears, so that VAT for January/February/March would be settled in April and VAT for April/May/June would be settled in July, etc.
Column G = G56
Column H = H56
Column I = I56
Column J = J56
Column L = J120
Column M = round((((M52 − M53)/4),0)
Column N = round((((N52 − N53)/4),0)
Column O = round((((O52 − O53)/4),0)
Column P = round((((P52 − P53)/4),0)

Line 121: When Amanda's business is taken over, it is possible that arrangements would be made to transfer the taxable losses to the new business so that losses in Amanda's first year could be offset against profits in the second year. However, this plan does not allow for this complication for the same reasons as before (see line 87). It is assumed that corporation tax is paid annually in arrears.

Column G = G87

Column H = G87 + H87

Column I = sum(G87.I87)

Column J = sum(G87.J87)

Column L = J121

Column M = M87

Column N = N87

Column O = O87

Column P = P87

Line 122: Not shown in Figure 2.3, because at this stage there are no dividends.

Line 123:

Column G = sum(G119.G122)

Column H = sum(H119.H122)

etc.

Line 125:

Column G = G128 − G112

Column H = H128 − H112

etc.

Line 128:

Column G = G130 + G131

Column H = H130 + H131

etc.

Line 130: The loans available in any one month are based on the asset backing available at the prior month.

Column G = E159

Column H = G159

Column I = H159

Column J = I159

Column L = J130

Column M = L159

Column N = M159
Column O = N159
Column P = O159
Line 131:
    Column G = G142
    Column H = H142
    etc.
Line 138:
    Column G = E138 + G93
    Column H = G138 + H93
    Column I = H138 + I93
    Column J = I138 + J93
    Column L = J138
    Column M = L138 + M93
    Column N = M138 + N93
    Column O = N138 + O93
    Column P = O138 + P93
Line 142:
    Column G = G139 − G141
    Column H = H139 − H141
    etc.

Figure 2.4 shows the calculation of the availability of loan. The amount that can be borrowed in the form of a loan will be dependent upon negotiations with banks. Usually, banks will require some form of security and how much they will lend against such security will again be subject to negotiation. As discussed in Chapter 1, it is never wise to give a bank a personal guarantee, nor is it sensible to offer security against personal assets, such as a house. Accordingly, the usual form of security is to offer the bank a fixed and floating charge against the assets of the business.

Each case will differ from the next, but Amanda's 5-year plan is put together on the basis that the amount the bank will lend will be equal to:

75% of net tangible assets +
80% of debtors +
20% of stock

	G	H	I	J		L	M	N	O	P
Amanda										
					Five Year Balance Sheet – Calculation of loans and interest (prior to equity investment)					
	Qu 1	Qu 2	Qu 3	Qu 4		Year 1	Year 2	Year 3	Year 4	Year 5
	£	£	£	£		£	£	£	£	£
Line Number	Prior Year £									
	Calculation of availability of loan									
156	10,313 75% of net tangible assets	9,454	8,594	483,047	470,000		470,000	418,646	367,847	993,356	869,113
157	94,800 80% of debtors	78,904	94,685	142,290	231,321		231,321	249,146	350,959	544,110	775,890
158	19,152 20% of stock	6,685	7,364	10,586	12,122		12,122	16,351	24,504	33,600	38,640
159	124,265	95,043	110,643	635,924	713,442		713,442	684,143	743,311	1,571,066	1,683,643
161	Interest	2,330	1,782	2,075	11,924		18,111	53,508	51,311	55,748	117,830

Figure 2.4 Case study – Amanda – 5-year plan – calculation of loans and interest (prior to equity investment)

The formulae for Figure 2.4, are as follows:

Line 156:
 Column G = G110 * 0.75
 Column H = H110 * 0.75
 etc.

Line 157:
 Column G = G115 * 0.8
 Column H = H115 * 0.8
 etc.

Line 158:
 Column G = G114 * 0.2
 Column H = H114 * 0.2
 etc.

Line 159:
 Column G = sum(G156.G158)
 Column H = sum(H156.H158)
 etc.

Line 161: As with line 130, it is assumed that the maximum loan available is based on the prior month's security. The interest rate charged would be subject to negotiation and would vary from one deal to the next, but it is assumed for this plan that Amanda and her advisers have agreed an annual interest rate of 7.5%.

 Column G = round(((E159 * 0.075/4)),0)
 Column H = round(((G159 * 0.075)/4)),0)
 Column I = round(((H159 * 0.075)/4)),0)
 Column J = round(((I159 * 0.075)/4)),0)
 Column L = sum(G161.J161)
 Column M = round((L159 * 0.075),0)
 Column N = round((M159 * 0.075),0)
 Column O = round((N159 * 0.075),0)
 Column P = round((O159 * 0.075),0)

Case study – Amanda – the deal structure

Amanda and her advisers have, at this stage, prepared the following:

(1) A 5-year plan Earnings Statement; and
(2) A 5-year plan Balance Sheet.

The amount of debt that will be available to the new business has also been established.

The next step is to look along the 'cash at bank' line (line 116) in Figure 2.3. By looking across at each column, we are looking for the column with the biggest overdraft figure. This will tell us how much equity, net of costs, we must raise to allow us to meet the objectives set in the plan.

Amanda's advisers told her that she would need to raise roughly £1 million and the costs associated with raising this money would equate roughly to 15% of the amount raised. This sum would cover all legal and accountancy costs associated with the deal.

Amanda's solicitor confirmed, what he had told her before, that the amount she required was too small for most venture capital firms that were focusing on much larger deals. He knew of many business angels who would be willing to invest the amount she needed, but the problem was that they would likely want to be heavily involved in the business and to be in the position to control it. This meant that they would likely want more than 75% of the equity.

If the share of the business that each party owned was based solely on the capital put in, then Amanda would only own a very small proportion of the new business. Clearly, at this level of ownership, she would have little incentive to carry on. However, her solicitor explained to her that she had been very lucky. He had found a seriously rich business angel from an oil-producing country who ran his affairs as if he were a venture capital firm. He employed experts in particular industries and these experts were appointed non-executive Chairman in the company in which he made an investment. In addition, his view was that the entrepreneurs who achieved high returns for him should be aptly rewarded. On the other hand, he was wary of making investments where the entrepreneur lacked total commitment to make the venture a success. To achieve both these ends, all his investments involved the use of a deal structure.

Amanda had told her solicitor that by taking into account the net worth of her business and additional borrowing she could raise, she could put £40 000 into this business. On the basis of this he had agreed with the business angel:

- The assets and liabilities of Amanda's original business would be transferred to the new company and the new company would pay Amanda the net worth of her business.

- The business angel would appoint a part-time non-executive chairman who would help her to grow the business. The salary of this non-executive chairman would be paid by the company.
- Amanda would be appointed Managing Director (an executive position) of the new company at a salary to be agreed.
- The deal would be structured financially, as below.

Amanda was advised that she should discuss this deal structure with her financial adviser so that she fully understood it and provided she agreed her solicitor would go ahead and draw up the legal documents.

All deal structures are different and subject to individual negotiation, but in each case the objectives remain the same:

(1) To offer the entrepreneur the incentive to work hard in the business, so that the investor gets a good return.
(2) To protect the investor in the event that the business does not proceed as planned for whatever reason.

The deal structure

The parties agreed that to prevent the business from coming under financial pressure early on, the loan would be reduced to £100 000 in the first year. Thereafter, it was to be reduced as cash flow would allow. The planned borrowings were calculated as shown in Figure 2.7. It was agreed that the remaining capital would be structured as below:

	Amanda	Business angel	Total
	£	£	£
25 pence ordinary shares (for £1)	10 000	15 000	25 000
10% £1 Cumulative redeemable preference shares		800 000	800 000
25 pence Convertible redeemable preference shares (for £1)		35 000	35 000
Share premium on ordinary shares	30 000	45 000	75 000
Share premium on convertible shares		105 000	105 000
Total provided by investors	40 000	1 000 000	1 040 000

Under this deal structure, Amanda owns 40% of the business for putting in just 3.8% of the capital, but there is a catch. She will achieve this objective only if everything goes according to plan. The terms of the deal structure are as follows:

- The cumulative redeemable preference shares can be redeemed in four equal instalments, provided the company has sufficient funds to do this, from the end of year two onwards.
- If by the end of year five any of the cumulative redeemable preference shares remain unredeemed, then all of the convertible redeemable preference shares will be converted to ordinary shares on a one-for-one basis.
- Provided all the cumulative redeemable preference shares have been redeemed at the end of year five, the parties should agree that they will make arrangements to sell the business within the following 12 months. The convertible redeemable preference shares will be redeemed at the rate of 2.8% of the gross selling price and any remaining shares of this class unredeemed will be converted to ordinary shares.

The effect of this deal structure can be worked out in advance, as the following two examples illustrate:

(1) All the cumulative redeemable preference shares are redeemed and the business is sold for £4 million during the year six.
112 000 of the convertible redeemable preference shares are redeemed, leaving 28 000 shares to be converted to ordinary shares.

	Amanda	Business angel	Total
Number of ordinary shares	40 000	88 000	128 000
%	31.25	68.75	100.00

(2) Things do not go as planned and only 600 000 of the cumulative redeemable preference shares are redeemed at the end of year five.
The business angel's 140 000 convertible redeemable preference shares are converted to ordinary shares, so that the percentage owned by each party is:

	Amanda	Business angel	Total
Number of ordinary shares	40 000	200 000	240 000
%	16.67	83.33	100.00

In addition, the business angel is a priority creditor in that the interest due to date on the remaining 200 000 cumulative redeemable preference shares will have to be paid and they will also have to be redeemed in full before the business can be sold and the net proceeds shared out.

(3) Things go really badly and none of the redeemable preference shares are redeemed at the end of year five.

The business angel's 140 000 convertible redeemable preference shares are converted to ordinary shares, so that the percentage owned by each party is:

	Amanda	Business angel	Total
Number of ordinary shares	40 000	200 000	240 000
%	16.67	83.33	100.00

In these circumstances, it is likely that the business would not be worth much and what value there was would go to the priority creditors. In this case, Amanda's shares would probably be worthless.

However, the business plan assumes that the business is successful and that the redeemable convertible preference shares will be redeemed in full by the end of year five. Based on this capital structure, the 5-year plan is revised. This is shown in Figures 2.5 and 2.6.

The actual cost of raising the capital is £165 000 and the bottom block of the Balance Sheet (Figure 2.6) is put together on the following basis:

	£	£
100 000 ordinary shares of 25 pence each		25 000
800 000 cumulative redeemable preference shares of £1		800 000
140 000 cumulative redeemable convertible preference shares of 25 pence		35 000
Share premium on ordinary shares		75 000
Share premium on convertible shares		105 000
		180 000
Less: cost of raising capital		165 000
Share premium account (net)		15 000

E										

Five Year Plan

Amanda — Earnings Statement

Line Number		Qu 1 £	Qu 2 £	Qu 3 £	Qu 4 £	Year 1 £	Year 2 £	Year 3 £	Year 4 £	Year 5 £
68	Turnover	150,000	180,000	260,000	410,000	1,000,000	1,750,000	2,450,000	3,700,000	5,200,000
70	Cost of sales	124,500	152,500	168,000	241,500	686,500	1,106,120	1,492,000	2,236,000	3,066,000
72	Gross profit	25,500	27,500	92,000	168,500	313,500	643,880	958,000	1,464,000	2,134,000
74	Distribution	5,000	7,200	13,000	20,500	45,700	87,500	200,000	364,000	532,000
75	Administration	11,145	15,546	38,196	51,257	116,144	193,612	254,491	444,748	596,418
77	Operating profit before Exceptional items	9,355	4,754	40,804	96,743	151,656	362,768	503,509	655,252	1,005,582
79	Exceptional items	0	0	25,000	0	25,000	0	0	0	0
81	Operating profit after Exceptional items	9,355	4,754	15,804	96,743	126,656	362,768	503,509	655,252	1,005,582
83	Interest	1,875	1,875	1,875	1,875	7,500	0	3,750	30,000	3,750
85	Profit/(loss) before tax	7,480	2,879	13,929	94,868	119,156	362,768	499,759	625,252	1,001,832
87	Corporation tax	1,870	720	3,482	23,717	29,789	90,692	124,940	156,313	250,458
89	Earnings	5,610	2,159	10,447	71,151	89,367	272,076	374,819	468,939	751,374
91	Preference dividend	0	0	0	8,000	8,000	8,000	6,000	4,000	2,000
93	Earnings available to equity holders	5,610	2,159	10,447	63,151	81,367	264,076	368,819	464,939	749,374

Figure 2.5 Case study – Amanda – 5-year plan – Earnings Statement

Amanda Five Year Plan

Balance Sheet

Line Number	Description	Days	Prior Year £	Qu 1 £	Qu 2 £	Qu 3 £	Qu 4 £	Year 1 £	Year 2 £	Year 3 £	Year 4 £	Year 5 £
106	Intangible Assets		25,000	25,000	25,000	25,000	25,000	25,000	25,000	25,000	25,000	25,000
108	Tangible assets		20,000	20,000	20,000	670,000	670,000	670,000	670,000	670,000	1,670,000	1,670,000
109	Depreciation to date		6,250	7,395	8,541	25,937	43,334	43,334	111,806	179,537	345,525	511,183
110	Net tangible assets		13,750	12,605	11,459	644,063	626,666	626,666	558,194	490,463	1,324,475	1,158,817
112	Total net fixed assets		38,750	37,605	36,459	669,063	651,666	651,666	583,194	515,463	1,349,475	1,183,817
114	Stock	20	95,761	33,425	36,822	52,932	60,609	60,609	81,753	122,521	168,000	193,200
115	Debtors	60	118,500	98,630	118,356	177,863	289,151	289,151	311,433	438,699	680,137	969,863
116	Cash at bank		220	817,580	808,613	18,309	161,391	161,391	221,225	423,378	50,048	273,108
117	Total current assets		214,481	949,635	963,791	249,104	511,151	511,151	614,411	984,598	898,185	1,436,171
119	Creditors	30	43,200	44,204	56,190	75,958	100,104	100,104	105,807	154,006	242,856	334,602
120	VAT		(2,380)	(1,855)	(3,710)	(119,490)	6,146	6,146	10,252	13,442	27,879	51,942
121	Corporation tax		0	1,870	2,590	6,072	29,789	29,789	90,692	124,940	156,313	250,458
122	Dividends		0	0	0	0	8,000	8,000	8,000	6,000	4,000	2,000
123	Total current liabilities		40,820	44,219	55,070	(37,460)	144,039	144,039	214,751	298,388	431,048	639,002
125	Net current assets/(liabilities)		173,661	905,416	908,721	286,564	367,112	367,112	399,660	686,210	467,137	797,169
128	Total assets less current liabilities		212,411	943,021	945,180	955,627	1,018,778	1,018,778	982,854	1,201,673	1,816,612	1,980,986
130	Less: long term loans		200,000	100,000	100,000	100,000	100,000	100,000	0	50,000	400,000	50,000
131	Total net assets		12,411	843,021	845,180	855,627	918,778	918,778	982,854	1,151,673	1,416,612	1,930,986
134	Share capital – Ordinary shares of 25p		50,000	25,000	25,000	25,000	25,000	25,000	25,000	25,000	25,000	25,000
135	Share premium account			15,000	15,000	15,000	15,000	15,000	15,000	15,000	15,000	15,000
136	10% £1 Cumulative Redeemable preference shares			800,000	800,000	800,000	800,000	800,000	600,000	400,000	200,000	0
137	Convertible Redeemable preference shares											
138	Capital reserves			35,000	35,000	35,000	35,000	35,000	35,000	35,000	35,000	0
139	Retained earnings		(37,589)	(31,979)	(29,820)	(19,373)	43,778	43,778	307,854	676,673	1,141,612	1,890,986
140	Total liabilities		12,411	843,021	845,180	855,627	918,778	918,778	982,854	1,151,673	1,416,612	1,930,986
142	Preference shares		0	835,000	835,000	835,000	835,000	835,000	635,000	435,000	235,000	0
143	Total equity		12,411	8,021	10,180	20,627	83,778	83,778	347,854	716,673	1,181,612	1,930,986

Figure 2.6 Case study – Amanda – 5-year plan – Balance Sheet

Figures 2.1 (base workings), 2.2 (earnings statement), 2.3 (Balance Sheet) and 2.4 (calculation of the availability of loan) are copied across into the next block.

If the base workings remain unchanged, then:

Figure 2.2 becomes Figure 2.5.
Figure 2.3 becomes Figure 2.6.
Figure 2.4 becomes Figure 2.7.

The formulae for Figure 2.5 are the same as that for Figure 2.2, except that line 83 is taken from line 66 (not line 161). Figure 2.5 is completed by inserting the preference dividend based on the deal structure.

The formulae for Figure 2.6 are the same as that for Figure 2.3. Figure 2.6 is completed by inserting the share capital and the share premium as per the deal structure.

Figure 2.6, line 143:
Each column is calculated using the same formula, so:
Column G = G140 − G142
Column H = H140 − H142
etc.

Figure 2.7 is completed following completion of the deal structure, as discussed above.

Amanda

Five Year Balance Sheet – Calculation of loans and interest

Calculation of availability of loan

Line Number	Days	Prior Year £		Qu 1 £	Qu 2 £	Qu 3 £	Qu 4 £	Year 1 £	Year 2 £	Year 3 £	Year 4 £	Year 5 £
156		10,313	75% of net tangible assets	9,454	8,594	483,047	470,000	470,000	418,646	367,847	993,356	869,113
157		94,800	80% of debtors	78,904	94,685	142,290	231,321	231,321	249,146	350,959	544,110	775,890
158		19,152	20% of stock	6,685	7,364	10,586	12,122	12,122	16,351	24,504	33,600	38,640
159		124,265		95,043	110,643	635,924	713,442	713,442	684,143	743,311	1,571,066	1,683,643
161		(24,265)	Less: Extra/Repayment	4,957	(10,643)	(535,924)	(613,442)	(713,442)	(634,143)	(343,311)	(1,521,066)	(1,683,643)
163		100,000	Loan	100,000	100,000	100,000	100,000	0	50,000	400,000	50,000	0
166		1,875	Interest	1,875	1,875	1,875	1,875	7,500	0	3,750	30,000	3,750

Figure 2.7 Case study – Amanda – 5-year plan – calculation of loans and interest

The Cash Flow Statement

In the days before the Accounting Standards Board (ASB) was set up, the preparation of published accounts was left to the interpretation of what was required by each board of Directors. As long as they complied with legislation and, for example, met with the requirements of what had to go into the Directors' Report, what accounts they presented was up to them.

Some companies did not publish a Cash Flow Statement and even if they did, it did not appear in a standard format; this was a glaring omission and the first major problem addressed by the ASB. Accordingly, in 1996 they published their first FRS (Financial Reporting Standard) – FRS 1 Cash Flow Statements. Upon publication of this standard, all companies, except those exempted, had to prepare a Cash Flow Statement in the prescribed format. These exemptions were:

(1) subsidiary undertakings where 90% or more of the voting rights are controlled within the group, provided that consolidated financial statements in which those subsidiary undertakings are included are publicly available;
(2) mutual life assurance companies;
(3) pension funds;
(4) open-ended investment funds, subject to certain further conditions;
(5) for two years from the effective date of the FRS, building societies that, as required by law, prepare a statement of source and application of funds in a prescribed format; and
(6) small entities (based on the small companies exemption in companies legislation).

(*Source*: FRS 1 – Issued by the ASB in October 1996.)

As we will see in Chapter 4, the Cash Flow Statement is the saviour as it is the one statement that cannot be manipulated. The Profit and Loss Accounts is based on a series of judgements, likewise the Balance Sheet, but not the Cash Flow Statement. Cash comes in and cash goes out; what has happened cannot be changed. As long as a company's cash book has been reconciled to the bank statement, the balancing figures in the Cash Flow Statement (opening and closing cash) will be correct.

The Cash Flow Statement is simply a summary showing how cash was generated and how it was spent in a given period. Once the Profit and Loss Account and Balance Sheet are in hand, the Cash Flow Statement can be produced entirely by using formulae.

To prepare a Cash Flow Statement, every line from the 'Operating Profit' downwards in the Profit and Loss Account and every line in the Balance Sheet must be used. The rules for preparing a Cash Flow Statement are simple:

(1) If the line used in the Profit and Loss Account does NOT also appear in the Balance Sheet (such as 'operating profit'), then the figure that goes in the Cash Flow Statement is the same as that shown in the Profit and Loss Account.

(2) If the line used in the Profit and Loss Account ALSO appears in the Balance Sheet (such as 'corporation tax'), then the figure that goes in the Cash Flow Statement is:

   Opening figure in Balance Sheet
   PLUS: figure in Profit and Loss Account
   LESS: Closing figure in the Balance Sheet;

(3) If the line used is NOT found in the Profit and Loss Account and appears ONLY in the Balance Sheet (such as 'stock'), then the figure that goes in the Cash Flow Statement is the DIFFERENCE between the opening and closing figure in the Balance Sheet.

The only remaining thing to work out for each line used is whether the figure calculated is money generated or money spent. Again, simple rules make this decision easy.

(1) If the figure is taken from the Profit and Loss Account only, then:
   'Operating profit' = cash generated and 'Operating loss' = cash expended
   All other lines = cash expended;

(2) If the figure is taken from the Balance Sheet, then:
   If assets increase, then cash has been expended; if assets decrease, then cash has been generated;
   If liabilities increase, then cash has been generated, if liabilities decrease, then cash has been expended.

On a Cash Flow Statement, cash generated is shown as a plus (+) sign, while cash expended is shown as a minus (−) sign.

Figure 2.8 shows the 5-year plan Cash Flow Statement. The formulae for Figure 2.8 are shown below, but note that the lines quoted relate to Figures 2.5 and 2.6.

Amanda — Five Year Plan

Cash Flow Statement

Line Number		G Qu 1 £	H Qu 2 £	I Qu 3 £	J Qu 4 £	L Year 1 £	M Year 2 £	N Year 3 £	O Year 4 £	P Year 5 £
	Reconciliation of operating profit to net cash inflow from operating activities									
180	Operating profit	9,355	4,754	15,804	96,743	126,656	362,768	503,509	655,252	1,005,582
182	Amortisation of intangible assets	0	0	0	0	0	0	0	0	0
183	Depreciation of tangible assets	1,145	1,146	17,296	17,397	37,084	68,472	67,731	165,988	165,658
185	(Increase)/decrease in stocks	62,336	(3,397)	(16,110)	(7,677)	35,152	(21,144)	(40,768)	(45,479)	(25,200)
186	(Increase)/decrease in debtors	19,870	(19,726)	(59,507)	(111,288)	(170,651)	(22,282)	(127,266)	(241,438)	(289,726)
187	Increase/(decrease) in creditors	1,529	10,131	(96,012)	149,782	65,430	9,809	51,389	103,287	115,809
189	Net Cash Inflow/(Outflow) from Operating Activitie	94,235	(7,092)	(138,429)	144,957	93,671	397,623	454,595	637,610	972,123
	CASH FLOW STATEMENT									
193	Net Cash Inflow/(Outflow) from Operating Activitie	94,235	(7,092)	(138,429)	144,957	93,671	397,623	454,595	637,610	972,123
195	Return on Investment									
196	Servicing of finance	(1,875)	(1,875)	(1,875)	(1,875)	(7,500)	0	(3,750)	(30,000)	(3,750)
197	Taxation	0	0	0	0	0	(29,789)	(90,692)	(124,940)	(156,313)
198	Capital expenditure	0	0	(650 000)	0	(650,000)	0	0	(1,000,000)	0
199	Dividends paid	0	0	0	0	0	(8,000)	(8,000)	(6,000)	(4,000)
201	Net Cash Inflow/(Outflow) before Financing	92,360	(8,967)	(790,304)	143,082	(563,829)	359,834	352,153	(523,330)	808,060
203	Financing – issue/repayment of shares	825,000	0	0	0	825,000	(200,000)	(200,000)	(200,000)	(235,000)
204	Financing – Issue/repayment of loans	(100,000)	0	1	0	(100,000)	(100,000)	50,000	350,000	(350,000)
205	Increase/(decrease) in Cash	817,360	(8,967)	(790,303)	143,082	161,171	59,834	202,153	(373,330)	223,060
	Reconciliation of Cash Flow with Cash Movements									
211	Opening Cash	220	817,580	808,613	18,309	220	161,391	221,225	423,378	50,048
212	Closing Cash	817,580	808,613	18,309	161,391	161,391	221,225	423,378	50,048	273,108
213	Movement in Cash balances	817,360	(8,967)	(790,303)	143,082	161,171	59,834	202,153	(373,330)	223,060

Figure 2.8 Case study – Amanda – 5-year plan – Cash Flow Statement

Line 180:

    Column G = G81

    Column H = H81

    etc.

Line 182: Nil (0) inserted on all lines, as intangibles were not amortised.

Line 183:

    Column G = G109 − E109

    Column H = H109 − G109

    Column I = I109 − H109

    Column J = J109 − I109

    Column L = sum(G183.J183)

    Column M = M109 − l109

    Column N = N109 − M109

    Column O = O109 − N109

    Column P = P109 − O109

Line 185:

    Column G = E114 − G114

    Column H = G114 − H114

    Column I = H114 − I114

    Column J = I114 − J114

    Column L = sum(G185.J185)

    Column M = L114 − M114

    Column N = M114 − N114

    Column O = N114 − O114

    Column P = O114 − P114

Line 186 uses the same formulae as line 185, except line 114 becomes line 115, so:

    Column G = E115 = G115

    Column H = G115 − H115

    etc.

Line 187:

    Column G = G119 + G120 − E119 − E120

    Column H = H119 + H120 − G119 − G120

    Column I = I119 + I120 − H119 − H120

    Column J = J119 + J120 − I119 − I120

    Column L = sum(G187.J187)

    Column M = M119 + M120 − L119 − L120

    Column N = N119 + N190 − M119 − M120

Column O = O119 + O120 − N119 − N120

Column P = P119 + P120 − O119 − O120

Line 189:

Column G = sum(G180.G187)

Column H = sum(H180.H187)

etc.

Line 193:

Column G = G189

Column H = H189

etc.

Line 195 is nil (0) on every line as there are no investments (shares in other companies) in the plan.

Line 196:

Column G = − G83

Column H = − H83

etc.

Line 197:

Column G = − E121 − G87 + G121

Column H = − G121 − H87 + H121

Column I = −H121−I87+I121

Column J = −I121−J87+J121

Column L = sum(G197.J197)

Column M = −L121−M87+M121

Column N = −M121−N87+N121

Column O = −N121−O87+O121

Column P = −O121−P87+P121

Line 198:

Column G = E108 − G108

Column H = G108 − H108

Column I = H108 − I108

Column J = I108 − J108

Column L = sum(G108.J108)

Column M = L108 − M108

Column N = M108 − N108

Column O = N108 − O108

Column P = O108 − P108

Line 199:

Column G = − E122 − G91 + G122

Column H = − G122 − H91 + H122

Column I = $-$H122$-$I91$+$I122
Column J = $-$I122$-$J91$+$J122
Column L = sum(G199.J199)
Column M = $-$L122$-$M91$+$M122
Column N = $-$M122$-$N91$+$N122
Column O = $-$N122$-$O91$+$O122
Column P = $-$O122$-$P91$+$P122

Line 201:
Column G = sum(G193.G199)
Column H = sum(H193.H199)
etc.

Line 203:
Column G = sum(G134.G137) $-$ sum(E134.E137)
Column H = sum(H134.H137) $-$ sum(G134.G137)
Column I = sum(I134.I137) $-$ sum(H134.H137)
Column J = sum(J134.J137) $-$ sum(I134.I137)
Column L = sum(G203.J203)
Column M = sum(M134.M137) $-$ sum(L134.L137)
Column N = sum(N134.N137) $-$ sum(M134.M137)
Column O = sum(O134.O137) $-$ sum(N134.N137)
Column P = sum(P134.P137) $-$ sum(O134.O137)

Line 204:
Column G = G130 $-$ E130
Column H = H130 $-$ G130
Column I = I130 $-$ H130
Column J = J130 $-$ I130
Column L = sum(G204.J204)
Column M = M130 $-$ L130
Column N = N130 $-$ M130
Column O = O130 $-$ N130
Column P = P130 $-$ O130

Line 205:
Column G = sum(G201.G204)
Column H = sum(H201.H204)
etc.

Line 211:
Column G = E116
Column H = G116
etc.

Line 212:

    Column G = G116

    Column H = H116

    etc.

Line 213:

    Column G = G212 − G211

    Column H = H212 − H211

    etc.

If we look at Figures 2.6 and 2.8, we can see that there is a very high cash balance in the first two quarters. The reason for this is that we have raised capital ahead of our planned capital expenditure in the third quarter. As explained earlier, the cash balances shown for later years are not likely to be accurate. However, it must be remembered that this is a 5-year plan; in later years the objective is merely to give a reasonable overview.

Capital structure summary and exit strategies

Small business starts with money put in by their owners and debt provided by banks. If the amount of debt available is limited, then such business may use hire purchase arrangements to finance the purchase of assets and/or debtor discounting and the like to finance working capital.

As a business expands and becomes profitable, it will become easier to take on debt, but such availability will not be limitless and there will come a point when continued growth is not possible. At this time, the owners of the business either have to shelve their growth plans or dilute their holding by taking on equity.

Some business owners attempt to sell only a small proportion of their equity by organising a sale through the EIS. The deal structures embedded in such schemes usually mean that investors pay a far higher price for their shares than the original owners, in return for tax relief. Whether a particular deal structure between the buyers and sellers is reasonable or not will be a matter of judgement, but from a buying perspective, the ability to fully understand a prospectus is paramount. A big disadvantage from a buyer's point of view, unless the buyer is a business angel, is that not being connected with the investment there is no possibility of influencing the way the business is run in what could probably be described as a high-risk venture.

Alternatively, small businesses might attempt to raise capital through venture capital or private equity funds, the latter including business angels. In investment terms, the big difference between this and the EIS is that the investor is usually in the position, through the deal structure, to control how the business in run.

Private individuals who have insufficient funds to become business angels or to participate in closed end funds run by the large venture capital companies can invest in VCTs. This vehicle, attracting tax relief, has the advantage over the EIS that their investment will be spread amongst several companies and they have a fund manager looking after things. Nevertheless, VCTs can be high-risk investments.

Those investing in venture capital will usually seek to exit from their investment in between 5 years and 10 years. Some investments will end in failure and will be relatively worthless, while others may be more successful. Moderately successful businesses might be sold through a trade sale, while the more successful could float on AIM, while the most successful could float on the full stock exchange.

Companies able to float on the full stock exchange will be assessed by credit rating agencies to assess their credit worthiness. Companies with a good credit rating will, in addition to obtaining secured debt from banks, be able to sell unsecured debt to the general public in the form of bonds. Companies with a poor credit rating will be able to sell debt to the general public only if they offer a high rate of interest and such issues are known as 'junk bonds'.

Large established companies able to raise both debt and equity without too much trouble will decide the proportion they wish to have of each. This is the subject of much academic debate, but the reality is that no two boards will have exactly the same view.

Basic tools of analysis

Once Amanda's company is up and running, she can compare her financial results with those of her competitors operating in the same sector. The basic tools of analysis to achieve this are straightforward and easy to calculate, but their interpretation is much more difficult. How the various ratios are calculated is shown below. All the ratios are based on Figure 2.9 – A Food Manufacturing Company. As discussed earlier, these ratios can be divided into four sections and remembered by the acronym – Pam Sir.

A Food Manufacturing Company					
Year ended	31 Dec 06	31 Dec 05	31 Dec 04	31 Dec 03	31 Dec 02
	£'000	£'000	£'000	£'000	£'000
Turnover	128,500	127,197	105,035	80,892	53,056
Cost of sales	96,700	97,244	77,795	56,530	36,245
Gross profit	31,800	29,953	27,240	24,362	16,811
Distribution and Administration	24,968	23,119	19,592	18,592	12,845
Operating profit/(loss) before amortisation	6,832	6,834	7,648	5,770	3,966
Goodwill/amortisation/impairment/exceptional	1,750	1,787	940	890	440
Operating profit/(loss)	5,082	5,047	6,708	4,880	3,526
Interest payable/(receivable)	2,503	3,100	3,077	1,894	732
Tax on profits	875	590	1,101	1,126	1,265
Earnings	1,704	1,357	2,530	1,860	1,529
Dividends	200	173	150	135	123
Retained profit/(loss) for the year	1,504	1,184	2,380	1,725	1,406
Number of ordinary shares ('000)	86,500	86,500	86,500	84,800	82,100
Year ended	31 Dec 06	31 Dec 05	31 Dec 04	31 Dec 03	31 Dec 02
	£'000	£'000	£'000	£'000	£'000
Intangible assets	32,206	33,956	35,743	31,700	22,963
Tangible Assets + other long term assets	61,660	67,400	66,896	41,637	25,600
Fixed Assets	93,866	101,356	102,639	73,337	48,563
Stock	9,720	10,100	8,600	6,600	3,942
Trade Debtors	21,417	30,114	19,894	15,267	10,541
Other debtors/current assets					
Cash at bank	4,456	4,751	2,464	4,361	4,405
Total Current Assets	35,593	44,965	30,958	26,228	18,888
Trade creditors	29,240	28,136	21,700	17,375	10,315
Other creditors	3,635	3,200	2,685	2,100	1,543
Bank Overdraft and Loans	4,200	9,200	5,000	4,200	3,145
Total Current Liabilities	37,075	40,536	29,385	23,675	15,003
Net Current Assets/(Liabilities)	(1,482)	4,429	1,573	2,553	3,885
Total Assets less Current Liabilities	92,384	105,785	104,212	75,890	52,448
Other long term liabilities (creditors)	7,200	7,105	6,716	6,200	5,153
Long term debt	50,000	65,000	65,000	40,000	20,009
Net Assets	35,184	33,680	32,496	29,690	27,286
Share capital	3,632	3,632	3,632	3,560	3,446
Share premium account	18,024	18,024	18,024	17,670	17,105
Other capital reserves	2,030	2,030	2,030	2,030	2,030
Profit and Loss Account	11,498	9,994	8,810	6,430	4,705
Other revenue reserves					
Equity shareholders' funds	35,184	33,680	32,496	29,690	27,286
Net (Debt)/Funds	(49,744)	(69,449)	(67,536)	(39,839)	(18,749)

Figure 2.9 A Food Manufacturing Co. – Profit and Loss Account and Balance Sheet

Performance ratios

What we are looking for is evidence that the company we are reviewing is innovating. This means that the company is sustaining growth by having a sustained research plan and developing new ideas and products. It is possible that growth comes about through the development of innovative concepts and sometimes this means simply bringing the existing products to the market in a novel way.

To sustain growth, companies must either be offering products as good as their competitors, but at cheaper prices, or be offering superior products at premium prices. Large companies can dominate the market by being the most cost effective, while small companies have to be innovative to survive.

There are many ways of achieving increased profitability in the short term, without spending money on research or being innovative, but such strategies cannot be maintained in the long term. Methods of achieving this include divesting unprofitable businesses, outsourcing and downsizing.

So, it is known that growth is the key to long-term success, but the objective of using performance ratios is to assess if growth is being achieved and whether it is likely to be sustainable or not.

Ratio – turnover compound growth

This ratio calculates the compound growth in turnover.

	2006	2005	2004	2003	2002
Turnover (£'000)	128 500	127 197	105 035	80 892	53 056
Compound growth (%)	24.7	33.8	41.1	52.5	

Ratio – gross profit percentage

This ratio calculates the gross margin as a percentage of sales.

	2006	2005	2004	2003	2002
Turnover (£'000)	128 500	127 197	105 035	80 892	53 056
Gross profit (£'000)	31 800	29 953	27 240	24 362	16 811
Percentage (%)	24.7	23.5	25.9	30.1	31.7

Ratio – gross profit compound growth

This ratio calculates the compound growth in gross profit.

	2006	2005	2004	2003	2002
Gross profit (£'000)	31 800	29 953	27 240	24 362	16 811
Compound growth (%)	17.3	21.2	27.3	44.9	

Ratio – operating profit (before extraordinary items) percentage

This ratio calculates the operating profit (before extraordinary items) as a percentage of sales.

	2006	2005	2004	2003	2002
Turnover (£'000)	128 500	127 197	105 035	80 892	53 056
Operating profit (£'000)	6832	6834	7648	5770	3966
Percentage (%)	5.3	5.4	7.3	7.1	7.5

Ratio – operating profit (before extraordinary items) compound growth

This ratio calculates the compound growth in gross profit.

	2006	2005	2004	2003	2002
Operating profit (£'000)	6832	6834	7648	5770	3966
Compound growth (%)	14.6	19.9	39.1	45.5	

Ratio – operating profit by employee

Some companies, often retail companies, divide their operating profit by the average number of employees employed during the year to calculate how much profit each employee has generated. The same calculation can be done for turnover and gross profit.

Ratio – return on capital employed

This ratio assesses how well the company is utilising the capital available to them.

	2006	2005	2004	2003	2002
Operating profit (£'000)	6832	6834	7648	5770	3966
Capital employed (£'000)	92 384	105 785	104 212	75 890	52 448
ROCE (%)	7.4	6.5	7.3	7.6	7.6

As companies make new investments, we would expect the ROCE to fall in the short term because it would take time for such investments to generate profit. However, after this initial fall, ROCE should increase as profits come through and should increase, at least in the short term, steeply upwards if new investments are not made. However, where no new investments were made over the years, we would expect stagnation to set in and profits to fall, forcing ROCE in a downward spiral. In our example, ROCE has not increased over the years, suggesting that the investments made in the earlier years were disappointing.

Asset management ratios

The purpose of asset management ratios is to assess how well the directors of the company are controlling the company's assets.

Ratio – current ratio

This ratio assesses the ability of the company to meet its short-term liabilities. Current assets are divided by current liabilities to calculate the ratio. This should be 1 or greater, as a ratio of less than 1 suggests that the company cannot meet its everyday liabilities without resorting to bank borrowings.

	2006	2005	2004	2003	2002
Current assets (£'000)	35 593	44 965	30 958	26 228	18 888
Current liabilities (£'000)	37 075	40 536	29 385	23 675	15 003
Ratio	0.96	1.11	1.05	1.11	1.26

Ratio – quick ratio

This ratio assesses the ability of the company to service its short-term liabilities without the need to sell stock or resort to bank borrowings. Again, this ratio should be 1 or greater, but a figure below this does not necessarily indicate that there is a problem. For example, a hospitality company, such as a hotel operator, will be able to negotiate credit terms with its suppliers but will expect its customers to pay on departure. The result of this is that such companies often have a quick ratio of less than 1, but can easily meet their short-term liabilities as they fall due.

	2006	2005	2004	2003	2002
CA (excl. stock) (£'000)	25 873	34 865	22 358	19 628	14 946
Current liabilities (£'000)	37 075	40 536	29 385	23 675	15 003
Ratio	0.70	0.86	0.76	0.83	1.00

Ratio – stock days

Here the objective is to calculate how many days' stock the company is holding. The formula to calculate this is stock divided by cost of sales, multiplied by 365. 'Cost of sales' strictly relates to the direct costs of achieving the sales and should not include allocated overheads, but the figure of 'cost of sales' in published accounts will include all costs associated with bringing the goods and services to the point they are available to the customer. Given this, the number of days calculated from published accounts will be lower than the real figure, but if we are consistent in calculating each year and peer companies in the same way, it should be possible to be able to make a valid judgement.

Stock days will vary by industry and the correct judgement can be made only if the particular industry norm is known, but any sudden increase from one year to the next warrants further investigation.

	2006	2005	2004	2003	2002
Stock (£'000)	9720	10 100	8600	6600	3942
Cost of sales (£'000)	96 700	97 244	77 795	56 530	36 245
Days	37	38	40	43	40

Ratio – debtor days

The idea here is to work out how long it is taking the company to recover its debts. A high number may indicate that the company is having credit control problems, while taking the worse case scenario it could mean that the company is taking sales before they are entitled to do so. The formula is debtors divided by sales plus VAT on the sales multiplied by 365. The sales shown in published accounts (other than certain 'retail' accounts, where sales plus VAT is shown, prior to VAT on sales being deducted) exclude VAT, so VAT must be added to calculate this ratio. However, there is no VAT on export sales, so to calculate sales plus VAT, it will be necessary to do two different calculations. If this split is unavailable and VAT is added to total sales, then the days calculated will be slightly lower than the true figure. On the other hand, the figure for 'trade debtors' (the figure we should be using) may not be available, so we have to use the figure shown as 'debtors' in the Balance Sheet. This will mean that our calculation will show debtor days to be higher than they really are. However, as with the stock calculation, consistency is the key to making the right judgement. Also, it must be noted that we are primarily looking for the change from one year to the next, not the absolute figure. Any figure taken in isolation would only be a concern if it were very high.

	2006	2005	2004	2003	2002
Debtors (£'000)	21 417	30 114	19 894	15 267	10 541
Sales + VAT (£'000)	150 988	149 456	123 416	95 048	62 341
Days	52	74	59	59	62

With regard to this example, the 2005 figure would cause concern, and had debtor days gone out further in 2006, then such concern would have become critical.

Structure ratios

The reason 'structure' ratios are calculated is to assess how risky the business is in terms of its gearing and its ability to meet key liabilities. It must be remembered that gearing is critical; companies are forced out of business when they cannot meet their liabilities as they fall due. Failure to make a profit does not cause a problem unless the losses are so great as to cause a cash problem.

Interest cover

This ratio shows whether (all other things being equal) the company is generating sufficient profit to meet interest payments as they fall due. Sometimes a company will be covenant with its bank that the interest cover ratio will be maintained above a particular figure, so 'interest cover' can be a key ratio.

	2006	2005	2004	2003	2002
Profit before interest (£'000)	5082	5047	6708	4880	3526
Interest (£'000)	2503	3100	3077	1894	732
Interest cover	2.0	1.6	2.2	2.6	4.8

In this example, the figure of 1.6 in 2005 would likely have caused the bank concern and may explain why there was no capital expenditure in 2006.

Gearing ratio

The gearing ratio expresses long-term debt as a percentage of total capital employed. Any figure greater than 50% is considered to be high geared and therefore high risk.

	2006	2005	2004	2003	2002
Long term debt (£'000)	57 200	72 105	71 716	46 200	25 162
Capital employed (£'000)	92 384	105 785	104 212	75 890	52 448
Gearing %	61.9	68.2	68.8	60.9	48.0

Debt to equity ratio

The debt to equity ratio is similar to the gearing ratio but in this case a figure greater than 100% is considered to be high geared.

	2006	2005	2004	2003	2002
Long term debt (£'000)	57 200	72 105	71 716	46 200	25 162
Equity (£'000)	35 184	33 680	32 496	29 690	27 286
Debt to equity %	162.6	214.1	220.7	155.6	92.2

Investor ratios

Investor ratios look at the company from the perspective of the investor; in other words, the holders of the equity shares.

Return on equity

Whereas the ratio 'return on capital employed' assesses what the company has achieved with the total capital available to it, the first investor ratio assesses how much the company has earned for its investors compared to the money they put in. That part of a company's profit that belongs to the owners of the business is called 'earnings' and this is compared with 'equity shareholders' funds.

	2006	2005	2004	2003	2002
Earnings (£'000)	1704	1357	2530	1860	1529
Shareholders' funds (£'000)	35 184	33 680	32 496	29 690	27 286
ROE (%)	4.8	4.0	7.8	6.3	5.6

Earnings per share

This ratio calculates how much each share has earned in a particular financial year. Earnings per share (EPS) is usually declared in pence if the share is quoted in sterling, or in cents if the share is quoted in euros.

	2006	2005	2004	2003	2002
Earnings (£'000)	1704	1357	2530	1860	1529
Number of shares '000	86 500	86 500	86 500	84 800	82 100
EPS (pence)	2.0	1.6	2.9	2.2	1.9

Price/earnings ratio

This ratio is calculated by dividing the current price of the share by the EPS. A P/E ratio of below 10 suggests that the market believes that there is likely to be very little earnings growth in the future, while a very small P/E ratio (7 or lower) suggests that the market believes that profitability will decline. As the P/E goes higher (15 and above), the market forecast is that the company will grow. A P/E of 100+ suggests the mammoth growth that is unlikely to be sustained. Indeed P/Es above 100, last experienced in the dot-com boom, is an indicator of a bubble that could burst at any moment.

	2006	2005	2004	2003	2002
Price of share (pence)	41.0	44.0	38.0	45.0	35.0
EPS (pence)	2.0	1.6	2.9	2.2	1.9
P/E ratio	20.5	27.5	13.1	20.5	18.4

Dividend cover

Some shareholders buy shares for income. In such cases, the amount of the dividend is important and especially how it is covered. If the dividend is not well covered, then there is the risk that it would be lowered in the future.

	2006	2005	2004	2003	2002
Earnings (£'000)	1704	1357	2530	1860	1529
Dividends (£'000)	200	173	150	135	123
Dividend cover	8.5	7.8	16.9	13.8	12.4

In this example, although the cover has been dropping, the dividend is well covered.

Dividend yield

	2006	2005	2004	2003	2002
Price of share (pence)	41.0	44.0	38.0	45.0	35.0
Dividend per share (pence)	0.23	0.20	0.17	0.16	0.15
Dividend yield (%)	0.56	0.45	0.45	0.36	0.43

This example is clearly not what could be described as an 'income share'!

Goodwill built into share

The idea here is to compare the value of the company as determined by the current share price with the value as shown in the Balance Sheet.

	2006	2005	2004	2003	2002
Number of shares '000	86 500	86 500	86 500	84 800	82 100
Price of share (pence)	41.0	44.0	38.0	45.0	35.0
Value of company (£'000)	35 465	38 080	32 870	38 160	28 735
Asset value (£'000)	35 184	33 680	32 496	29 690	27 286
Goodwill	281	4400	374	8470	1449
Goodwill (%)	0.8	13.1	1.2	28.5	5.3

The key ratios

The next chapter includes corporate governance and looks at some of the strategies developed to ensure that companies produce accurate accounts, especially in the light of high-profile cases such as Enron. The fact is though that Enron was an isolated example where the directors of the company acted fraudulently; accounts are usually inaccurate due to errors of judgement rather than criminal activity.

The difficulty for investors is, that while ratio analysis can draw attention to problem areas, they are not privy to the internal management accounts and therefore have to make judgements based on limited information. Nor can investors know whether a particular management team is on top of the problem or not; if they are, the problem indicated by the adverse ratio could go away. However, there are a few cases that crop up each year where the adverse ratio has predicted a major problem area before it has become a public knowledge.

The key ratios to look at with a view to spotting potential disasters are all asset management ratios and are to do with stock, debtors and cash.

Cash is king

If a company is making a profit, it should be generating cash. If it is not, this is an indicator that something is wrong. The company may spend more than it earns to buy assets to grow the company and, of course, this is acceptable, but growth must follow this expenditure. Also, this expenditure must improve cash generation in the long term, so eventually even growing companies should generate cash. However, where companies are not buying assets, but merely consuming cash to fund short-term increases in working capital due to growth, this can result in 'overtrading' and liquidity problems. So, if a company consistently, year on year, spends more money than it is generating, then it is an indicator that something may be wrong. This, of course, is especially dangerous where the company was highly indebted before the growth took place.

Jarvis plc is a prime example of what can happen when overtrading takes place. At the company's year end close at 31 March 2000, intangible assets accounted for 87% of equity shareholders' funds (£179 million) and net debt stood at £118 million. In its 2001 financial year, the company generated £42 million against earnings of £15 million, so all seemed well, except that the dividend was covered only 1.1 times. However, it was the 2002 result that should have caused readers of accounts some concern. Turnover went up by 29% compared to the previous year and although stock days and debtor days were virtually unchanged, net debt went up to £80 million, despite earnings doubling to £31 million. At the same time, the company was being blamed for the crash at Potters Bar and although the company denied this allegation, it came on top of a weak Balance Sheet.

Many companies suffer problems of the type faced by Jarvis plc (accusations of doing something wrong in the course of business) and no business is without risk, but when things go wrong it is the companies that are indebted that are the most vulnerable. Jarvis's shares trading at around 334 pence in 2002 ended below one penny a few years later. So, cash is king.

The first test that needs to be carried out is the 'Cash Test'. To do this, 'Net Cash Inflow from Operations' (operating activities in UK GAAP accounts) in the Cash Flow Statement is compared to the 'Operating Profit' in the Profit and Loss Account. 'Net Cash Inflow from Operations' should nearly (see exceptions below) always be *higher* than the 'operating profit', because the cash flow figure is simply operating profit plus depreciation plus amortisation plus or minus movement in working capital. If the cash flow figure is lower than operating profit, the cause may be overtrading and/or poor asset management. The calculation of stock days and debtor days might provide the necessary clues.

This simple calculation can be illustrated from Figure 2.10 – Cash Flow Statement for A Food Manufacturing Company:

	2006	2005	2004	2003
Operating profit (£'000)	5082	5047	6708	4880
Net cash inflow from op. act (£'000)	22 848	8629	10 671	9311

As can be seen from the debtor days ratio, there was a potential problem with debtor days in 2005, yet this was insufficient to cause the above test to fail. Accordingly, where it does fail, every effort must be made to establish the reason.

Of course, there are exceptions to every rule. A house builder's stock days might be high because the land bought for future development is included in stock, for example. Therefore, it is likely that the correct judgement will be made only if through appropriate research what could be considered the norm is established for each industry.

Cash Flow Statement for: A Food Manufacturing Company			
31 Dec 06	31 Dec 05	31 Dec 04	31 Dec 03
£'000	£'000	£'000	£'000

Reconciliation of operating profit to net cash inflow from operating activities

	31 Dec 06 £'000	31 Dec 05 £'000	31 Dec 04 £'000	31 Dec 03 £'000
Operating profit	5,082	5,047	6,708	4,880
Amortisation of intangible assets	1,750	1,787	1,585	1,148
Depreciation of tangible assets	5,740	6,690	4,164	2,560
(Increase)/decrease in stocks	380	(1,500)	(2,000)	(2,658)
(Increase)/decrease in debtors	8,697	(10,220)	(4,627)	(4,726)
Increase/(decrease) in creditors	1,199	6,825	4,841	8,107
Net cash inflow from operating activities	22,848	8,629	10,671	9,311
CASH FLOW STATEMENT				
Net cash inflow from operating activities	22,848	8,629	10,671	9,311
Return on investment	0	0	0	0
Servicing of Finance	(2,503)	(3,100)	(3,077)	(1,894)
Taxation	(467)	(98)	(531)	(581)
Capital expenditure	0	(7,194)	(35,051)	(28,482)
Dividends paid	(173)	(150)	(135)	(123)
Net cash inflow/(outflow) before financing	19,705	(1,913)	(28,123)	(21,769)
Financing – issue of shares	0	0	426	679
Financing – issue/(repayment) of loans	(15,000)	0	25,000	19,991
Increase/(decrease) in cash	4,705	(1,913)	(2,697)	(1,099)
Reconciliation of cash flow with movements in cash				
Opening cash	(4,449)	(2,536)	161	1,260
Closing cash	256	(4,449)	(2,536)	161
Movement in cash balances	4,705	(1,913)	(2,697)	(1,099)

Figure 2.10 A Food Manufacturing Co. – Cash Flow Statement

Stock days

Stock days in the hotel and catering industry will be relatively low, as companies operating bars, restaurants and hotels are likely to have only a few days' stock of food and only a few weeks' stock of drink. A review of accounts of five companies in this sector resulted in stock days being in the range 6–16 days, so when SFI plc's accounts for the year ended 31 May 2001 came out with 32 days' stock it could be described as somewhat surprising. However, these accounts did not really have an adverse impact on the market and the shares continued to trade at around £2. The following year's accounts, for the year ended 31 May 2002, should have raised even more eyebrows, as stock days went out to 43 days. Months later it was revealed that stock had been overstated and the company ceased trading.

Debtor days

Debtor days will vary from industry to industry. A retailer selling largely for cash will have only a few debtor days, an industrial company may have debtors at around 60 days, while other companies have to offer longer periods of credit. Companies specialising in computer software often have long debtor days. A particular contract might include stage payments, but the customer is likely to hold a fair percentage of the contract price back until there is sufficient evidence that the software works. Accordingly, debtor days at around 100 days might not be too alarming for a software company.

Isoft plc is a computer software company and at its year ended 30 April 2003, their accounts showed debtor days at 106 days, a little high against the norm, but not alarmingly so. However, the calculation of debtor days from the following year's accounts showed debtor days up to 223 days. Now, both these figures (106 days and 223 days) were based on total debtors as shown in the accounts and would have included debtors other than trade debtors, so we cannot ascertain what the trade figures actually were. However, it was the comparison between the two years that would have caused concern.

The market was clearly not concerned as the shares continued to trade in the range of 350 pence–450 pence. However, the company announced later that it was changing the way it calculated the sales value of ongoing contracts and the share price fell back to 50 pence.

Case study – Amanda' completion meeting

Finally, after months of hard work, everyone is meeting in a boardroom located in Amanda's firm of solicitors. Amanda is with her solicitor and sat opposite are the proposed non-executive chairman of the new business, a representative of the business angel and the business angel's solicitor. In front of them is a mountain of legal documents that covers:

- The setting up of the new company, including articles and memorandum of association.
- The sale of Amanda's old business to the new company.
- The subscription agreement setting out the terms of investment, including the deal structure.
- Agreement between the new company and the non-executive chairman.
- Amanda's contract of employment.

Eventually, all the documents are signed and Amanda is back in business.

Discussion Questions

The Profit and Loss Account of ABKZ Retail plc is shown below for the year ended 31 December 2005 and for the year ended 31 December 2006. Also shown is the Balance Sheet at these dates. ABKZ Retail Limited is a clothes retailer servicing the younger end of the market.

You are given the following information:

(1) The line in the Profit and Loss Account headed 'Goodwill' is wholly amortisation of intangible assets.
(2) There were no intangible assets purchased in 2006.
(3) No tangible assets were sold in 2006.
(4) Included in 'Distribution and Administration' for 2006 is depreciation of tangible assets amounting to £20.33 million.

The requirement for this question:

(1) Prepare the Cash Flow Statement for ABKZ Retail plc for the year ended 31 December 2006, using the shell provided.

Profit and Loss Account of ABKZ Retail plc		
Year ended	31 Dec 06	31 Dec 05
	£'000	£'000
Turnover	675,780	548,640
Cost of sales	604,520	489,720
Gross profit	71,260	58,920
Distribution and Administration	42,200	38,880
Operating profit/(loss) before amortisation	29,060	20,040
Goodwill/amortisation/impairment/exceptional	6,900	4,920
Operating profit/(loss)	22,160	15,120
Interest payable/(receivable)	(3,400)	(8,000)
Tax on profits	7,900	5,040
Earnings	17,660	18,080
Dividends	7,920	6,600
Retained profit/(loss) for the year	9,740	11,480
Number of ordinary shares ('000)	91,300	83,000
Balance Sheet		
Year ended	31 Dec 06	31 Dec 05
	£'000	£'000
Intangible assets	12,660	19,560
Tangible Assets + other long term assets	105,330	101,160
Fixed Assets	117,990	120,720
Stock	115,240	56,160
Trade Debtors	37,030	34,560
Other debtors/current assets		
Cash at bank	21,580	44,400
Total Current Assets	173,850	135,120
Trade creditors	90,400	67,080
Corporation tax	5,840	5,160
Dividends due	6,336	5,280
Total Current Liabilities	102,576	77,520
Net Current Assets/(Liabilities)	71,274	57,600
Total Assets less Current Liabilities	189,264	178,320
Other long term liabilities (creditors)	34,600	39,840
Long term debt		
Net Assets	154,664	138,480
Share capital	47,256	42,960
Share premium account	23,628	21,480
Other capital reserves	0	0
Profit and Loss Account	83,780	74,040
Other revenue reserves		
Equity shareholders' funds	154,664	138,480

Profit and Loss Account of ABKZ Retail plc

	31 Dec 06
	£'000

Reconciliation of operating profit to net cash inflow from operating activities

Operating profit

Amortisation of intangible assets
Depreciation of tangible assets

(Increase)/decrease in stocks
(Increase)/decrease in debtors
Increase/(decrease) in creditors

Net cash inflow from operating activities

CASH FLOW STATEMENT

Net cash inflow from operating activities

Return on investment
Servicing of Finance
Taxation
Capital expenditure
Dividends paid

Net cash inflow/(outflow) before financing

Financing – issue of shares
Financing – issue/(repayment) of loans

Increase/(decrease) in cash

Reconciliation of cash flow with movements in cash

Opening cash
Closing cash

Movement in cash balances

Financial reporting and IFRS

In Chapter 3, we do not meet Amanda, although it can be assumed that her business is progressing. This chapter looks at published accounts and the standards that impact such accounts. The message that comes across is that despite more and more regulation and the desire to ensure all companies follow the same standards, the production of a set of accounts requires those responsible to make a series of judgements, where no two people are likely to come to exactly the same conclusion.

The topics covered are the following:

- Accounting is a series of judgements
- Auditors, their responsibility and the limitations of an audit
- International Financial Reporting Standards
- Revenue recognition
- Research and development
- Share-based payments
- Intangible assets
- Investment property and investment property under development (case study – UNITE Group plc)
- Dividends
- Salary-related pension schemes
- Financial derivatives
- Leases
- Minor adjustments (IFRS vs. UK GAAP)
- Corporate governance
- The Report of the Directors
- The Directors' Remuneration Report
- Optional (non-statutory) reports
- Annual report – summary
- Enron and the Sarbanes-Oxley Act
- Shareholders' power

Accounting is a series of judgements

Accounts are never black and white, but many shades of grey as they have to be based on a series of judgements. The problem investors have is to evaluate exactly what shade they are looking at when reviewing a particular set of accounts, because judgement is always clouded by human nature.

The problems often start with unrealistic expectations. The 'market' seems to believe that companies should endlessly grow in terms of sales and profitability, although it does not show the same level of concern about cash generation. Reality, usually, is often different; companies operate in cycles where their fortunes tend to go up and down. Directors know that an announcement reporting a declining growth percentage or a statement suggesting that 'profits will not meet market expectations' could result in their company's share price being savaged. So, the pressure to perform starts at the top.

This pressure percolates down the organisation, so that managers can be subjected to the carrot and stick routine. High remuneration is linked with a high standard of performance where mistakes are not allowed. So if things go wrong, managers are tempted to bend the rules; the more punitive an organisation is, greater is the likelihood that some will crack. Sometimes the pressure is self-induced but the point is that it is usually pressure that causes managers to stray from the straight and narrow. Sometimes, though, it may be simply the case that a particular manager wants to impress the senior management and will go to any lengths to achieve this. It is impossible, in the final analysis, to know for certain what motivates employees to bend the rules, but when they do, it can be disastrous for shareholders.

Most organisations produce monthly management accounts, so non-performing managers can be found out well before financial accounts have to be published; so an under-pressure manager might be tempted to add in (say) two days' sales from the following month to the current month. The plea to the branch accountant might be the promise that things will be put right at the end of the following month. But two days becomes four days and so on. Of course, the opposite might happen. If monthly sales are ahead of plan, then the manager might hold sales back, in case things go wrong sometime in future. Of course, such indiscretions could be relatively minor and not necessarily significant. In other cases, they could be more serious.

On 26 February 2007, McAlpine (Alfred) plc announced that they had uncovered a serious accounting problem. The company said that in the previous week they had discovered a systematic misrepresentation of production volumes and sales over a number of years, by a number of senior managers at their Slate subsidiary.

The company reported that those involved sought to conceal the financial implications of their action through the pre-selling of slate at substantially discounted prices in deliberate and possibly fraudulently behaviour. Their actions had led to suspensions pending further investigation. The company added that independent accountants would be brought in to conduct a detailed forensic analysis that would likely take 4–6 weeks.

The effect of the above announcement was that the company's share price fell 22% from 613.5 pence to 476.5 pence. The key question is whether or not this disaster could have been predicted from the accounts. The answer is, of course, nothing could be predicted with certainty, but when such events happen the accounts usually throw up the same clue, which is that 'cash inflow/(outflow) from operations' is lower than 'operating profit', when it should be the other way around (see Chapter 2).

The last published accounts of McAlpine (Alfred) plc stated:

	6 months to 30 June 2006	6 months to 30 June 2005	12 months to 31 December 2005
	£'m	£'m	£'m
Profit before interest and tax	17.4	17.3	41.9
Cash inflow/(outflow) from operations	(10.9)	7.6	27.9

However, as stated in Chapter 2, accounting inaccuracies are usually the result of flawed judgements, rather than fraudulent activity. Either way, it will be the duty of directors of the company to ensure that their accounting records meet the required standards, which means that they give a true and fair view of the start of affairs of their company. Their financial statements must comply with the appropriate Companies Acts, European legislation of stock exchange rules.

In preparing such financial statements, the directors are required to:

- select suitable accounting policies and apply them consistently;
- make *judgements and estimates* that are *reasonable and prudent*;
- state whether applicable accounting standards have been followed, subject to any *material* departures disclosed and explained in the financial statements;
- prepare the financial statements on the going concern basis unless it is inappropriate to presume that the company will continue in business.

The directors also have a general responsibility for taking such steps that are *reasonably* open to them to safeguard the assets of the company and to prevent and detect fraud and other irregularities.

At the end of the financial year, the directors will have gathered in all the information available to them, including details of minor indiscretions if there are any and if they have come to light, and will then be faced with a series of judgements, including:

- the carrying value of intangible assets;
- stock;
- debtors;
- contingent liabilities.

The carrying value of intangible assets. When a company buys another for a price greater than the tangible assets acquired, this gives rise to 'goodwill'. This is shown as an asset in the Balance Sheet, but its inclusion in the Balance Sheet is dependent upon the goodwill having a genuine value. This means that the 'goodwill' must generate future income streams, otherwise it will have to be impaired, meaning that it will have to be partially or wholly written off, as the case may be. As we cannot predict the future accurately, we are relying on judgements made by the directors. To argue with directors' judgement, the auditor would have to be able to prove that the directors were being unreasonable or imprudent.

Stock. At each year end, an 'age' analysis of stock will reveal slow moving stock, or stock that is out of specification, even in a small way. Will this stock be sold in the following year? Who knows? A cautious director might want to write off the bulk of this stock, while another, taking a more imprudent approach, might take the view that somehow the company will find a buyer for it. What actually happens will likely be different from either view.

Debtors. At the year end, an established customer owes a large amount and is 60 days overdue. The concern is that this customer has a good record of paying on time. The optimistic view would be that as the customer has always paid in the past, he will do so in future, while the pessimist will believe that there has to be something wrong. Who is correct? The directors cannot tell for certain, either way; it comes down to being a matter of judgement.

Contingent liabilities. A debtor will not pay your invoice for £100 000 and is suing you for £900 000 on the basis that your product, allegedly being faulty and out of specification, has damaged many batches of his production. Your legal team, having seen only your evidence, believes that you have a 60% chance of winning, but advises you to write off the debt and offer an equal amount in compensation. They advise you that in their view there is a 90% probability that the debtor would accept this compromise, but the 10% downside risk is that he will use your offer to demonstrate your guilt. Beyond that, they cannot advise you and have told you that the recommendation they have made does create a risk profile, for which they cannot be responsible. It is your decision. So what do you do and how much do you reserve in the accounts? Again it is a matter of judgement.

The judgements detailed above were simply required to meet the 'prudence concept' that neither profits nor assets should be overstated and liabilities should be not be understated. However, under IFRS as all costs and assets must be stated at 'fair value', the directors are required to make even more judgements.

The Auditors' Report and their responsibilities

Under company law, independent auditors have to review the annual report and accounts and give their *opinion* as to whether the financial statements give a true and fair view of the state of affairs of the company and have been properly prepared in accordance with the Companies Act 1985 and Article 4 of the IAS Regulation.

They check whether the company has kept proper accounting records and report if they have not received all the information and explanations required for their audit. They ensure that the Directors' Report is consistent with the accounts and that the Corporate Governance Statement reflects compliance with the nine provisions of the 2003 FRC Combined Code specified by the Listing Rules of the Financial Services Authority (FSA). However, the auditors cannot be in the position to confirm that corporate governance procedures cover all risks. They do, however, have the responsibility to give *reasonable* assurance that the accounts are free from *material* misstatement, whether caused by fraud or other irregularity or error.

Auditors conduct their audit in accordance with International Standards of Auditing issued by the Auditing Practices Board. An audit includes an examination, *on a test basis*, of evidence presented to them by the company. It also includes an assessment of the *significant estimates and judgements* made by the Directors in the preparation of the financial statements, and of whether the accounting policies are appropriate to the company's circumstances, consistently applied and *adequately* disclosed.

By law, auditors have a responsibility only to the company and its members, the shareholders. Their report is made solely to the company's members, as a body, in accordance with section 235 of the Companies Act 1985. This means that if a member of the public, not being a member of a particular company at the time, bought shares in that company on the strength of a recently published Annual Report, he or she would not have a claim against the Auditors, even if the accounts that formed part of the Annual Report turned out to be wholly false.

The limitations of the Independent Auditors' Report

Auditors have a duty to review only the mandatory parts of an annual report and while they will look at optional reports they only have to ensure that these do not contain *apparent* misstatements or material inconsistencies. In other words, they get involved only if they believe a particular report is grossly misleading. What this means is that it is perfectly acceptable in a Chairman's Report to write two pages of glowing prose while limiting the downside to two lines, provided this downside does not contain anything untruthful.

What the key words in the Independent Auditors' Report actually mean

So, we know that directors and auditors are primarily responsible for the accounts and mandatory disclosures, but we need to examine some of the key words. These are the ones shown above in italics, as discussed below.

Opinion. The auditors are not saying that the audited accounts are accurate. Put simply, nobody knows what 'accurate' is, as the accounts have been compiled after making a number of judgements. What they are saying is that they are simply stating an opinion. The value of an opinion must be much less than a statement of fact.

True and fair view. It is difficult to know what this exactly means. How do you know what the 'truth' is and whether it is 'fair', given that the accounts are based on judgements and estimates.

Reasonable (or 'reasonably'). The dictionary definition of 'reasonable' is 'having sound judgement; moderate; ready to listen to reason; not absurd; within the limits of reason; not greatly less or more than might be expected'. The difficulty here is that we are going round in circles, as we are back to 'judgement'.

Material. This is a key word. It means 'significant' in accounting terms. The test is whether the error or omission is material or not. Company A has omitted a batch of invoices of value £80 000 that has been counted as stock. The error has come to light only as the year-end accounts are being signed off. The profit declared in these accounts was £100 000. In such a case, the error is clearly material and the accounts would have to be corrected. Company B has made the mistake in the same circumstances, but has declared profits of £8.9 million. Company B's accounts have been printed. In this case, the error would not be deemed to be material, the accounts would be unaltered and the adjustment made in the following year.

On a test basis. This means that the auditors, by virtue of cost and time limitations, cannot test everything and they have to make a judgement as to what they are going to test. If they get unlucky and miss something significant, or relatively significant, then the get-out clause in their report is the statement that 'an audit includes an examination, on a test basis, ...' However, over time the potential for missing something will reduce as eventually all areas will be tested. The point the auditors are making is that while they will make every effort to test everything that needs testing, it is impossible to check everything in a single audit.

Significant. See 'material'.

Estimates and judgements. The auditors will often make it clear that they are reliant upon the judgements made by the directors (see above).

Adequately. The dictionary definition of 'adequate' is 'sufficient or barely sufficient; satisfactory (often with the implication of being barely so); proportionate.'

Apparent. This means that any misstatement must be obvious. The auditors cannot be held responsible for minor errors and for statements that are open to different interpretations.

It must be appreciated that the auditors are doing a very difficult job, and while they might be expected to unearth a major fraud, minor mistakes will sometimes be made and will remain unnoticed. Auditors to some extent have to rely on the honesty of the directors and will obviously continue to believe unless one of their tests proves otherwise. The vast majority of companies are honestly run and where management and auditors differ will usually be over matters of judgement.

What happens when directors and auditors cannot agree

If auditors make recommendations to the directors in respect of the annual report or accounts and the directors choose to ignore them, then the auditors are faced with a dilemma. The only sanction they have is to 'qualify' the accounts, which means that they state their concerns in their report. Such an action is the nuclear option; the company's share price would collapse and the directors would recommend to the shareholders that the company change their auditors.

So, if the directors are determined, for example, to inflate the profit in a small way, then it comes down to negotiation. How far can the directors go before the auditors draw the line and qualify the accounts? Who will blink first?

More often than not, in these cases it comes down to compromise. For example, the directors are adamant that the carrying value of the goodwill is justified, but the auditors are not convinced. As a compromise, what they might say is that in return for agreeing this year's accounts, the directors must agree to write-off 'x' amount next year, if sales in the particular sector do not reach 'y'.

In the final analysis, the 'accuracy' (if there is such a thing) of all accounts come down the judgement of directors and auditors and if these two parties cannot agree to, it will come down to negotiation. Accordingly, published accounts can vary from being ultra-cautious to excessively optimistic, but, of course, the vast majority are somewhere in the middle. But at the extreme end of the middle band, you will find variations between the cautious and the imprudent.

It has to be said that examples where the accounts of companies in Europe have been either totally imprudent or fraudulent are extremely rare. Nevertheless, it was recognised that European counties and the companies within them have varying interpretations on how accounts should be put together not only from a judgemental point of view, but also in the way they were presented. Accordingly, it was felt that it was difficult for investors to compare different companies, especially if they were based in different countries. To correct this situation, the International Accounting Standards Board (IASB) developed international accounting standards (IAS) and IFRS. Such standards impacted financial reporting in the United Kingdom on 1 January 2005.

International Financial Reporting Standards

Accounts prepared under the historical cost convention had two pillars of integrity, the matching concept and the prudence concept. The matching concept applied the principle that in a given period, sales and the costs associated with those sales must match, giving rise to accruals and prepayments. The prudence concept was unequivocal; profits could not be taken before they were earned and companies had to create a provision to account for any potential liability. These two concepts ensured that provided accounts were honestly prepared, the 'profit and loss' account would show a profit or loss that was prudent. What 'prudent' in this context meant was that taking into account that the profit or loss was struck after making a series of judgements, it was very unlikely that the profit was overstated or loss understated.

The historical cost convention, therefore, produced a Profit and Loss account that could usually be relied upon and using this document to calculate earnings per share allowed investors to assess the trend over time. However, the downside of the historical cost convention was that if the accounting standards were applied literally, key liabilities (usually long-term liabilities), namely pension liabilities and liabilities relating to financial derivatives, could be missed off the Balance Sheet.

As discussed in the following chapter, companies can be valued by assessing future potential income streams and the asset value of the company. Investors found that they could make valid investment judgements from the Profit and Loss Account only to be caught out by not knowing the true liabilities of the company. The Cash Flow Statement helped in that if assets were overstated, the company would not be generating the cash their operating profit suggested should be. But there was no way of assessing what the missing liabilities might be as they would only come to light at the time they had to be settled.

The ASB concluded that the way to resolve this problem of missing liabilities was to move from historical costing (assets and costs are recorded at their transactional values) to 'fair value' accounting.

All companies who are members of either Le Capital Investissement, the British Venture Capital Association or the European Private Equity & Venture Capital Association have agreed to value their investments using fair value principles. These organisations have produced a booklet 'International Private

Equity And Venture Capital Valuation Guidelines', which defines the concept of 'fair value':

> Fair Value is the amount for which an asset could be exchanged between knowledgeable, willing parties in an arm's length transaction.
>
> The estimation of Fair Value does not assume that the Underlying Business is saleable at the reporting date or that its current shareholders have an intention to sell their holdings in the near future.
>
> The objective is to estimate the exchange price at which hypothetical Market Participants would agree to transact.
>
> Fair Value is not the amount that an entity would receive or pay in a forced transaction, involuntary liquidation or distressed sale.
>
> Although transfers of shares in private businesses are often subject to restrictions, rights of pre-emption and other barriers, it should still be possible to estimate what amount a willing buyer would pay to take ownership of the investment.

These organisations own assets in the form of investments that they plan to dispose of in the medium to longer term. Accordingly, as a matter of course, they will seek to establish 'fair value' on an ongoing basis to enable them to make the key decision of staying with a particular investment or disposing it of. Do nothing in the long term is not an option. In other words, if there was no market for a particular investment, because for example there would never be a willing buyer, then that investment would have to have a 'nil' valuation. So investment companies should be able to establish 'fair value' because they hold assets that they intend to sell and would not have bought them in the first place if they knew there was no market for their assets.

However, the concept of 'fair value' under IFRS goes further and insists that a 'fair value' calculation be made even where there is no market for the asset. Some academics argue that this is perfectly valid and that estimating fair values will become a culture. Dimitris N. Chorafas writes:

> Fair value: This will, in all likelihood, be the most significant impact of IFRS. Fair value of assets and liabilities that have not been traded will become a culture, uncertainty over its measurement when no market exists for certain issues notwithstanding.
>
> (*Source*: IRFS, Fair Values and Corporate Governance (2006), p. 59, Dimitris N. Chorafas, Elsevier)

However, the contrary view is that calculating fair values where there is no discernable market could lead to assets being overstated and that in such circumstances it would be more prudent to use historical cost values. In addition, it could be argued that in applying fair value this way the safeguards inherent in historical cost accounting have been abandoned, in that the matching concept and the prudence concept no longer apply. For example, bookmakers often take bets ante-post for events that take place after the company's year end. Under UK GAAP, these were treated as payments in advance (creditors in the Balance Sheet) and had no impact on the Profit and Loss Account. Under IFRS, such payments in advance are treated as financial instruments and accordingly must be valued a 'fair value'. But it is absolutely impossible to estimate this, as the results of the events betted on cannot be reliably predicted. All the bookmakers can do is make an assessment taking into account the ante-post bets already lost through already declared non-runners and the overall betting margin usually achieved. This means that the bookmaking company will be forced to take a profit before it is earned, something that can hardly be described as being prudent.

A further difficulty is that there is no longer a distinction between a real liability and the one that could be described as imaginary. A 'real liability' is one where the liability will eventually have to be settled and an 'imaginary liability' is one that is never settled in the books of the company for which accounts are to be prepared.

At the beginning of 2007 a brief questionnaire was sent to the Finance Director of 100 FTSE 350 companies. Two of the questions were:

- From an investor point of view, do you believe that IFRS provides better information than UK GAAP?
- In the last complete financial year, how much extra have you spent complying with IFRS than you would have spent producing accounts under UK GAAP (if any)?

There were eighteen respondents (18% of sample) and while such a low response rate might not be statistically sufficient to form a judgement, only three (17%) voted in favour of IFRS. They gave the cost of implementing IFRS in the range of zero (we have used internal resources and have not quantified the cost) to £2 million. The average was £384 000.

Some respondents volunteered opinions and the three given below were representative of the overall view:

In favour: 'I think it very important that we have International Standards so that companies in different companies can be compared.'

Against: 'I do not believe that IFRS provides any better information but at least there is a greater consistency between all European companies. The Investors have struggled to understand the impact of IFRS upon companies and spend even more time reviewing cash flows.'

Against: 'Not quite the contrary, IFRS has resulted in considerable pollution of reporting. A point which it seems the IASB is now starting to recognise since it has observed that the merging of cash and value based items is not helpful. We have maintained our split of "Trading" and "Other Items" in our Income Statement – an approach which is non-compliant with IFRS but which it is possible the standards will change to!!'

The point made by the respondent about merging of cash and value-based items is the same as the point about a real liability (cash) and an imaginary liability (value-based). An example of an 'imaginary liability' is 'share-based payments', where the 'fair value' of share options must be charged to the Income Statement, with the credit going to 'equity' in the Balance Sheet. But if no entry was made for share-based payments, then although the 'retained earnings' would be higher, the figure for 'equity' would be the same. The effect of this 'share-based payments' entry, therefore, is that it is a one-sided entry (debit) only. Even worse, as companies continue to show 'diluted earnings per share', it means that this calculation has been subject to a double hit for the same thing, firstly the cost of the option and secondly the dilution.

Apart from imaginary liabilities, the worst aspect of IFRS is the abandonment of the prudence concept, as under this current standard, profits are taken into the Income Statement before they are earned. Such imaginary profits are then taxed. The accounts for the 'Big Yellow Group plc' demonstrate this absurdity; having to comply with IFRS, their Consolidated Income Statement for 31 March 2006 showed profits of £118.547 million and taxation of £35.112 million, giving earnings per share of 82.10 pence. However, 'to give a clearer understanding of the Group's underlying trading performance', a note in the accounts shows 'an "adjusted" earnings per share of 8.91 pence'. In his 'Financial Review', the Finance Director points out 'the group's actual cash tax liability for the year is, however, nil, as . . . .'

So we are left in the position that IFRS has improved matters by forcing companies to provide a Balance Sheet that includes all known liabilities, but has made matters worse by changing a Profit and Loss Account from a document where earnings per share could be extracted to establish a trend over the years to an Income Statement that is subject to so much volatility that it becomes potentially meaningless. However, the good news is that the 'Cash Flow Statement' can be adjusted to assess what the earnings per share should really be and this combined with a better Balance Sheet means that investors have, overall, improved tools to work with. How 'earnings per share' can be validated is illustrated in Chapter 4.

In Chapter 2, Figures 2.3 and 2.4 showed the Profit and Loss Account, Balance Sheet and Cash Flow Statement for 'A Food Manufacturing Company' using a UK GAAP format. Figures 3.1–3.3 show the same accounts for 2006 as they would appear under IFRS. Note that as the format is different, the numbers are also different. The format differences are explained below:

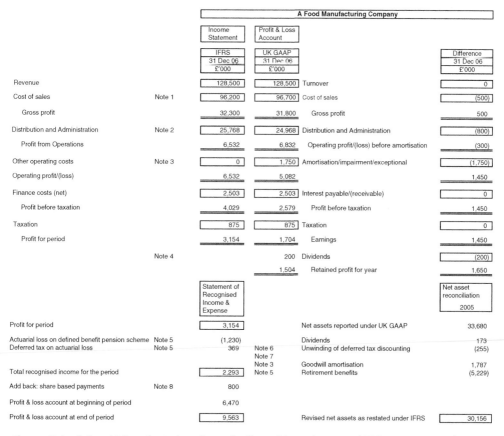

		Income Statement	Profit & Loss Account		Difference
		IFRS 31 Dec 06 £'000	UK GAAP 31 Dec 06 £'000		31 Dec 06 £'000
Revenue		128,500	128,500	Turnover	0
Cost of sales	Note 1	96,200	96,700	Cost of sales	(500)
Gross profit		32,300	31,800	Gross profit	500
Distribution and Administration	Note 2	25,768	24,968	Distribution and Administration	(800)
Profit from Operations		6,532	6,832	Operating profit/(loss) before amortisation	(300)
Other operating costs	Note 3	0	1,750	Amortisation/impairment/exceptional	(1,750)
Operating profit/(loss)		6,532	5,082		1,450
Finance costs (net)		2,503	2,503	Interest payable/(receivable)	0
Profit before taxation		4,029	2,579	Profit before taxation	1,450
Taxation		875	875	Taxation	0
Profit for period		3,154	1,704	Earnings	1,450
	Note 4		200	Dividends	(200)
			1,504	Retained profit for year	1,650

		Statement of Recognised Income & Expense			Net asset reconciliation 2005
Profit for period		3,154		Net assets reported under UK GAAP	33,680
Actuarial loss on defined benefit pension scheme	Note 5	(1,230)		Dividends	173
Deferred tax on actuarial loss	Note 5	369	Note 6	Unwinding of deferred tax discounting	(255)
			Note 7		
			Note 3	Goodwill amortisation	1,787
Total recognised income for the period		2,293	Note 5	Retirement benefits	(5,229)
Add back: share based payments	Note 8	800			
Profit & loss account at beginning of period		6,470			
Profit & loss account at end of period		9,563		Revised net assets as restated under IFRS	30,156

Figure 3.1   A Food Manufacturing Co. – Profit and Loss Account (IFRS vs. UK GAAP)

A Food Manufacturing Company					
		Balance Sheet	Balance Sheet	(UK GAAP Balance Sheet is in IFRS Format)	
		IFRS 31 Dec 06 £'000	UK GAAP 31 Dec 06 £'000		Difference 31 Dec 06 £'000
Assets					
Non-current assets					
Goodwill	Note 3	35,743	32,206	Goodwill	3,537
Other intangible assets	Note 1/9	1,700	0	Other intangible assets	1,700
Property, plant and equipment	Note 9	59,260	60,460	Tangible assets	(1,200)
Deferred tax asset	Note 3	2,610	0		2,610
Investments	Note 10	1,100	1,200	Investments	(100)
		100,413	93,866		6,547
Current assets					
Inventories		9,720	9,720	Stock	0
Trade and other receivables		21,417	21,417	Debtors	0
Cash and cash equivalents		4,456	4,456	Cash	0
		35,593	35,593		0
Total assets		136,006	129,459	**Total assets**	6,547
Liabilities					
Current liabilities					
Trade and other payables	Note 4	28,867	29,240	Trade creditors	(373)
Current tax liabilities		3,635	3,635	Other creditors	0
Borrowings		4,200	4,200	Bank overdraft and loans	0
		36,702	37,075		(373)
Non-current liabilities					
Long term borrowings		50,000	50,000	Long term debt	0
Financial instruments	Note 11	103			103
Retirement benefit obligations	Note 5	8,700			8,700
Deferred tax liabilities	Note 6	255			255
Other provisions for liabilities & charges		7,200	7,200	Other long term liabilities	0
		66,258	57,200		9,058
Total liabilities		102,960	94,275	**Total liabilities**	8,685
Net assets		33,046	35,184	**Net assets**	(2,138)
Equity					
Called up share capital		3,632	3,632	Share capital	0
Share premium account		18,024	18,024	Share premium account	0
Revaluation reserve					0
Other reserves		1,827	2,030	Capital reserves	(203)
Retained earnings	(as fig. 3.1)	9,563	11,498	Retained earnings	(1,935)
Total shareholders' equity		33,046	35,184	**Total shareholders' equity**	(2,138)

Figure 3.2   A Food Manufacturing Co. – Balance Sheet (IFRS vs. UK GAAP)

The Income Statement

The Income Statement replaces the Profit and Loss Account; the only real format difference between the two being that the former does not show dividends, so that the bottom line is 'profit after tax'. In the Profit and Loss Account, 'profit after tax' was the same as 'earnings' and represented the profit that belonged to shareholders, which, in theory at least, could be distributed to shareholders. This is no longer the case because as non-monetary adjustments are now appearing in the Income Statement, profit after tax does not necessarily represent earnings that could be described as distributable. Figure 3.1 illustrates the differences between the Profit and Loss Account (UK GAAP) and the Income Statement (IFRS).

	IFRS Style
Cash Flow Statement for	31 Dec 06
A Food Manufacturing company	£'000

Reconciliation of profit to net
cash inflow from operating activities

Profit after taxation	**3,154**
Taxation	875
Interest	2,503
Operating profit	**6,532**
Depreciation of tangible assets	5,740
Share based payments	800
(Increase)/decrease in stocks	380
(Increase)/decrease in debtors	8,697
Increase/(decrease) in creditors	1,199
Cash generated from operations	**23,348**
Interest paid	(2,503)
Tax paid	(467)
Net cash inflow from operating activities	**20,378**
Investment in development costs	(500)
Net cash outflow from investing activities	**(500)**
Repayment of bank loans	(15,000)
Dividends paid to shareholders	(173)
Net cash outflow from financing activities	**(15,173)**
Net increase in cash and cash equivalents	**4,705**

Reconciliation of cash flow with
movements in cash and cash equivalents

Opening cash and cash equivalents	(4,449)
Closing cash and cash equivalents	256
Movement in cash and cash equivalents	**4,705**

Figure 3.3 A Food Manufacturing Co. – Cash Flow Statement (IFRS vs. UK GAAP)

The Balance Sheet

The Balance Sheet under UK GAAP style and IFRS style changes both in format and terminology. In essence, IFRS uses American terminology. The differences are:

	UK GAAP	IFRS
Current assets manufactured for sale or bought for resale	Stock	Inventory
People who owe the business money	Debtors	Receivables
People the business owe money to	Creditors	Payables

The UK GAAP Balance Sheet was designed to show the 'total capital employed', and after deducting long-term debt this agreed with 'shareholders' funds', so the format was:

Fixed assets at cost less cumulative depreciation = Net fixed assets
Current assets less current liabilities = Working capital
Net fixed assets plus working capital = Total capital employed.
Total capital employed less long-term debt = Net assets.
Share capital plus share premium plus capital reserves plus cumulative Profit and Loss Account = Shareholders' funds.
Net Assets = Shareholders' funds.

The IFRS Balance Sheet is much more informative, with the following information available on the face of the Balance Sheet, rather than in the notes under UK GAAP

- Goodwill is separated from 'other intangible assets'.
- The deferred tax asset is not netted off with the deferred tax liability.
- Investments are shown separately.
- Current tax liabilities and borrowings are shown separately and not simply lumped together with 'trade and other payables'.
- Provisions have to be evaluated so that they are shown correctly as current or non-current (formerly known as 'fixed' under UK GAAP) liabilities.
- Retirement benefit obligations are included in non-current liabilities.

The format under IFRS also changes:

Non-current assets plus current assets = Total assets
Current liabilities plus non-current liabilities = Total liabilities

Total assets less total liabilities = Net assets
Net assets = Total shareholders' equity.

Figure 3.2 illustrates the differences between the Balance Sheet under UK GAAP and the Balance Sheet under IFRS.

The Cash Flow Statement

The Cash Flow Statement is much clearer under IFRS than it was under UK GAAP and is easier to follow. The main difference between the two statements is that under UK GAAP, 'operating profit' (profit before interest and tax) is reconciled to 'net cash inflow from operating activities', whereas under IFRS, 'profit after tax' is reconciled with 'net cash inflow from operating activities.'

Under IFRS, the starting figure is 'profit after taxation', to which interest and tax (as shown in the Income Statement) are added to get to 'operating profit'. From this figure, non-cash charges such as depreciation and share-based payments are added and then movement in working capital is either added or deducted, as the case may be, to arrive at 'cash generated from operations'. This figure represents what 'cash inflow from operating activities' was under UK GAAP. Finally, the actual interest and the tax paid are deduced from 'cash generated from operations' to arrive at 'cash inflow from operating activities' under IFRS style.

This is simpler than it was under UK GAAP, because we now have just three sections:

Net cash inflow/(outflow) from operating activities
Net cash inflow/(outflow) from investing activities
Net cash inflow/(outflow) from financing activities

The sum of these three sections is the same as the increase/(decrease) in cash and cash equivalents.

With regard to the Cash Flow Statement, the only other difference between UK GAAP and IFRS is that the former reconciles to 'cash', whereas the latter reconciles to 'cash and cash equivalent'. A 'cash equivalent' is a financial instrument where the value is known and secure and can be converted to cash within 3 months of the Balance Sheet date.

Figure 3.3 illustrates the differences in Cash Flow Statement under UK GAAP and IFRS. In our 'Food Manufacturing Company' illustration, there are no 'cash equivalents' and accordingly unlike the Income Statement and the Balance Sheet, the numbers between the two systems match. This is because all the changes made by IFRS are book entries that have no impact on cash.

These differences in the Income Statement and the Balance Sheet are explained below and match with the 'note numbers' shown in the accounts.

Revenue recognition

There are two aspects of revenue recognition, what it is and when you recognise it. In normal circumstances, revenue is recognised when the goods or service has been supplied and the customer, subject to the agreed credit terms, legally has to pay . But there can be complications. An engineering company might be working on a large project where the terms are (say) 20% deposit on order, interim payment of 30% when half complete, 40% on delivery and 10% when fully commissioned, meaning that the equipment is working satisfactorily on the customer's site. Revenue and expenses would be recognised in proportion to the stage completed on a contract, but in such circumstances, when to declare the revenue will be a matter of judgement.

Another example could be a manufacturer developing software for a huge organisation that could take several years to complete. In such cases, stage payments are usually negotiated, but again when to take the revenue takes a considerable amount of judgement and over the years some computer companies have either collapsed or seen their share price fall when it was admitted that revenue had been taken early.

Of course, in all cases where revenue is taken early, the giveaway is ever expanding debtor days. To reiterate what has been stated earlier, debtor days being too high, taking into account the particular industry and competition, means that either sales have been taken early or credit control is poor. Either way, investing in companies with such a profile is risky, although some do recover.

For banks, revenue becomes 'income' where income is defined as interest receivable less interest payable, plus other income where applicable such as income from trading activities, fees, commissions and insurance premiums. For insurance companies, revenue becomes net premiums earned plus net investment return and other operating income.

For bookmaking companies, revenue under UK GAAP was the amount wagered by bettors. Cost of sales was the amount returned to bettors for winning bets, leaving 'gross win' from which the costs associated with these bets were deducted to arrive at the gross profit. The costs associated with betting include such things as costs associated with running betting shops, betting taxes, software supplier costs and data rights.

Under IRFS, what used to be 'gross win' is now defined as revenue and to assess bookmaking companies for investment purposes we are reliant upon them giving their gross take figure (what used to be 'revenue' under UK GAAP) as well. The reason for this is that the percentage returned to bettors will vary from one accounting period to another, depending upon the results. In the long term, the gross win figure will settle down to that expected based on in-built margins (in the same way the number of 'heads' or 'tails' will get closer to 50% of the total, the more times a coin is spun), but any 6-month period could be some way off the mean. For this reason, when judging trends in bookmaking companies, UK GAAP revenue is more important than IFRS revenue.

Research and development (notes 1 and 9)

How to deal with expenditure on research and development is one of those areas where a considerable amount of judgement is called for. It could be argued that from a prudent point of view, such expenditure should be written off to the Income Statement, while others might argue that as the expenditure will generate future income streams, it should be capitalised. IFRS attempts to clarify the position by declaring that research costs (cost associated with developing an unknown product) should be written off while development costs should be capitalised as an intangible asset. Development costs are those associated with bringing a new product from the research stage to getting it to a state where it is ready to be sold. In our example, £500 000 of development costs that would have been written off, following a judgemental decision, have been capitalised.

Share-based payments (notes 2 and 8)

If we examine 'share-based payments', we find that the concept is flawed from practically every aspect examined. Under historical cost accounting, what was charged into the accounts was the exact value of the transaction. If a director or manager a got an exceptionally good deal on a commodity purchase, then the accounts reflected the achievement. On the other hand, if a poor manager paid too much for an item, again the accounts reflected what had actually happened. Anyone with a knowledge of the type of transactions entered into could assess whether the management of a particular company was up to the job or not.

Now, under IFRS, we have moved from recording the actual cost of transaction to recording transactions at 'fair value', the main difficulty being how you assess the fair value. It is all rather subjective.

Probably, the most subjective of all the IFRS rules is the concept of charging the Income Statement (and crediting 'equity') with the 'fair value' of share options, where directors and other senior employees are granted such options. Traditionally, directors and in some cases senior employees have been granted share options giving them the option of purchasing the company's shares at price prevailing at the date of the grant some time in future. Often the future is any time between (say) 5 years hence and 10 years from the date of the grant.

Share options are designed both to provide an incentive for the employee to perform well and to protect the company from having the employee headhunted and poached by another. This is achieved by having a clause to the effect that if the employee leaves the company prior to the first exercise date, then all share options held would lapse.

The beauty of share options is that it is a classic win–win play. If, in future, the company's share price has increased, then the director or the employee holding the option will exercise it. In response, the company will issue more shares, and as the entry for this will be debit 'cash received', credit 'share capital' and credit 'share premium', rather that costing the company, it will strengthen its Balance Sheet. The only losers will be the other shareholders who will have their shareholding diluted, but they will not be unhappy as it would have simply taken the edge off the gains they must have made. In addition to this, shareholders will have realised that if the directors and other senior employees had not been given the incentive in the first place, then there might not have been any gains. Clearly, 95% plus of gain is better than 100% of no gain at all. This is illustrated below.

A company's latest accounts for their year ended 31 December 2006 show a share capital comprising 105 000 000 ordinary shares of 0.1 pence each that have been issued for 25 pence each. On 31 December 2003, the directors were granted options to buy 4 250 000 0.1-pence ordinary shares for £1 per share anytime between 31 December 2009 and 31 December 2012, provided they remain an employee of the company on 31 December 2007 and provided that the company's earnings per share (as a percentage of the issue price to get a like for like calculation) is more than 10% higher than the sector averages in each of the five years 2003–2007.

The company declared earnings of £36 million, shareholders' equity was valued at £175 million and the company's ordinary shares were quoted at 540 pence at their year end. At this stage there is no guarantee that the share options will have any value because the hurdle set for 2007 cannot have been achieved. So shareholders can reasonably assume that either the share price will go higher and the directors will be able to exercise their options or if things do not work out as per plan, then they will not become diluted.

If shareholders assume the best, then it is a simple matter to calculate the effect of potential dilution:

	Without dilution	With dilution
Number of shares	105.000 million	109.250 million
Market price of share	540 pence	
Market price of company	£567.000 million	£567.000 million
Add: issue of shares		£4.250 million
Value of company	£567.000 million	£571.250 million
Market price of share	540 pence	523 pence

Note that the above calculation assumes that the goodwill built into the share price, being the difference between the market price and the asset value per share (shareholders' funds divided by the number of ordinary shares), remains the same after dilution.

Another way of calculating dilution is to calculate the diluted earnings per share:

	Without dilution	With dilution
Number of shares	105.000 million	109.250 million
Earnings	£36.000 million	£36.000 million
Earnings per share (pence)	34.3	33.0

If the difference between the basic and the diluted earnings per share (1.3 pence) is multiplied by the basic P/E ratio of 15.74, we get a valuation of 20.5 pence. This compares with the difference of 17 pence, based on market values. This difference (3.5 pence) is the effect of the directors subscribing £4.25 million for shares. So whichever way it is looked at, the effect of dilution on shareholders is between 17 pence and 20.5 pence. Nothing to get really exited about!

Published accounts show the potential diluted effect of share options and all seemed well. But along comes the ASB that determines that the hypothetical cost of share options must be recognised in the accounts, the problem being, of course, the impossibility of calculating the 'fair value' of such transactions.

In most cases, companies use either Monte Carlo option pricing model or the Black-Scholes option pricing model (sometimes both), with the latter model being used in the majority of cases. Now while the use of the Black-Scholes option pricing model might appeal to some academics, from investors' point of view the model has significant flaws.

The book by Lowenstein 'When Genius Failed – The Rise and Fall of Long Term Capital Management' (Harper Collins, 2001) describes how the model is based on the assumption that a stock price will follow a random walk in continuous time (p. 66) but as random events such as the flip of a coin are independent of each other, markets have memories (pp. 72 and 73).

He writes:

> Early in 1998, Long Term began to short large amounts of equity volatility (equity vol)....and it set the fund ineluctably on the road to disaster. Equity vol comes straight from the Black-Scholes model. It is based on the assumption that the volatility of stocks is, over time, consistent.

The professors running Long-Term Capital Management calculated that, using the Black-Scholes model, the options market was pricing in volatility of around 20% when in fact actual volatility was only about 15%. Now, being followers of the efficient market hypothesis, they believed that markets had got it wrong and that accordingly option prices would fall. What they had not understood was that investors can act in a way they believe is perfectly rational, which to academics trained in mathematics and financial economics appear completely irrational.

What had happened was that investors were panicking because they believed equity prices were about to fall back sharply. The market was capitalising on such panic by selling products at a price, of course, that protected investors against the downside risk of share prices falling back. The salesman's patter might have read 'invest in our fund; if the market goes up we will pay you 75% of the increase in the index (the index the fund was being linked to), but if it goes down you lose nothing. The worst that can happen is you get your money back.'

If the market went down, then institutions selling these products would not make any profit, so they bought options to protect themselves. Demand for such options accordingly increased, pushing up the price. The difference between the actual option prices and the prices determined by the Black-Scholes model was simply the cost of panic in the market. Now, the efficient market hypothesis believes that an efficient market will quickly correct irrational factors such as panic, but it does not. Human beings, once in panic mode, stay panicking long after it is rational to do so and certainly even after the options expired.

The point in the above example is that the vital constituent of the Black-Scholes model that future volatility can be assumed from historical records is not necessarily realistic. Mathematical models that assume that future results will always fit inside a normal bell curve are bound to fail in the long term, because the future is always about the unexpected. After all, the future is the spice of life and what makes the requirement of judgement (as against 'mathematical certainty') a consistent feature.

The effect of volatility on the Black-Scholes model can be seen from the table below. In each case, the share is currently priced at 692 pence and the strike price (the price at which the option holder can buy the share) is 692 pence. The option has an expected life of 5 years or 8.5 years, the risk-free rate is assumed to be 4.3% and the dividend yield is expected to be 2.0%.

Assumed volatility (%)	Black-Scholes option price (pence)	
	5-year term	8.5-year term
0.1	66.1	101.0
10.0	92.3	124.9
20.0	141.3	179.3
22.0	151.3	190.5
27.0	176.2	218.5
30.0	191.1	235.1
35.0	215.5	262.2
40.0	239.5	288.4
45.0	263.0	313.7
50.0	285.8	337.8

In effect, the Black-Scholes model assumes two things, neither of which holds true:

- Markets are perfect, every investor is equally knowledgeable and will act rationally.
- The historical volatility of a share is a good predictor of future volatility as it is constant.

However, the key point is that you can never mathematically model human behaviour, because with human beings you are dealing with uncertainty, rather than risk.

Nevertheless, companies have been forced to charge their Income Statement with the theoretical cost of share options, based on the rules laid down by IFRS 2, even though from investors' point of view the amounts involved are not material and will lead to an unnecessary volatility in earnings.

For the purpose of share-based payments, there are three key dates: grant date, vesting date and exercise date. The grant date is the date at which the share options were granted (31 December 2003 in the above example); the vesting date is that date at which the employees are unconditionally entitled to the share options (31 December 2007 in the above example) and the exercise date is the earliest date at which the options can be exercised (31 December 2009 in the above example).

For IFRS 2, the key date is the vesting date for this is the date at which the value of the share option becomes fixed and charged to the Income Statement on a permanent basis. In the meantime, for share options granted on or after 7 November 2002, companies have to accrue for the cost of the share option from the grant date to the vesting date. In our example, this would mean the following:

- At 31 December 2004, calculate theoretical option cost for 4.25 million shares and divide by 4.
- At 31 December 2005, calculate same option (using latest data) and divide by 2. From this, take away the 2004 accrual to arrive at the 2005 accrual.
- At 31 December 2006, calculate same option (again using latest data) and divide by three-quarters. From this, take away the 2005 accrual to arrive at the 2006 accrual.
- At 31 December 2007, calculate same option (using latest information available). From this take, away the 2006 accrual. This charge in the Income Statement will now become permanent and will not be changed.

Now if in 2009, disaster struck the company and the share price fell to (say) 90 pence, then the share options could not be exercised. Clearly in such cases, there is no cost to the company, yet the charge to the Income Statement would stand. This has to be irrational, but the argument the ASB use is that share options have been granted for services provided. Again, it could be argued that such reasoning is illogical. The Directors are paid a salary for services rendered and receive share options along with other incentives to achieve an above-average performance. If, for example, a director's contract stated that he would receive a bonus of 1% of basic salary for every one percentage point the company's share price beat the FTSE 100 index and if the company's closing share price fell below that index, then there would be no bonus paid.

There is a basic rule in management accounting that states that the benefit of a particular report must exceed the cost of producing it; otherwise, there is no point in preparing it in the first place. Investors might reasonably question whether the benefit of IFRS 2 to them is greater than the costs involved in getting together the necessary data, especially because the charge has minimal impact on earnings per share.

The accounts of 30 companies, with accounting year ends of 31 January 2006 or later, were examined. These companies were selected at random, slightly adjusted to ensure that a full range based on size was included. The capital employed by these companies ranged from £34 million to £713 162 million. The cost of share options charged to their Income Statement was added to their stated earnings, from which an 'earnings per share' excluding share options was calculated and compared to the actual earnings per share.

The results are as below:

	Earnings per share		%
	Excluding share options (pence)	Actual (as accounts) (pence)	
1	169.63	168.27	99.2
2	148.59	147.23	99.1
3	113.47	113.26	99.8
4	71.94	70.46	97.9
5	55.53	51.77	93.2
6	46.62	42.72	91.6
7	45.04	44.21	98.2

	Earnings per share		%
	Excluding share options (pence)	Actual (as accounts) (pence)	
8	42.74	41.71	97.6
9	42.41	41.64	98.2
10	35.85	35.04	97.7
11	34.17	33.86	99.1
12	28.69	28.13	98.0
13	27.50	27.12	98.6
14	25.21	25.11	99.6
15	24.42	23.70	97.1
16	17.33	17.14	98.9
17	15.34	15.27	99.5
18	13.55	12.71	93.8
19	12.77	12.74	99.8
20	10.77	10.55	98.0
21	10.38	10.38	100.0
22	8.72	8.52	97.7
23	8.03	8.03	100.0
24	6.99	6.44	92.1
25	5.43	5.19	95.6
26	3.86	3.83	99.2
27	3.35	2.96	88.4
28	2.64	2.40	90.9
29	(0.98)	(1.02)	96.8
30	(11.51)	(11.90)	96.6

A further point to consider is that the option price as calculated by the Black-Scholes model could not, even by stretching the imagination, be deemed to be a 'fair value' price. Given that 'fair value' is deemed to be 'the amount with which an asset could be exchanged between knowledgeable, willing parties in an arm's length transaction', the first thing to evaluate is who the willing parties might be. The most likely parties would be whoever wanted to buy the option and banks, those operating through traders would be the likely sellers. Now, let it be assumed that despite its flaws. the Black-Scholes model is the most accurate model available. What this model would tell us would be, in betting terms, the break-even price; in other words, the price at which neither party could expect to make a profit. But we know that the sellers always aim to make a profit, so that the option price they would quote would probably be around 40% plus above the Black-Scholes computation.

It could not be argued otherwise because banks always build in a profit margin into the financial derivatives they sell, yet they find willing buyers, in the same way as bookmakers find willing punters despite their profit margin built into the odds. All these lead to the inescapable conclusion that IFRS 2 is pretty pointless. In our example (Figure 3.1), the cost of share options is assumed to be £800 000. Note 2 shows the charge while note 8 demonstrates that the credit is found in equity.

Intangible assets (notes 1 and 3)

An intangible asset is defined as the one that cannot be seen or touched, but according to IAS 38 (see note accompanying IFRS vs. UK GAAP summary) it is defined as 'an identifiable non-monetary asset without physical substance'. The key words must be 'physical substance' because although computer software can usually be seen in the form of a disc, what you see cannot be substantial enough to demonstrate what you get. Accordingly, under IFRS, computer software that can be used independently of a particular hardware configuration is deemed to be an intangible asset, rather than a tangible asset as it was under UK GAAP.

It could be argued that this decision is somewhat illogical, given the other types of intangible asset:

- Goodwill, being the difference between the price paid for a business and the fair value of the net assets in that business.
- Development costs, including the cost of tooling.
- The costs of setting up and maintaining brands, provided these costs are external to the company.

These intangible assets can only be deemed to be assets and therefore Balance Sheet items if the expenditure is expected to generate future income streams. In all these cases, if the expenditure does generate income streams, then they are likely to continue to do so as long as the company is in business. Accordingly, these assets are deemed to have indefinite useful lives.

For most companies, the largest intangible asset is usually 'goodwill', a type of asset with an indefinable lifespan, which was therefore deemed indefinite.

Under UK GAAP, it was felt prudent to assume that these assets would have a lifespan of 20 years and accordingly these would be amortised at the rate of 5% per annum. However, under IFRS, such intangible assets cannot be amortised. Instead, a judgement has to be made as to the fair value of the intangible asset. This may be defined as the higher of market value of the asset less costs associated with selling the assets and the 'value in use' of the asset. The 'value in use' takes into account predicted future income streams and discount rates that reflect the market conditions and the risks involved. All of which must be judgemental and to some extent subjective.

If the fair value of the intangible asset is less than the amount shown in the Balance Sheet, then it is 'impaired' to bring it back to the correct value. This impairment is charged to the Income Statement, with the corresponding credit reducing the value of the intangible asset.

Intangible assets must be tested annually and their fair value adjusted accordingly. If in the following year, the fair value of the intangible asset is greater than it was, then the impairment is reversed to bring it back to its correct valuation. This time, the Income Statement would be credited and the asset debited. However, the value of the intangible asset cannot be greater than its original cost, so there cannot be overall negative impairment.

Given valuations can go up and down; it again means that the volatility will result in it being difficult to interpret the Income Statement. As can be seen, the vast majority of intangible assets will no longer be amortised, but will instead be impaired as appropriate, and it is this that makes computer software stand out. Most companies rightly believe that computer software has a finite life and where it is developed for a particular company cannot have a market value in the accepted sense of the word. In addition, computer software is not installed to generate future business, but rather to enable the company to organise its administration effectively. Accordingly, most company's write-off their software over 3 years and accordingly amortise it. On the basis that software will not work without the associated hardware, it would seem logical to treat both as a tangible asset.

In our example (Figure 3.1), it is assumed that the fair value of the intangible asset is the same value as the carrying value and accordingly no impairment is required. The amount charged under UK GAAP reflected the annual charge for amortisation. In Figure 3.2, 'other intangible assets' is assumed to include software and development costs.

Investment property and investment property under development (Case Study: UNITE Group plc)

This is an area where there has been a significant change from UK GAAP to IFRS, and this is explained succinctly in UNITE Group plc's annual accounts for 2005.

UNITE Group plc is a company based in Bristol, which has a core strategy of building and maintaining student accommodation at universities. The company's primary focus is to build modern and safe student accommodation in a relaxed atmosphere, thereby creating a community environment. Typical of this vision is 'The Heights' complex in Birmingham, a new concept of student village that houses 911 students and incorporates a large common room, a quiet room and a gym. The company is expanding and has property under development as well as completed property.

UNITE Group plc's 2005 accounts explain the following.

Investment property and investment property under development

Under IFRS, completed investment property (accounted for under IAS 40) is held separately from investment property under development (accounted for under IAS 16).

Completed investment property is carried at fair value under IAS 40, which equates to the market value previously applied under UK GAAP. There is therefore no equity impact arising from the change to IFRS in respect of these properties.

Investment property under development is carried at fair value under IAS 16, which differs slightly from the directors' valuations previously applied under UK GAAP. This has resulted in additional value being recognised in both opening and closing balance sheets. IFRS fair values for both the above classes of property have been calculated by the Group's external valuers.

Under UK GAAP, all revaluations of property were made directly in equity (unless values fell below cost). Under IFRS, investment properties under development continue to be accounted for this way but completed property valuation movements are recognised in the Income Statement. In addition, when a property under development is completed and transferred to investment property, the difference between its fair value at that date and its previous carrying value is recognised in the Income Statement. This has resulted in an increase in the profit of £20.869 million under IFRS (2004).

(*Source*: Reproduced from UNITE Group plc's 2005 accounts, with kind permission from the Board of UNITE Group plc.)

UNITE Group plc's accounts for 2005 showed a revaluation surplus in the Income Statement of £23.377 million, so that the overall profit of £32.310 for the year equated to an earnings per share of 28.7 pence. When this calculation was adjusted by removing valuation gains, movements in ineffective hedges and movements in deferred tax, brought about by IFRS (as against UK GAAP) earnings per share, fell to just 3.0 pence (Figures 3.4 and 3.5).

These accounting standards do raise issues that are worthy of debate. Based on UNITE Group plc's accounts, it would seem that UK GAAP is more prudent than IFRS, but far more importantly, in recording a profit before it is earned, the concept of prudence is thrown out of the window.

		Unite Group plc		
Consolidated Income Statement for the year ended	Notes	31 Dec 2006	31 Dec 2005	31 Dec 2004
		£'000	£'000	£'000
Revenue	1 [U2]	110,636	113,799	74,623
Cost of sales	1 [U2]	(49,889)	(54,864)	(24,678)
Administrative expense – goodwill impairment				(2,515)
Administrative expense – other		(19,751)	(15,671)	(14,284)
Profit/(loss) on disposal of property		(5,397)	2,534	23
Net valuation gains on investment property	1 & 2 [U8]	60,817	23,377	20,869
Net operating profit before net financing costs		96,416	69,175	54,038
Loan interest and similar charges	1 [U6]	(53,599)	(44,212)	(38,098)
Changes in fair value of ineffective hedges	1 [U6]	5,014	(4,317)	0
Finance income		1,551	1,541	1,137
Net financing costs	1 [U6]	(47,034)	(46,988)	(36,961)
Share of joint venture profit	1 [U11]	9,180	5,944	30
Profit before tax		58,562	28,131	17,107
Tax credit	1 [U7]	12,921	4,179	233
Profit for the year		71,483	32,310	17,340
Earnings per share – Basic	1 [U20]	58.4	28.7	15.8
Earnings per share – Diluted	1 [U20]	57.8	28.3	15.6

Note 1. In Unite Group plc's accounts various notes explain the above figures. The number in (square brackets) is the note number in this company's accounts for 2005, as follows: Figures in (brackets) below indicate corresponding note numbers in 2006.

Note 2 gives segmental analysis for sales and cost of sales;
Note 6 (7) provides details of interest costs, including amounts capitalised
Note 7 (8) demonstrates how the tax charge and deferred tax is calculated, including showing that tax on unrealised gains is deferred;
Note 8 (5) shows how the valuation of investment property and property under development has moved from the prior year (see script);
Note 11 (6) provides full details of subsidiares and joint ventures; and
Note 20 (10) explains that the basic and diluted earnings per share falls to 3.0p (loss 11.6p in 2006) when IFRS type adjustments are taken out.

Unite Plc's Income Statements for 2004 to 2006 are reproduced by kind permission of the Unite Group plc Board

Figure 3.4 UNITE Group plc – Income Statement for 2004 to 2006

Consolidated Balance Sheet as at		Unite Group plc		
		31 Dec 2006	31 Dec 2005	31 Dec 2004
		£'000	£'000	£'000
Assets				
Investment property		656,969	1,028,747	991,460
Investment property under construction		124,980	80,004	119,732
Property, plant and equipment		9,533	19,303	15,971
Investments in joint ventures		106,287	18,861	817
Intangible assets		5,216	5,465	4,753
Other receivables		4,973	8,618	6,079
Total non-current assets		907,958	1,160,998	1,138,812
Property under development	Note 1	12,093	0	0
Inventories		22,982	13,418	13,401
Trade and other receivables		70,165	66,011	26,246
Cash and cash equivalents		55,143	30,297	37,582
Total current assets		160,383	109,726	77,229
Total assets		1,068,341	1,270,724	1,216,041
Liabilitites				
Borrowings and financial derivatives		(63,563)	(124,541)	(106,153)
Trade and other payables		(78,594)	(73,559)	(71,675)
Total current liabilities		(142,157)	(198,100)	(177,828)
Borrowings and financial derivatives		(403,181)	(644,671)	(665,925)
Deferred tax liabilities		(41,816)	(45,255)	(50,479)
Total non-current liabilities		(444,997)	(689,926)	(716,404)
Total liabilities		(587,154)	(888,026)	(894,232)
Net Assets		481,187	382,698	321,809
Equity				
Issued share capital		30,763	30,435	27,825
Share premium		173,008	169,957	141,324
Merger reserve		40,177	40,177	40,177
Retained earnings		218,035	129,508	96,113
Revaluation reserve		18,053	17,531	16,370
Hedging reserve		1,151	(4,910)	0
Total equity		481,187	382,698	321,809

Note that In Unite Group plc's Balance Sheets (as reproduced above) there are acompanying notes providing details of each line.

Note 1. In 2006, UNITE Group plc created the a 'UK Student Accommodation Fund' in which the company owns a 39% stake and acts as a property and fund manager. It is likely that this fund will acquire the Groups future developments and accordingly property under development that will be sold to this fund are classified as current assets. This revised business model will allow the group to reduce its borrowings.

Unite Plc's Balance Sheets for 2004 to 2006 are reproduced by kind permission of the Unite Group plc Board

Figure 3.5 UNITE Group plc – Balance Sheet for 2004 to 2006

The issues here are that the Income Statement should reflect the profit generated in the period, while the Balance Sheet should show a true and fair valuation for assets and liabilities. Given that judgements are required to calculate fair value, it will be relatively certain that the figure calculated will turn out to be incorrect.

Anyone who has ever tried to sell a house will know that no two estate agents or valuers will come up with the same valuation on the property. Establishing the true market price is not an exact science and coming up with the answer relies upon educated guesswork. The problem under IFRS is that if traditional company valuation methods are used; a small error in property valuation will lead to completely unrealistic company valuations. This can be illustrated below with UNITE plc's 2005 accounts:

Average no. of shares ('000)	Earnings (£'000)		Net Assets (£'000)
		Properties	1 108 751
		Other	(726 053)
112 633	32 310		382 698

Earnings per share	28.7 pence	Asset value per share	339.8 pence

Price of share at 31 December 2005 = 400 pence

P/E ratio	13.9	Goodwill in share valuation 60.2 pence

Now if the property valuation had overvalued the properties by a mere 2.5%, then the picture would change:

Average no. of shares ('000)	Earnings (£'000)		Net Assets (£'000)
		Properties	1 081 032
		Other	(726 053)
112 633	4591		354 979

Earnings per share	4.1 pence	Asset value per share	315.2 pence

Price of share at 31 December 2005 = 400 pence
Price of share based on P/E ratio of 13.9 = 57 pence
Price of share based on maintaining goodwill = 375 pence

What this shows is that even very minor errors in valuation can have a dramatic effect on the Income Statement, and given the uncertainties in valuation, earnings per share calculated in this way simply cannot have much validity.

Of course, it is not suggested that there are any inaccuracies in the valuation of UNITE Group plc's accounts either for 2005 or 2006; the example above is merely to show the dramatic effect that minor variations in valuations can have on these types of company's accounts.

In addition, it should be noted that investors would base their valuation of companies such as UNITE Group plc on asset values, rather than on income. Nevertheless, this does demonstrate that including unrealised profits in Income Statements does not help investors to make rational decisions.

Dividends (note 4)

Most companies pay a dividend to their shareholders, usually twice a year. The interim dividend paid on the first six months is often between a quarter and one-third of that expected for the year.

At the end of each financial year, the directors meet to decide what the final dividend will be. In doing so, they take several factors into account:

- What they can afford to pay, given the results.
- The expectation of shareholders.
- How much of the earnings they want to hold back to pay for future growth.
- If the dividend is cut, how such action would impact the company's share price.

If a company is doing well, then the directors' decision is an easy one; they simply increase the dividend and explain that this decision reflects the strength of the company. However, if the company is doing badly, then the directors face a dilemma. Do they put a brave face on things and pay an increased dividend saying that this decision is based on their confidence that things will get better, or do they come clean? Dishonesty will hold up the share price in short term and will risk a middle- to long-term crash, while honesty usually leads to a short-term crash, but a very quick recovery.

The shareholders need to know three things from the accounts:

- Whether or not the company is generating sufficient cash to pay the dividend;
- What the dividend yield is, based on the current share price;
- What the dividend cover is.

From UK GAAP accounts, such information was easily deduced, but under IFRS, shareholders will have to scramble around the notes and then do their own calculations to elicit the information they require. It has been argued that those responsible to IFRS must be academics who practice the art of theoretical abstract in a scholarly way, but who have not deemed the needs of investors as paramount in their thinking. The decision to drop dividends from the Income Statement would seem to support this view.

Under the matching concept, the cost of the dividend was included in the Profit and Loss Account because the cost related to the period in which the income was taken. But once the matching concept has been abandoned, we are in the realms of legalistic phenomena. The argument goes like this. If, say, a company has a year end of 31 December 2006, the accounts will have been prepared by 28 February 2007. In early March 2007, the directors will meet to agree a dividend. Having done so, the accounts will be finalised and will go off to the printers. They will be despatched early April telling shareholders what the recommended dividend is and telling them that this will be one of the resolutions that will be put before the annual general meeting to be held in mid-May.

The argument put forward by those determining accounting standards is that as the dividend was not in public knowledge before April, it could not be a 'fair value' liability before that time and certainly when the company closed its accounts on 31 December 2006, there was no liability. Strictly, of course, the dividend does not become a liability until the shareholders have voted to accept the dividend as recommended by the directors, though it has to be said that it is extremely rare to find shareholders voting to refuse the dividend.

So, if there is no liability at the date of the accounts, then the dividend will not go into the accounts. This seems rather strange because of the liabilities that appear in the Balance Sheet; the liability for the final dividend is just about as accurate as it gets, even though in legal terms there is no liability. But there will be 'legal liabilities' in the Balance Sheet, which are based on judgements that turn out to be more inaccurate than the dividend liability. This is clearly an example where IFRS has been designed to hinder investors, even if unwittingly so, rather than to help them. With regard to note 4 of Figure 3.1, the dividend is omitted in the IFRS accounts.

Salary-related pension schemes (note 5)

Having whinged about IFRS, this is one area where the new standards get full marks, despite protests coming from some companies. The concept behind a salary-related pension scheme is that employees and their employer will contribute a set percentage of the employee's salary. The money saved this way would be invested for the long term by the trustees of the scheme.

Under these schemes, employees could, for example, receive a pension that is equal to the number of year's service, divided by (say) 80, multiplied by the best of the last three years' salary. Pensions are often subject to inflationary increases year on year, subject to a set formula.

Whether the sums add up in the end is dependent upon a number of factors, including the following:

- The success or otherwise of the investments
- The longevity of the members receiving a pension
- The number of people leaving the scheme early

At any one time, it is possible to calculate the surpluses or deficits in the scheme by calculating the value of the investments on the one hand and actuarial liabilities on the other.

In the 1970s, salary-related pension schemes built up huge surpluses, because investment returns were good and people left their pension schemes to seek other jobs. In those days, if an employee had a relatively short number of year's service, then that employee would receive only a return of his or her contributions on leaving the employment. Often, the amount returned was relatively small.

The most generous pension schemes (other than those for members of parliament who encourage restraint upon everybody apart from themselves) were for those employed in the civil service. These were usually non-contributory (i.e. the employee made no contribution) and inflation-proof. By the early 1980s, inflation was running riot and it was apparent to the government of the day that unless drastic action was taken they might have to default on pensions. So, getting inflation down became a priority and as the dual objective was to reduce the power of the unions, the method chosen was to deliberately create a high level of unemployment. This meant that hundreds of thousands of people lost their jobs and with inflation coming down, many pension schemes saw their surpluses increase.

Some 'entrepreneurs' took advantage of this phenomenon. What they did was to look for honestly run companies that had built up surpluses in their pension scheme. They then made audacious takeover bids for these companies arguing that the current management team was sleepwalking to nowhere. Once these entrepreneurs had gained control, they had a wholesale culling of employees aged 50 or more, paying allegedly generous redundancy payments. This increased the surplus in the company's pension scheme, which was then transferred to the company. The company's pension scheme was therefore nei- ther in surplus nor deficit and the company had a pot of money that was used to pay a huge dividend. The company was then sold.

The reason they could do this was that there was no way that pension funds could be ring fenced. The company had a legal duty to pay pensions as they fell due in accordance with the terms of the scheme. If therefore they had to make good pension deficits legally, the other side of the coin was that they could take out surpluses.

The directors with higher scruples nevertheless could not see the point of having pension schemes with huge surpluses, so they took 'holidays'. What this meant was that although the employees continued to contribute, the company did not. Of course, although the company again made contributions once the surplus was gone, what many had not thought of was that there were swings and roundabouts and that sometimes surpluses were required to cover future deficits.

It is true to say that governments' refusal to pass legislation to ring-fence pen- sion schemes is one of the scandals of our time. A small number of companies have been forced into liquidation because they could not meet their pension liabilities, leaving pensioners will little or no pension after years of saving for one.

By the twenty-first century, many companies realised that the combination of no surpluses to carry forward in their pension scheme, reduced investment returns and people living longer meant that it was unlikely such schemes would ever move into surplus. So what they did was to close salary-related schemes to new employees and instead offer them a money purchase scheme. Under these schemes, both the employee and the employer make regular contributions, where neither party take a holiday. The money saved and then invested builds up a 'pot' that is then used to finance the employee's pension. This time the pension fund is ring-fenced because there cannot be any surplus or deficit; the pension is entirely dependent upon the value of the pot at the date of retirement.

Many companies are now finding that their salary-related pension schemes are in deficit, but as the company's pension scheme did not form part of its accounts, such deficits did not show up under UK GAAP. Under IFRS, companies at each year end must show details of their pension scheme showing both assets and liabilities.

On the assets side, companies show the amounts held in their pension scheme, comprising equities, bonds, gilts and cash, together with the expected return on these financial instruments. The liabilities are shown as the present value of the scheme's liabilities, as computed by the company's actuaries. Where liabilities exceed assets it means there is a deficit and companies show their funding plan to meet such deficit.

Companies sometimes address this deficit by making regular payments into their pension fund. When this happens, the payment will be shown in the Cash Flow Statement, but not in the Income Statement. There may be some charge somewhere in the Income Statement relating to pensions and pension liabilities, but often the disclosures are difficult to interpret. This is yet another reason why the Income Statement as presented under IFRS is not investor friendly as far as shareholders are concerned. Investors are primarily interested in 'earnings' defined as the profit available to them and it must be obvious that the net profit shown in the Income Statement does not belong to them if a chunk had to be paid out to reduce the deficit in the company's pension scheme. However, at least such deficit is shown in the Balance Sheet, so it is now known. In Figure 3.1, note 5 demonstrates these fundamental changes.

Financial derivatives (note 11)

The companies dealing in financial derivatives can be classified into two categories: hedgers and gamblers. Many manufacturing and trading companies, especially if involved in trading, worldwide are subject to three types of risks: credit risk, currency risk and interest rate risk. These companies will almost certainly be involved in hedging activities, where the sole aim is to limit risk. But limiting risk is not costless, so hedging costs money.

The companies taking on the risk, in turn for reward, are banks and institutions. These are the gamblers, but, like bookmakers, banks like the odds in their favour. Insurance companies, on the other hand, tend to calculate their premiums to give lower margins, but make up for this by the returns they achieve on their investments built up over the years.

However, the activities of banks and insurance companies with regard to financial derivatives are very complex and not within the scope of this book. We are concerned solely with hedging activities.

Credit risk

Credit risk is to do with a bank holding the company's liquid assets defaulting and/or the company's debtors being unable to pay for a variety of reasons. The probability of a major bank defaulting is extremely low, but nevertheless this risk is managed by having accounts with more than one bank. Large companies with many customers can stand the odd one defaulting, so they will take no action to limit this risk. Smaller companies who rely on a relatively small numbers of customers will take out insurance to cover both their UK and foreign customers.

Currency risk

Imagine a company has contracted to buy a quantity of a particular raw material costing $1 million in total, for delivery and payment in 6 months time. The material is to be used to manufacture 1000 tonnes of a chemical with a selling price of £900 per tonne. Other raw materials used to manufacture the chemical are paid in sterling and amount to £107 per tonne. At the time the order for the main material was placed, the exchange rate was $1.95 to £1.00, so that the total raw material cost is £620 per tonne, giving a margin of £280 per tonne.

The company might take the currency risk and do nothing and there could be three possible outcomes:

- The pound weakens so there are less dollars to the pound, in which case the raw material price increases, which could put the company into a loss-making situation.
- The exchange rate does not change much, so the margin is roughly maintained.
- The pound strengthens the dollar again, thereby reducing the material cost per tonne and increasing the company's profitability.

However, the company is a chemical manufacturer, not a currency trader, and therefore will not want to take risks. Accordingly, imagine it has two options:

- To buy $1 000 000 forward at a fixed rate of $1.891 to £1.00 in 6 months from the date of the contract; or
- Buy an option to buy $1 000 000 at the spot rate of $1.950 anytime between the date of the contract and 6 months later at a cost of £24 000.

If the company opts for the forward contract, the raw material cost will increase by £16 per tonne, reducing the overall margin to £264 per tonne, but this would be guaranteed. On the other hand, if the company chose to buy the option, then the worse case scenario is that the raw material cost would increase by £24 per tonne. The risk of taking the option, rather than the forward contract, would be £8000, a gamble that would pay off if the spot rate went to $1.981 to £1.00, or higher.

Now let us imagine that at the company's year end, three months from the date of the contract, the spot rate was $2.00 to £1.00 and the company had bought the option. The trend is that the dollar is weakening and the Finance Director believes that it will continue to do so; accordingly, he does not want to exercise the option at the company's year end. The question is: what goes into the accounts?

There can be several views as to how these events might be treated:

- As the spot rate at the date of the contract was $1.95 to £1.00 and margins were worked out on this basis, then the £24 000 cost of the option should be written off to administrative expenses. This is the most prudent view.
- As the company does not take risks, the margins to be taken in the following year should take account of the forward rate (fixed rate) of $1.891 to £1.00. Therefore, only £8000 should be charged to administrative expenses, this being the difference between the worst possible and contracting at the forward rate.

The difficulty here is that different companies could not be relied upon to come up with the same interpretation, so the IASB felt it necessary to be prescriptive for the sake of consistency. They determined that financial derivatives should be valued at 'fair value'. In our example, the 'fair value' of our financial derivative would be £12 821, being the difference of $1 000 000 at the strike price of $1.95 to £1.00 and the closing price of $2.00 to £1.00.

Interest rate risk

Companies often borrow money at a fixed number of percentage points over base rate, which means they have a variable rate of interest as the base rate can change. Guessing what the base rate might be in future is, of course, a gamble. Companies can hedge this risk by swapping their variable rate borrowings for a fixed rate loan. Obviously, at the time the deal is struck, there will be a cost to the company, which will be equal to the bank's (the one agreeing the swap) valuation of the risks involved, together with their profit margin. Again under

IFRS, all these derivatives must be assessed at the year end and valued at their perceived 'fair value'.

In Figure 3.2, the figure shown as 'financial instruments' represents a liability in connection with foreign currency hedging, not recognised under UK GAAP.

Leases

Leases are another area that has been open to a high level of judgement in the past. These financial instruments are particularly interesting because their popularity really took off because of stealth taxes introduced in the early 1980s. In the Labour era of the late 1970s, corporation tax was at an extremely high level, primarily because the then Labour government wanted to encourage growth by regeneration. They wanted to encourage companies to invest in new capital equipment and to encourage increased productivity through better training. As such, companies received 100% capital allowances against capital expenditure and were paid training grants, all of which went to offset their corporation tax bill.

Politics never seems to be honest and Margaret Thatcher focussed on the rate of corporation tax, promising to slash it and free the companies to spend their money as they saw fit. At the time, companies drooled over the thought of a vastly reduced rate of corporation tax. What they forgot was that freedom meant that training allowances were to be abolished and capital allowed were to be reduced to 25% reducing balance. The companies that were investing heavily for the future suddenly found that they were paying more corporation tax than they would have done when a higher rate was applied.

So what was to be done? The answer was to lease capital equipment, rather than buy it. Obviously, leasing was more expensive as the company leasing the equipment had to make a profit, but as the cost of lease payments were deductible for corporation tax purposes, net of tax leasing was cheaper than buying.

Quite naturally, the government of the day got very cross over this, as they always do when clever accountants come up with a legal tax avoidance scheme, as against an illegal tax evasion scheme. So this loophole was closed. Now the determining factor is whether or not under the terms of the lease the lessee effectively owns the asset, where owning means taking on all the risks and rewards associated with it. If the lessee does effectively own the asset, then it is a finance lease. If it is a finance lease, then under IFRS, it must be capitalised at the lower of 'fair value' or the present value of the lease payments, having separated the capital element from the interest to be charged over the term of the lease. It will then be depreciated in the normal way in accordance with a particular company's accounting policy. So the asset leased in this way will appear as an asset in non-current assets and the corresponding liability will be included in non-current liabilities. Finance leases are treated as capital expenditure for tax purposes, meaning that neither the fair value of the asset nor depreciation is tax deductible. Instead, the normal capital allowances are applied.

If the lessee does not effectively own the asset, then it is deemed to be an operating lease. In such cases, the monthly rental is charged to the Income Statement. Under IFRS, lease incentives such as payment holidays must be spread over the whole term of the lease.

Minor adjustments

In addition to the above, there are minor changes in the way IFRS accounts are prepared, compared to UK GAAP. In respect of Figure 3.2, many of the changes referred above will have an impact on the deferred tax calculation. In addition, as stated earlier, under IFRS, deferred tax assets and deferred tax liabilities are not netted off (notes 3 and 6). Another minor change is the valuation of investments (note 10). As discussed in Chapter 2, two prices are given for quoted stocks and shares: the bid price at which the broker will buy your share and the ask price at which he will sell you the share. The difference between these two prices is known as the spread and the centre point of the spread is the mid price. Under UK GAAP, investments were valued at the mid price, but under IFRS, they are valued at the (more prudent) bid price. The reduction in value of the investments under IFRS, as note 10, reflects this change.

IFRS vs. UK GAAP summary

To date (March 2007), there have been eight IFRS issued:

IFRS 1. This covers the arrangement for migrating from UK GAAP to IFRS. In effect, companies must show two complete years in which they account both ways and explain the differences between the two.

IFRS 2. Share based payments. This standard has been discussed in detail earlier in this chapter.

IFRS 3. Business combinations. This standard states that when one entity takes over another, the transaction must be accounted for using the purchase method. All the assets and liabilities of the acquired business must be valued at fair value at the date of the transaction and goodwill calculated on this basis.

IFRS 4. Insurance contracts. This standard aims to ensure that the accounts for insurance companies make it clear that at the date of the company's year end, insurance contracts in place could result in significant claims in future that the insurer is currently unaware of. In other words, the published accounts must make shareholders aware of the risks involved. However, insurance companies are specifically prohibited from making provisions against possible future catastrophes that do not relate to existing contracts.

IFRS 5. Non-current assets held for sale and discontinued operations. Where appropriate, profits/losses relating to discontinued operations must be shown separately on the Income Statement. If an asset is being held for sale and it is available for sale at the company's year end, then it must be valued at the lower of its carrying amount and fair value less costs to sell. This is exactly the same as the traditional valuation of stock that is the lower of cost and net realisable value, with net realisable value being defined as selling price, less the cost of getting the product to the customer.

IFRS 6. Exploration for and evaluation of mineral resources. This standard allows companies to capitalise the cost of searching for minerals, oil, natural gas and other non-regenerative resources as an asset, but insists that at each accounting period, these assets are tested for fair value and are impaired as necessary.

IFRS 7. Financial instrument: disclosures. This standard makes companies to disclose their financial instruments and their associated risks and state how the management manages such risks.

IFRS 8. Operating segments. Most companies produce internal management accounts that enable the management to make key decisions. On this basis, each company must decide what its operating segments are and must produce separate Income Statements for each operating statement and a separate Balance Sheet, as appropriate.

(*Source*: Technical Summaries prepared by IASC Foundation Staff.) Details of the eight IFRS's, as above, are summaries of a much larger extracts produced by IASC Foundation Staff, which have not been approved by the IASB. This also applies to the description of IAS 38. It must be noted that this chapter is written with the objective of providing an overview from an investor's perspective. Readers with responsibility for implementing IFRS should refer to the full International Financial Reporting Standards.

The Income Statement under IFRS is helpful in separating profit/loss between continuing and discontinued operations, but overall it is a disappointment as it cluttered up the non-monetary adjustments that make it, in isolation, difficult to interpret. The decision to omit the proposed dividend also hinders investors.

Apart from investments, where a more prudent position is taken, an IFRS Balance Sheet will show assets at a higher asset value than a UK GAAP Balance Sheet, because assets and liabilities are shown at fair value. However, the differences, overall, should not be that great and in any event the IFRS Balance Sheet should project the more accurate picture, as well as providing more detailed information.

The IFRS Cash Flow Statement will balance to the same numbers as the UK GAAP Cash Flow Statement (except the former includes 'cash equivalents'). In addition, the IFRS format is easier to understand.

Corporate governance

Within the limitations of human error and human nature, most published accounts give a reasonable approximation to profitability, assets, liabilities and cash flow. Assuming accounts have been put together honestly, the Cash Flow Statement should be the most accurate statement, the reason being that it is reconciled to something tangible, being cash and cash equivalents held by the company.

However, corporate governance is not about the accuracy of the accounts, but rather how the directors conduct themselves. In particular, shareholders need to be confident that they will get their fair share of the company's profits and not see the directors take the lion's share for themselves.

In the past, there have been a number of concerns, all based on the 'old pals' act, where the pals were the executive directors, non-executive directors and auditors, all of whom might be said to have a conflict of interest.

For example, the directors might suggest to the auditors that they accept the numbers put before them, reminding them that the company has paid several thousands of pounds in consultancy fees, on top of the audit fee, all of which might be lost to them in future. So, in this example, we clearly have a conflict of interest.

Of course, in the majority of cases there was no conflict of interest because the accountancy firm's consultancy arm acted independently of its auditing arm. But the problem was, how could this be proved, even if it is true? Did not both arms meet up at the local hostelry for lunch?

Then there was the problem of non-executive directors not really doing their job. The Managing Director of a company might suggest to his non-executive directors that executive salaries should increase by 25%, adding, 'of course, we would not object to your fees going up by the same percentage'.

To alleviate these problems, the regularity authorities introduced the 'Combined Code' setting out what is good governance and best practice. The following is what one might see in a Corporate Governance Report.

Duties of the Board of Directors

Duties listed might include:

- Approval of Board Appointments
- The roles of Chairman and Chief Executive and how their duties have been segregated, together with the roles of other executive directors
- Details of non-executive directors, together with a statement showing how the executive directors can confirm that the non-executive directors are truly independent
- The induction and training offered to new non-executive directors to ensure that they know sufficient about the company to make informed decisions
- Establishment of various committees, such as the Audit Committee and Remuneration Committee, setting out their constitution
- Strategy and corporate objectives
- Business plans, forecasting procedures and variance analysis
- Performance monitoring of the board and senior management
- Setting approval limits for employees, in terms of what each senior employee can commit the company to with regard to revenue and capital expenditure
- Approval of major contracts, outside the approval limits set for employees

- Approval of internal control and accounting procedures and the publication of annual accounts
- Risk identification and evaluation
- Health and safety
- Environmental sustainability
- Dialogue with institutional shareholders on a meeting basis and keeping smaller private investors in touch by updating the company's website

The Audit Committee

The Audit Committee will usually comprise solely non-executive directors and if this is not the case the 'Corporate Governance' Report will usually state the reasons. The Audit Committee is responsible for recommending the appointment of the external auditors and for ensuring that the appointee will not be granted consultancy work, unless such consultancy can be seen to be directly linked to the audit. For example, a company might ask their auditors to advise on tax matters and the implementation of IFRS and such consultancy could not conflict with the audit or compromise the auditors in any way.

The Remuneration Committee

Like the Audit Committee, the Remuneration Committee should be made up on non-executive directors. Their role is to determine remuneration policy with regard to the executive board and will make recommendations with regard to salary, conditions of employment, the award of share options and other benefits.

The Nominations Committee

Non-executive directors usually outnumber executive directors in the Nominations Committee. If a company has such a committee, it will meet up at least once a year to consider the size, structure and composition of the Board. It will also oversee retirements from the Board and recommend changes or new appointments, as necessary.

Board and Committee membership

The Corporate Governance Report will list the members of the full board and the constitution of each committee. Some reports indicate how often each met and also details of attendance records.

The Report of the Directors

The Report of the Directors is a statutory report, in which the following information are provided:

- Principal activity
- Results and dividends
- Business Review (brief, often referring to fuller report found elsewhere)
- Share capital – a list of all shareholders holding 3% or more of the company's shares
- Directors' interest – a list showing how many shares each director holds
- Suppliers payment policy (usually says that payment is made to agreed terms, but this does not quite seem believable in every case)
- Amount that has been paid out for charitable and political purposes, if at all, with full disclosure required for the latter
- Directors' responsibilities (if not included under 'corporate governance')
- The recommendation to reappoint the current auditors or (rarely) to change auditors
- Notice of the Annual General Meeting, specifying date, place and time
- If there is any doubt whatsoever, confirming that business is assumed to be a 'going concern'

If the company in question is an investment trust, then further information are provided:

- Details of tax and investment company status
- Regulation, indicating, for example, that the company is regulated by the FSA.
- Management arrangements – cover such matters as to how management fees and 'carried interest' are charged.

Probably, the most interesting aspect of the legal requirements for disclosures in the 'Report of the Directors' is the requirement to specify the 'principal activity'. This requirement goes back to many decades and is rumoured to originate when limited liability companies were first legalised. In the early days, there was no requirement to state what the principal activity of the company was, and it is rumoured that some companies were set up as a front to prostitution. Apparently, it all came to a head when the Church of England inadvertently found itself investing in and profiting from prostitution. So something had to be done . . . .

The Directors' Remuneration Report

Some people moan about the remuneration some directors reward themselves, but it is certainly transparent as the 'Directors' Remuneration Report' is a legal requirement.

The following information are usually found in this report:

- Details of the 'Remuneration Committee' (or reference to its constitution as shown under 'corporate governance')
- The company's remuneration policy
- Details of annual incentive plans and long-term incentive plans
- Company policy on directors' contracts of employment
- Company policy with regard to share options
- List of directors, each one showing their salary/fees, benefits (company car, BUPA, etc.) bonuses and total remuneration
- Disclosure details of directors' pensions schemes
- List of directors, each one showing details of share options

Share options are shown in detail and the following will be shown for each director (as applicable):

- Date of grant
- Option price
- Date from which exercisable
- Expiry date
- Number of share options held at beginning of accounting period
- Number of share options exercised during the year
- Number of share options granted during the year
- Number of share options held at the end of the accounting period

Optional (non-statutory) reports

The Chairman, Chief Executive, Finance Director or indeed any other director may choose to write a report for the benefit of the shareholders. In addition, most companies include in their Annual Report 'promotional' pieces that are designed to encourage shareholders to appreciate the company they have invested in.

Annual Report – Summary

A few years ago an 'Annual Report' would be a relatively thin document comprising simply a little promotional material, annual accounts and the 'Report of the Directors', but ever increasing regulation has meant that these documents have become thicker and thicker. Of course, it is the shareholders who end up paying for all the regulation and there must come a point where it becomes self-defeating from a cost benefit point of view.

Of course, it is totally reasonable to expect highly paid directors to act in a manner consistent with their remuneration, but do we need to cut down so many forests to provide every shareholder all the details? Surely the following statement in the Report of the Directors would suffice:

> We the directors do hereby declare that we have adhered to all the appropriate rules and regulations, including all matters relating to corporate governance, and have made the appropriate decisions with regard to business and risk in a professional, competent and honest manner. Details of our salaries/fees, benefits, bonuses and share options are shown below.

But it could have been worse. At one time, the ASB was pursuing the concept of introducing a report that would enable shareholders to assess the strategies adopted by the company and the potential of such strategies to succeed. This report was to be called an 'Operating and Financial Review' (OFR) and should (according to the proposal published by the ASB):

- have a forward-looking orientation;
- complement as well as supplement the financial statements;
- be comprehensive and understandable
- be balanced and neutral; and
- be comparable over time.

The OFR should include key elements of the disclosure framework that should cover:

- the nature, objectives and strategies of the business;
- the development and performance of the business, both in the period under review and in future;
- the resources, risks and uncertainties and relationships that may affect the entity's long-term value; and
- the position of the business including a description of the capital structure, treasury policies and objectives and liquidity of the entity, both in the period under review and in future.

The ASB recognised that if the proposal became a standard, then some guidance would be useful to directors. The ASB also recognised that the preparation of an OFR would require a fair amount of judgement on the part of the directors.

One had to wonder how many shareholders would have the ability to judge from an OFR whether a company's strategy was likely to be successful or not and to some it appeared that directors would soon be unable to do their jobs properly as they were slowly becoming submerged in red tape. No doubt, the latter people were relieved to learn that the concept of an OFR never became a legally enforceable standard. However, across the pond, they were not so lucky.

The Sarbanes-Oxley Act

There is no doubt that the collapse of Enron in the United States was so calamitous that we did not witness a financial wave, but a tsunami. Here we had a company that according to Gary Hamel was revolutionary and extraordinarily entrepreneurial. He wrote:

> Since 1984, when it was formed out of a merger between two sleepy natural gas pipeline companies, Enron has invented a handful of radical new business concepts. In so doing the company has reinvented itself several times over. By the mid 1990's, Enron had transformed the wholesale natural gas business from an inefficient and highly regulated bureaucracy into an extraordinarily efficient market. It had changed electric power grids from stodgy old-boys' clubs into flexible energy markets that meet the ever-changing needs of energy-hungry customers. It had revolutionised international power plant development, creating entrepreneurial solutions to some of the most perplexing energy problems in the third world.

> (*Source*: 'Leading the Revolution' Gary Hamel, Harvard Business School Press (first edition, 2000), p. 211.)

Unfortunately, one of the radical new business concepts developed by some of the senior Enron executives was to hide its liabilities off Balance Sheet. Whenever phenomenal growth in revenue and profitability is not accompanied by a mountain of cash, there is the risk that something is wrong somewhere. In Enron's case, what was wrong was that the whole thing was a sham.

If one counts the number of limited liability companies in the United States and United Kingdom, it has to be said that scandals such as Enron are extremely rare and can happen only where directors are acting dishonestly. In any event, the legal system in the United States was robust enough to ensure that the main perpetrators of the Enron scandal received long prison sentences. On this basis, it might have been concluded that the law was strong enough to act as a deterrent to dissuade directors of other companies to follow suit.

However, it was concluded that the law had to be strengthened; so on 30 July 2002 the Sarbanes-Oxley Act was signed into law. The concept behind this Act was no doubt admirable as the objective was to ensure that the highest standards of corporate governance are being maintained. However, the Act could be described as onerous and like 'taking a sledgehammer to crack a nut'.

In all, there are 11 'titles' being major sections and each 'title' has an average of seven sections. This gives approximately 80 sections, most of which require some action by the company.

Anybody wanting to get to grips with *the Sarbanes-Oxley Act* should read the book by Michael F. Holt with that title (Elsevier, CIMA Publishing, 2006). In this book, Mr Holt lists the action needed to be taken by companies. The examples below give a mere flavour of the tasks involved (all taken from Mr Holt's book):

- Section 102: Obtain written confirmation that the company's auditors are registered.
- Section 103: Obtain written confirmation that the company's auditors comply with the quality control and ethics rules of the Board.
- Section 105: If the company has a non-US accounting firm and is listed in the US, ensure by written confirmation that the auditing firm does and will conform to the requirements of the Act.
- Section 203: Retain records on an annual basis of the participants in the audits for the company and check that this requirement is observed (audit partner rotation).
- Section 406: Generate a suitable Code of Ethics and insert it in the Policies and Procedures Manual. Ensure that the CEO and other financial officers are aware of it, sign it, and agree to abide by it.

On pages 111–113 of his book, Mr Holt provides a checklist for things that management need to do to comply with the Act. In all he lists 32 sections, some of which require more than one action and as can be seen from the example above, some actions require a considerable amount of time and expertise.

The most expensive part of the Act as far as the companies will be concerned is section 302, which covers corporate responsibility for financial reports, and section 404, which covers management assessment of internal controls. Companies must therefore set up complicated internal control systems to comply with this legislation. Mr Holt defines 'internal control' within the context of the Act as:

A process, effected by an entity's board of directors, management and other personnel, designed to provide reasonable assurance regarding the achievement of objectives in the following **categories.**

(a) Effectiveness and efficiency of operations (Operations)
(b) Reliability of financial reporting (Financial Reporting)
(c) Compliance with applicable laws and regulations (Compliance)

The three categories have five components:

(1) Control environment
(2) Risk assessment
(3) Control activities
(4) Information and communication
(5) Monitoring

One of the key problems faced by companies is that some of the components are contrary to each other. For example, a risk assessment might believe that there is a risk of fraud and theft if the company's accountant and his staff are responsible for both producing the accounts and controlling the company's liquid resources. So the decision is made to separate the accounting and treasury functions. This can be further complicated where the treasury function is centralised to make the most of the cash resources available to the group as a whole. Now, instead of a cash book, each company accountant will have only details of intracompany transactions. This means that a key control function is lost, namely reconciling the accounts with cash movements and explaining the appropriate difference.

Another problem is that it is extremely difficult to have a control system that is so brilliant that it prevents serious fraudsters, acting in unison, from discovery in the short term. This is especially the case where the accounting function and treasury function are separated. How directors can be held totally responsible in such circumstances is difficult to envisage. It could be argued that companies would get better results if they prioritised recruitment and the motivation of staff.

It costs companies millions of dollars to comply with the Sarbanes-Oxley Act and some smaller companies simply cannot afford to do it and are delisted from the US stock markets. It has to be said that the overall cost to corporate investors (large pension funds and the like) of companies having to comply with this Act will likely be far more than the savings made by avoiding another 'Enron', given that something as bad as this calamity is extremely rare.

Shareholders' power

Although it might appear that directors are all powerful, the real power lies with shareholders. It is the shareholders who must pass ordinary (50% or more of the vote required) and special (75% or more of the vote required) resolutions at the Annual General Meeting. Shareholders must sanction the appointment of directors and auditors. That said, the real power lies with institutional investors as they have the voting power; in reality, the private shareholder is impotent. From information gleaned from an Annual Report, the private investor has just two choices, hold or sell his or her shares.

Given the power of institutional investors, many directors have developed policies in the area of what they define as 'investor relations'. Institutional investors can find themselves being wined and dined and given the hard sell. Whether this clouds their judgement or not is open to speculation, but the actions resulting from such meetings can be dramatic. If the institutional investor has been persuaded that a particular company is going forward, then he might buy some more of that company's shares pushing up the price. On the other hand, if he or she is disillusioned and feels the only way forward is regime change, then selling a wad of shares might be considered. Either way, such events can provide private investors with a headache, given they are solely reliant upon the information put out by the company, which, for obvious reasons, must be factual and cannot prejudge the current mood of institutional investors. Accordingly, it is even more important for private investors to assess correctly the information available to them.

Discussion Questions

1. The Auditor's Report will give 'reasonable assurance that accounts are free from material misstatement.' In this context define what 'reasonable' and 'material' means.

2. Give two examples of where IFRS has abandoned the 'matching concept'.

3. Under IFRS, what is the definition of 'fair value'?

4. What is meant by 'merging cash and value-based items'?

5. What is 'stocks', 'debtors' and 'creditors' known as under IFRS?

6. What is the difference between a deferred tax asset and a deferred tax liability under UK GAAP compared with IFRS?

7. Where would you find computer software in UK GAAP accounts and IFRS accounts?

8. How are 'research and development' costs treated under IFRS?

9. What major liability was often hidden in UK GAAP accounts, but must be shown in IFRS accounts?

10. Explain how investments are treated differently under UK GAAP and IFRS.

11. In an IFRS Cash Flow Statement, if you wanted to find the equivalent of what would have been shown as 'net cash inflow from operating activities' in a UK GAAP Cash Flow Statement, where would you find it?

12. An IFRS Cash Flow Statement reconciles to 'cash and cash equivalents' whereas a UK GAAP Cash Flow Statement reconciles to 'cash' only. What is the definition of 'cash equivalent'?

13. In what way is 'investment property' and 'investment property under construction' treated (a) the same and (b) differently in IFRS accounts?

14. Name three types of risks faced by most companies with regard to 'financial instruments'.

15. Explain the difference between an 'operating lease' and a 'finance lease'.

16. To maintain good corporate governance, name three sub-committees that a board of directors usually set up and explain what is important about their constitution.

17. In the 'Report of the Directors', all shareholders are listed if they hold a particular percentage (or higher) of the equity of the company. What is this minimum percentage?

18. In a set of published accounts, apart from the accounts themselves, name four statutory reports that you would always find and two non-statutory reports that you might find.

19. What major US legislation came about because of the Enron scandal?

20. At a company's Annual General Meeting, shareholders vote for both ordinary and specials resolutions. What is the minimum percentage in favour of such resolutions to enable them to be carried?

Assessing risk and valuing companies

In Chapter 4, Amanda sells her business and collects £1 million, net of tax, making 25 times her original investment. This chapter illustrates how Amanda might invest some of her £1 million, through understanding risk, how to interpret published accounts and how to apply different valuation techniques. The points made are backed up by four case studies, using real companies as examples.

The topics covered are the following:

- The acquisition of Amanda's company
- Risk (in general)
- Portfolio theory
- The experiment
- Risks associated with taking on unique risk
- Assessing company performance
- Basic checks
- Valuation techniques (earnings multiple, net asset valuation, discounted cash flow (DCF) and industry benchmarks)
- The BVCA Code of Conduct
- Final review
- Investment companies – case study – HgCapital Trust plc
- Why the market sometimes got it wrong
- Restructuring – case study – Topps Tiles plc
- Profit warnings? – case study – Paddy Power plc
- Take-over bids – case study – Morrison (William) Supermarkets plc

Amanda – Case Study – The acquisition of her company

With the help of her advisers, both internally and externally, Amanda's business progressed fairly steadily. One day the Chairman advised Amanda that he had been approached by a competitor who was considering to make an offer for the entire share capital of her company.

Following consultation with their external advisers, Amanda and her Chairman agreed that the business would be put up for sale with the objective of attracting other bidders, thereby creating a bidding war. Eventually a bid was received that was deemed acceptable and Amanda's solicitor explained the procedures that had to be followed. She was told that she would be asked questions about her business and that while she must answer truthfully, she must not disclose any information without first discussing it with her solicitor. She followed her instructions to the letter and eventually the deal went through netting Amanda £1 million. However, a clause in the contract meant that she had to stay in the business for 12 months from the date of the contract to ensure that the new owners of the business were fully acquainted with it.

Choice of investments

Imagine that you have been left £16 000 in a will and have this amount of money to spend. You want to buy a new car costing £16 000, but your existing car is still serving you well, so why not save the money? Do nothing by hiding the money in the house and a year later the car you want to buy might cost £16 400. So you need to do something with the money to stay ahead of inflation.

So where do you invest your money? You could buy a government bond or a fixed interest bond in a building society and assuming an interest rate of 4% your £16 000 would be worth £16 640 by the end of the year. But now you would have to pay tax and assuming the standard rate on savings of 20%, tax of £128 will put your net interest down to £512. But as due to inflation, the car you want to buy has increased to £16 400, the true interest gained (interest less inflation) is a mere £112, or 0.7%.

The investment described above will be relatively risk-free and it is unlikely that the £16 000 capital will be lost, but the true return is minuscule. So we must look for a method of investment that will give a higher return.

We could buy 16 000 £1 tickets on the following week's national lottery, and if we hit the jackpot, we might win £2 million or more, but as the odds for achieving this are approximately 14 million to 1, the chances are we will lose our money. So we need to understand the concept of risk.

Risk

According to Ross Westerfield and Jaffe, 'Corporate Finance' (4th edition) Irwin (1996) there is no universally agreed-upon definition of risk and that being the case risk means different things to different people. In this book, 'risk' is defined as the probability of losing all or part of an investment.

In financial theory, investors are deemed to be risk-averse. In this context, a risk-averse investor would prefer to avoid fair value gambles, where fair value gamble is one with a zero expected return. An example of a zero expected return is betting on the spin of a perfectly balanced coin where the stake and potential winnings are equal. A positive expected return is one where the gambler would expect to win in the long term, while a negative expected return is where the gambler would expect to lose in the long term. Betting on horse racing would have a small negative expected value, while betting on the National Lottery would have a large negative expected value. The difference between betting on horse racing and lotteries is that while it could be argued there is a skill to the former, there is no skill in the latter as the numbers are drawn at random.

If a gambler betting on horse racing believed that his skill was such that the number of winners he could select were 10% greater than the number he would expect to select at random and that by betting on the exchanges there was only a 2.5% spread, then it could be argued that he would have a positive expected value, even after paying commission.

In the long term, betting in stocks and shares has, in the past, produced a positive expected value, but we must consider the skill element in this activity. If you believe there is no skill in selecting stocks and shares, you must follow 'portfolio theory' (detailed below), but if you believe there is a skill to it, then there is no point in simply buying on an unstructured basis.

The key word, as always, is long term, because in the short term, stock markets can be very volatile, as the figures below illustrate:

Year (1st January)	FTSE 100 index	Year (% change)	Cumulative (% change)
1997	4129.0		
1998	5202.5	26.0	26.0
1999	5878.9	13.0	42.4
2000	6930.2	17.9	67.8
2001	6222.5	(10.2)	50.7
2002	5217.4	(16.2)	26.4
2003	3940.4	(24.5)	(4.6)
2004	4476.9	13.6	8.4
2005	4814.3	7.5	16.6
2006	5618.8	16.7	36.1
2007	6220.8	10.7	50.7

The above table tells you that anyone having a portfolio of shares matching the FTSE 100 index would have achieved a compound capital growth of 3.125% per annum on top of the dividend income they received over the years. This table also tells you the importance of *timing* when making investments, for as can be seen, anyone starting their portfolio in 2000 would still be suffering.

According to financial theory, a risk-averse investor would invest in stocks and shares because they offer a positive expected value in the long term, but they would not take unnecessary risks. Ross et al. (1996) state that risk can be measured by volatility. The spread or dispersion of a distribution is a measure of how much a particular return can deviate from the mean return. If the distribution is very spread out, the returns that will occur are very uncertain. By contrast, a distribution whose returns are all within a few percentage points of each other is tight and the returns are less uncertain. Volatility is measured by calculating the variance and its square root, the standard deviation.

As can be deduced from the above table, investing in the FTSE 100 index would be considered very uncertain, given a mean return of 4.9% with returns varying from +26.0% to −24.5%.

Portfolio theory

Such volatility is compounded when we consider that individual stocks within the portfolio of the FTSE 100 will themselves vary, sometimes quite dramatically. So investors investing in stocks and shares are taking considerable risks and can be expected to do so only if the overall return they receive is greater than the risk-free rate. The difference between the expected return and the risk-free rate is known as the risk premium.

The risk associated with shares is divided into two distinct categories:

- Portfolio risk, market risk or systematic risk
- Diversifiable risk, unique risk or unsystematic risk

Portfolio risk, market risk or systematic risk is the risk associated with the market as a whole, as demonstrated by the volatility of the FTSE index. Diversifiable, unique or unsystematic risk relates to the potential volatility associated with an individual share. Now it is accepted following the publication of the paper 'How Many Stocks Make A Diversified Portfolio' (*Journal of Financial and Quantitative Analysis,* September) by Meir Statman in 1987 that it is possible to diversify away diversifiable, unique or unsystematic risk. The concept is that by diversifying into different sectors and different stocks, you will be able to eliminate such risk, leaving you with only the risk of portfolio, market or systematic risk. 'Drury (Management and Cost Accounting, 6th edition, Thomson)' gives an example of how diversification works, by suggesting that if you wanted to invest in a company manufacturing ice cream, you could also invest in a raincoat manufacturer. If bad weather impacted upon the ice cream manufacturer, then the raincoat manufacturer would do well, to compensate. If there were a long hot dry summer, then the ice cream manufacturer should have a bonanza, while the raincoat manufacturer might suffer. Either way, it would be unlikely that both stocks would suffer. The number of stocks required to diversify away unsystematic risk is debatable, as different authors offer varying opinions, but between 15 and 30 seems to be the range.

However, there are two significant problems with portfolio theory, the first being like all theories it is often more difficult in practice. It is doubtful whether it is possible to select 15 or even 30 stocks to exactly match the market as a whole, but of course, it may be possible to get relatively close to this goal. But the greater problem with portfolio theory can be disclosed by a question. Why would any rational investor want to diversify away unique risk? For example, rather than investing in an ice cream manufacturer and a raincoat manufacturer, why not instead invest in a water company whose revenue will stay roughly the same regardless of whether it rains or not.

In terms of risk, which is the greater, market risk or unique risk? The answer is that market risk will usually be the greater risk. When the market falls, nearly all of the portfolios go with it; we have to be very unlucky if the majority of our portfolio is in poor-performing companies. To appreciate this, it is necessary to understand the difference between having a diverse portfolio and diversifying away unique risk. The former means 'not putting one's eggs in one basket' and attempting to invest in the best companies in each sector, so that if a particular sector is suffering, it will not affect the whole portfolio. The latter means attempting to invest to achieve the market average, for if you truly diversify away unique risk, the market average is what you must be left with.

This book suggests that diversifying away unique risk is irrational and that the objective must be to invest in the best companies, but have a diverse portfolio. The logic for this assertion is that the market is made up of several companies that follow the 20–60–20 rule. That is that 20% will be superbly managed, 60% will be well managed, while the bottom 20% will not be so well managed. In every year, some companies gain significant value for their shareholders, while others turn out to be a disaster. The market for an average year can be illustrated, using the £16 000 being invested, as below:

	Whole market (average year)			%
	Investment (£)	Closing value of investment (£)	Profit/(loss) (£)	
Company A	1 600	2 560	960	60.0
Company B	1 600	2 320	720	45.0
Company C	1 600	2 192	592	37.0
Company D	1 600	1 720	120	7.5
Company E	1 600	1 680	80	5.0
Company F	1 600	1 600	0	0.0
Company G	1 600	1 552	(48)	(3.0)
Company H	1 600	1 440	(160)	(10.0)
Company J	1 600	1 408	(192)	(12.0)
Company K	1 600	728	(872)	(54.5)
Total market	16 000	17 200	1 200	7.5

For illustrative purposes, it is assumed that dividends pay for transaction costs and that the figures above show capital gains and losses only. Again, for illustrative purposes, it is assumed that by investing in companies C, E, F and J, it is possible to diversify away unique risk. This is shown below:

	Selection eliminating unique risk (average year)			%
	Investment (£)	Closing value of investment (£)	Profit/(loss) (£)	
Company C	4 000	5 480	1 480	37.0
Company E	4 000	4 200	200	5.0
Company F	4 000	4 000	0	0.0
Company J	4 000	3 520	(480)	(12.0)
Total	16 000	17 200	1 200	7.5

If we look at the 'whole market' above, we can be confident that if the following year is an average year, then the market will end up as illustrated. What we do not know, of course, is which companies will be exceptionally good, which will be average and which will turn out to be losers. What we must try to do, though, is to avoid investing in the worst 20%. How do we do this? The answer is by analysing the last published accounts to assess the risks involved. How this is done is explained in Chapter 2 and later in this chapter. If we are successful, then it can be very rewarding. Suppose, for example, we had vested £2000 in each of companies A–H, rather than £1600 in each of the 10 companies, then our annual return would increase from 7.5% to 17.7%, a significant improvement.

We know that the risk of market failure is far greater than the risk of a portfolio of individual companies failing, but it is also true that when the market falls, it is the weakest companies that go to the wall. The companies that are heavily in debt may not be able to withstand the combination of falling sales together with an interest rate increase, while those in a better financial state will suffer, but recover. So when the market has a bad year, it may look like:

		Whole market (bad year)		%
	Investment (£)	Closing value of investment (£)	Profit/(loss) (£)	
Company A	1 600	1 840	240	15.0
Company B	1 600	1 760	160	10.0
Company C	1 600	1 720	120	7.5
Company D	1 600	1 440	(160)	(10.0)
Company E	1 600	1 360	(240)	(15.0)
Company F	1 600	1 240	(360)	(22.5)
Company G	1 600	1 200	(400)	(25.0)
Company H	1 600	1 008	(592)	(37.0)
Company J	1 600	512	(1 088)	(68.0)
Company K	1 600	0	(1 600)	(100.0)
Total market	16 000	12 080	(3 920)	(24.5)

Again, the effect of diversifying away unique risk can be illustrated as follows:

		Selection eliminating unique risk (bad year)		
	Investment (£)	Closing value of investment (£)	Profit/(loss) (£)	%
Company C	4 000	4 300	300	7.5
Company E	4 000	3 400	(600)	(15.0)
Company F	4 000	3 100	(900)	(22.5)
Company J	4 000	1 280	(2 720)	(68.0)
Total	16 000	12 080	(3 920)	(24.5)

This time, avoiding the bottom 20% of companies reduces the loss from 24.5% to 9.6%.

There will be years when the 'bulls' beat off the 'bears' and the market as a whole flourishes. However, even in these years, some companies will have to cease trading because they ran out of cash and the banks declined to support further. For example, 2006 was a very good year for the stock market as a whole, but that did not stop Farepak Food and Gifts Limited going into administration leaving approximately 125 000 of the poorest in the society going without the Christmas festivities they were expecting (Farepak website, December 2006).

For the illustration of a good year for the stock market, we have not shown any company being completely wiped out, but nevertheless the mix of fortunes will remain:

	Whole market (good year)			%
	Investment (£)	Closing value of investment (£)	Profit/(loss) (£)	
Company A	1 600	2 992	1 392	87.0
Company B	1 600	2 720	1 120	70.0
Company C	1 600	2 640	1 040	65.0
Company D	1 600	2 000	400	25.0
Company E	1 600	1 960	360	22.5
Company F	1 600	1 920	320	20.0
Company G	1 600	1 632	32	2.0
Company H	1 600	1 552	(48)	(3.0)
Company J	1 600	1 544	(56)	(3.5)
Company K	1 600	1 200	(400)	(25.0)
Total market	16 000	20 160	4 160	26.0

For the third time it is assumed that unique risk can be diversified away:

	Selection eliminating unique risk (good year)			
	Investment (£)	Closing value of investment (£)	Profit/(loss) (£)	%
Company C	4 000	6 600	2 600	65.0
Company E	4 000	4 900	900	22.5
Company F	4 000	4 800	800	20.0
Company J	4 000	3 860	(140)	(3.5)
Total	16 000	20 160	4 160	26.0

This time, eliminating the bottom 20% of companies improves the return to 36.1%. So as can be seen, if it were possible to avoid investing in the worst 20% of companies, the annual return that could be achieved would be far better than the market as a whole. But can it be done?

The experiment

Hemscott is a website dedicated to providing financial information. In 2003/2004, Tom Stevenson was Hemcott's head of research and in that capacity he wrote about the systematic approach to selecting shares. He regularly reviewed systems such as Jim Slater's price/earnings to growth (PEG) ratio, Michael O'Higgins high-yield approach and David Dreman's contrarian low price/earnings ratio (PER) method. Using these systems of selecting shares and using Hemcott's database, he drew up four shortlists from the FTSE Small Cap index. These were the following:

- The five with the lowest PERs
- The five producing the highest yields
- The five with the lowest price/tangible asset book value ratios
- The five with the lowest price/cash ratios

Ten months later at the end of June 2004, Tom Stevenson noted that although some shares produced amazing results in each category, there were also heavy losers. Overall, each section achieved net gains of 16%, 29%, 23% and 46% compared with an 8% gain for the market as a whole in the same period.

Again using Hemscott's database, he produced a list of the top five shares in each category as at the end of June 2004. These were:

- The lowest PERs – Chaucer Holdings, Cox Insurance, Goshawk Insurance, Molins and Jarvis
- The highest yields – Beattie (James), Molins, Hardy Underwriting and Ultraframe;
- The cheapest price/tangible asset ratio – Goshawk Insurance, Lavendon, Molins, Tops Estates and UNITE Group;
- The lowest price/cash flow – Hitachi capital, Ashtead, Lavendon, Danka and Beazley.

As can be seen, there were some duplications, so the original list of 20 companies came down to 16:

Ashtead Group, Beattie (James), Beazley, Chaucer Holdings, Cox Insurance, Danka, Goshawk Insurance, Hardy Underwriting, Hitachi Capital, Jarvis, Lavendon, Molins, Regent Inns, Tops Estates, Ultraframe and UNITE Group.

Based on the previous experiences described by Tom Stevenson for the 2003 selected companies (range: gain of 213% to loss of 96%), it seemed likely that the companies listed for 2004 would do either spectacularly well or excruciatingly bad. The question was: Could analysis of the latest published accounts distinguish between the two extremes?

On 1 July 2004, the latest published accounts for each of the 16 companies were examined. Because of timing constraints (analyse the accounts and write an article based upon the analysis), none of the accounts was reviewed in detail, which would be the case if investing real money had been envisaged. Instead, the exercise was simply an experiment to see if the accounts would give obvious clues without carrying out time-consuming reviews.

Three companies out of the sixteen were eliminated because they failed one or more of the tests described in Chapter 2. These were: Cox Insurance, Jarvis and Molins. Another four companies were eliminated because the latest accounts showed negative earnings. More time spent on these companies might have revealed reasons why future earnings could be better, but that was outside the scope of the rules laid down. Negative earnings took out Ashtead Group, Danka, Goshawk Insurance and UNITE Group.

The remaining nine companies were analysed and were placed in the following order:

(1) Tops Estates, (2) Chaucer Holdings, (3) Hitachi Capital, (4) Hardy Underwriting, (5) Beattie (James), (6) Beazley, (7) Ultraframe, (8) Lavendon, (9) Regent Inns

The top four shares were selected and backed against the whole 16 shares, based on £4000 being invested in each of the selected four shares compared with £1000 being invested in each of the 16 shares; the test to run over the 10 months (to be consistent with Tom Stevenson's selected timeframe) ended on 30 April 2005. The article was written on 1 July 2004 and was published in the October 2004 edition of 'Financial Management' (*Journal of Chartered Institute of Management Accountants*).

The results of this test were published in the June 2005 edition of 'Financial Management' (**selected companies in bold**, *rejected on test in italics*):

	Opening share price, 1 July 2004 (pence)	Closing share price 30 April 2005 (pence)	Percentage of capital returned[a]
Jarvis	*78.00*	*10.25*	*13.1*
Danka	63.00	16.50	26.2
Ultraframe	127.50	51.50	46.6
Beazley	96.50	88.00	91.5
Molins	*175.00*	*162.50*	*92.9*
Beattie (James)	126.50	116.50	94.9
Hardy Underwriting	**237.50**	**212.50**	**100.0**
Goshhawk Insurance	40.25	42.50	105.6
Chaucer Insurance	**48.00**	**56.00**	**118.2**
Cox Insurance	*71.50*	*92.00*	*129.4*
Hitachi Capital	**197.50**	**256.50**	**131.4**
Tops Estates	**332.00**	**442.50**	**134.5**
UNITE Group	197.50	285.00	145.6
Lavendon	125.00	184.50	149.4
Regent Inns	43.50	80.50	185.1
Ashtead Group	27.50	86.75	315.5

[a] Percentage takes into account dividends paid in the period (excluded if ex-dividend).

The four selected shares showed a profit of £3363.67 in the period on the investment of £16 000 (£2842 after transaction costs) compared to the profit of £2796.44 for the whole market (£2283 after transaction costs), giving a gross percentage profit of 21.0% and 17.5%, respectively, compared to the FTSE 100 index increasing 7.6% in the same period.

However, the methodology used for this experiment was flawed in that it used only one valuation method, that being valuation based on earnings. To evaluate insurance companies, the methodology should include an assessment of the risks associated with underwritten policies that were still live. In addition, property investment companies such as Tops Estates and UNITE Group are primarily valued on net asset values (NAVs) and not earnings (see UNITE Group's accounts in Chapter 3). In the latter case, it was the potential for increased property values in the future rather than the lack of earnings that should have been the key feature of any valuation.

Six months later, the overall 16 shares were performing much better than the four that had been selected. What this tells you is that reviewing a set of accounts once, making a decision and forgetting about it is not a rational strategy. Once a share is purchased, that company's accounts must be reviewed every 6 months.

This review should assess whether or not the methodology used for a particular company was the right one and should also look for clues in the latest accounts to see if the company is progressing or not. The old adage that 'you should buy into a good company and stay with it' is valid only if the company is continuing to perform. If a review of subsequent accounts cannot detect a problem, then by all means stay with a share even if the price is going down, but if the accounts reveal a reason why the share price is falling, then selling might be the best strategy.

Although the method of selecting companies had successfully eliminated the four worst-performing companies, it had also failed to spot the four companies that were going to show the greatest improvement. The reason why these winners were missed was a combination of using only one valuation methodology (as detailed above) and not looking at the potential for future earnings to improve. But further analysis revealed that the investment rule that states companies failing the tests shown in Chapter 2 (and later on in this chapter) should be avoided was largely validated. However, although it is not impossible that there will be exceptions to this rule, given the probabilities such companies may best be avoided.

The fate of the bottom four and top four companies is shown below:

	Share price (pence)			
	1 July 2004	30 April 2005	31 March 2006	5 April 2007
Bottom four				
Jarvis	78.00	10.25	0.20[a]	0.18[a]
Danka	63.00	16.50	20.00	16.00
Ultraframe	127.50	51.50	38.75	[b]
Beazley	96.50	88.00	118.00	161.50

[a] Based on restructuring where investors received one new ordinary share for every 400 old ordinary shares.
[b] Taken over by Latium Holdings Limited; price not known.

	Share price (pence)			
	1 July 2004	30 April 2005	31 March 2006	5 April 2007
Top four				
Ashtead Group	27.50	86.75	223.00	153.75
Regent Inns	43.50	80.50	97.50	113.75
Lavendon	125.00	184.50	280.00	416.00
UNITE Group	197.50	285.00	450.00	535.00

Risks associated with taking on unique risk

The benefits of taking on unique risk can be substantial, as detailed above, but there must be associated risks. The greatest risk is that a selected company will go badly wrong and be wound up, with the result that the investor will lose the total investment. A smaller risk is that despite financial analysis being accurate, the share price does not meet expectations in the short term. For this reason, buying and selling stocks and shares is less risky than buying and selling options, but because of leverage, options could provide the greatest profit. In simple terms, the greater the risk, the greater the potential for profit, the greater the potential for making a loss.

The example below explains. You have analysed a company and believe that the share price should be £10, compared to the current market price of £8, with a call (right to buy) at the current price anytime up to three months from the contract date at an option price of 40 pence per share. If you have £10 000 to spend, then ignoring transaction costs yon can either buy 1250 shares or 25 000 options.

If your analysis proves to be spot on and within 3 months the share price moves up to £10, then:

Owning the shares

Sell the shares for £10	Sales 1 250 × £10 = £12 500
Less: cost of shares	£10 000
Profit	£2500

Do not own the shares

Cost of option	£10 000
Exercise option – 25 000 shares at £8	£200 000
Cost of shares	£210 000
Sale of shares: 25 000 at £10	£250 000
Profit	£40 000

However, three other results can be imagined, price moves down (say) £2, price stays the same, or price moves up £2, but after three months it has expired. Now, the bigger picture can be reviewed:

	Share purchase Profit/(loss) (£)	Share option Profit/(loss) (£)
Price moves up £2 within 3 months	2500	40 000
Price moves up £2 after 3 months	2500	(10 000)
Price does not move	–	(10 000)
Price goes down £2	(2500)	(10 000)

Of course, put (right to sell) options can be even more dangerous. The situation can be imagined where the analysis of the latest accounts suggests that the company in is serious trouble and might not survive in the long term, so a put option is bought. Within 3 months, the company is in serious trouble and its shares are suspended. The analysis is spot on. However, the put option is worthless because you cannot buy the shares, so you cannot exercise the option.

Companies are never forced out of business for merely making a loss. The problems arise only when they have insufficient cash to meet their liabilities and their bankers refuse to bail them out. Failure to make a due payment to Revenue & Customs will often be fatal. For this reason, companies with huge debt and failing to generate a reasonable level of cash must be considered a higher risk than those companies either without debt or with little debt.

As explained in Chapter 2, companies whose working capital ratios are very much adverse when compared to their competitors must be considered to be a higher risk than such competitors. In such cases, the market might have discounted the share price to take account of this risk, but it has to be a matter of judgement as to whether such discount is reasonable or not.

Companies heavily indebted and not generated cash at reasonable levels, together with companies with adverse working capital ratios, are deemed to be high-risk companies, the rest are considered medium-risk companies. What investors choose to invest in will be dependent upon their risk profile. This book is designed for the risk profile shown in bold (below).

Some investors choose to invest in companies they think will grow, others might buy for a relatively high dividend yield. Many investors will aim for a combination of these attributes.

Risk profile	Investment type
Enjoys a high level of risk and expects very high returns (all or nothing)	Invest in options
A risk taker expecting to be rewarded for bravery	Invest in stocks and shares in high-risk companies
	May also invest in venture capital and biotechnology companies not yet in profit
Not a risk taker by nature, but will take some risk to beat the market	**Invest in stocks and shares in medium-risk companies**
	May try to predict takeover targets
Risk-averse	Invest in tracker funds, to eliminate unique risk
Do not take any risks	Invest in Government risk-free bonds

Assessing company performance

The accounts of 20 companies with a year end of 31 December 2005 or later were added together. All the accounts were prepared using the rules laid down by IFRS. The companies selected covered a broad range of industries as the objective was to find most, if not all, of the idiosyncrasies that can be found in a set of published accounts. The sum of the numbers was divided by 20 to arrive at a mean and the results are shown as a fictitious company – Con Glomerate plc.

Figure 4.1 shows the Income Statement (said to be for the year ended 31 December 2006). Figure 4.2 shows the Balance Sheet (said to be at 31 December 2006). Figure 4.3 shows the Cash Flow Statement (again said to be for year ended 31 December 2006).

The problem we have with these accounts is that the Income Statement as prepared under IFRS may not give us an earnings figure and consequently an 'earnings per share' figure that we can effectively use to judge performance. Of course, here we are in the realms of judgement because opinions are bound to differ. Indeed, if opinions did not differ, then we would not have a market. Some will argue that an IFRS Income Statement gives a true and fair view

Con Glomerate plc

Income Statement for year ended 31 December 2006

	£'000
Turnover	**1,311,510**
Cost of sales	1,116,443
Gross profit	195,067
Distribution costs	37,340
Administration costs	89,089
Net valuation (gains) on investment property	(9,154)
Operating profit	**77,792**
Interest payable	10,659
Profit before tax	**67,133**
Tax	19,028
Net profit	**48,105**
Number of ordinary shares ('000)	145,230
Earnings per share (pence)	**33.1**

Figure 4.1   Con Glomerate plc – Income Statement for year ended 31 December 2006

of earnings for investment purposes; others including the writer of this book argue otherwise.

So the adjustments recommended below represents the writer's view and although reasons for such views will be given, readers are invited to form their own opinions. To make the adjustments, it is necessary to look at the Cash Flow Statement (Figure 4.3).

Con Glomerate plc

Balance Sheet at 31 December 2006

	£'000
Goodwill	103,215
Other intangible assets	7,495
Tangible assets	221,609
Investments and deferred tax	34,776
Fixed assets	367,095
Inventories	202,579
Trade and other receivables	108,225
Current tax	376
Other current assets	3,375
Cash and cash equivalents	33,906
Current assets	348,461
Total assets	715,556
Trade and other payables	181,376
Financial liabilities	50,140
Provisions	1,965
Current tax liabilities	10,918
Current liabilities	244,399
Financial liabilities (long term debt)	184,017
Deferred tax	12,624
Pension deficit	20,134
Provisions	5,733
Other payables	7,173
Non-current liabilities	229,681
Total liabilities	474,080
NET ASSETS	241,476
Share capital	27,430
Share premium account	63,402
Other reserves	13,899
Retained earnings	136,745
EQUITY SHAREHOLDERS' FUNDS	241,476

Figure 4.2   Con Glomerate plc – Balance Sheet at 31 December 2006

211

Con Glomerate plc

Reconciliation between Operating profit
and Cash Inflow from operating activities

	£'000
Operating profit	**77,792**
Depreciation	15,100
Amortisation and impairment	4,977
Share options (IFRS 2)	918
Exceptional (gains)/losses	(3,164)
Movement in long term provisions	(2,417)
Dividend paid to minority interests	(175)
Revaluation gains on investment property	(9,154)
Defined benefit charge to Income Statement	203
Cash contribution to defined benefit scheme	(3,138)
(Increase)/decrease in stock	(17,224)
(Increase)/decrease in debtors	(14,198)
Increase/(decrease) in creditors	(34)
Interest paid	(8,828)
Tax paid	(11,168)
Cash inflow from operating activities	**29,490**

Figure 4.3 Con Glomerate plc – Part Cash Flow Statement for the year 31 December 2006

Exceptional gains

Companies may choose what depreciation rates they use and a gain on a sale of
an asset might merely reflect that it has been depreciated too quickly. Of course,
it could be depreciated equally too slowly and this is why Revenue and Customs
do not allow gains and losses to be used in corporation tax computations. The
figure in brackets in the Cash Flow Statement indicates that the gain was only
a 'paper' gain that did not generate cash. Accordingly, for assessment purposes
it should be ignored.

Revaluation gains on investment properties

As discussed earlier, property companies are assessed primarily on NAVs and
while it makes sense to have up to date valuations in the Balance Sheet,

declaring a profit in the Income Statement when clearly no such profit has been earned seems illogical. Accordingly, again for assessment purposes such profits should be ignored.

Share options

The cost of share options can be considered a mythical cost that simply will not happen in the context that cash will never be expended. Therefore, the cost of 'share options' should be added back to profits.

Defined benefit charge to Income Statement

The problem here is one of consistency and to achieve this we are going to charge the Income Statement with what we believe the charge should be, but after arriving at 'shareholders' operating profit'. Therefore, the actual charge is added back to profits to arrive at 'Real Operating Profit'. The effect of these adjustments is to reduce the 'operating profit' of £77 792 000 to a 'Real operating profit' of £66 595 000 (Figure 4.4).

The next step is to add 'depreciation' and 'amortisation and impairment' to the 'Real operating profit' of £66 595 000 to arrive at 'Operating profit before depreciation and amortisation and impairment' of £86 672 000 (Figure 4.4).

What we want to work out next is the tricky bit, what the 'true' earnings really are. In other words, we want to assess how much profit is available to shareholders and accordingly what the 'true' earnings per share really are. As discussed before, the real problem with the IFRS Income Statement is that the profit declared from one year to the next can be subject to significant volatility, when what we need to establish is the trend over time.

So from 'Operating Profit before depreciation and amortisation and impairment', we must take off those costs that will allow the company to stay in business and that must include making due allowance for known liabilities.

Depreciation

Depreciation is the charge to the Income Statement that takes into account that assets are being consumed and consequently are reducing in value over time. Applying the concept of 'fair value' might mean that assets are being depreciated unevenly and this will prevent the establishment of a trend. However,

Con Glomerate plc

**Calculation of REVISED (adjusted) 'earnings'
(profit belonging to shareholders)**

	£'000
Operating profit	77,792
Exceptional (gains)/losses	(3,164)
Revaluation gains on investment property	(9,154)
Share options (IFRS 2)	918
Defined benefit charge to Income Statement	203
Real 'operating profit'	**66,595**
Depreciation	15,100
Amortisation and impairment	4,977
Operating profit before depreciation and amortisation	**86,672**
Depreciation (Actual from Cash Flow Statement)	(15,100)
Amortisation (10% of intangibles)	(11,071)
'Shareholders' operating profit	**60,501**
Interest (Actual from Income Statement)	(10,659)
Pension deficit (10% of Balance Sheet figure)	(2,034)
Tax at 28% (from April 2008)	(16,486)
Dividend paid to minority interest	(175)
'Shareholders' earnings	**31,147**
Number of ordinary shares ('000)	145,230
Earnings per share (pence)	**21.4**

Figure 4.4   Con Glomerate plc – revised Earnings Statement (revised Figure 4.1)

such variations on assets normally depreciated are not thought to be significant, so no adjustment will be made.

Amortisation

Under UK GAAP, goodwill was amortised at the rate of 5% per annum. Under IFRS, goodwill is not amortised, but it is subject to an annual review and impairment as necessary. The difficulty with this decision is that readers of published accounts are reliant upon the directors having excellent judgement, but, more problematically, will experience extreme volatility in earnings.

It could be argued that although under UK GAAP goodwill was amortised, 5% per annum was too low a rate. The world changes rapidly in 20-year cycles. Twenty years ago, desktop computers had been in the United Kingdom for about 4 years and although they were novel at the time, their memory when compared to today was infinitesimal. Twenty years before that, only the largest of companies had computers. Such computers were located in large air-conditioned hanger-type rooms and could only slowly process punch cards. The currency in the United Kingdom was £sd, where 12 pennies made one shilling and 20 shillings made one pound. Calculators did not exist and all calculations were done by specialist comptometer operators who first converted £sd to decimals, did the calculations and converted back again.

The point of this story is to justify the view that goodwill will not last for an infinite time and that any goodwill today will not likely have much value in 20-years time as the world has moved on. Accordingly, in Figure 4.4, goodwill and other intangible assets have been amortised at the rate of 10%, again based on the values given in the Balance Sheet. Taking off depreciation and amortisation leaves a 'Shareholders' operating profit' of £60 501 000 (Figure 4.4). From this is deducted 'interest', being the actual figure taken from the Income Statement (Figure 4.1).

Pension deficit

The 'pension deficit' shown as a non-current liability in the Balance Sheet is the difference between the liabilities of the company's salary-related pension scheme in respect of the scheme's members and the fair value of the assets held by the pension fund to meet these liabilities.

This figure will change each year and some volatility is impossible to avoid. However, this liability should be recognised and it is assumed that over 10 years the company will fund the deficit. Accordingly, 10% of this deficit is charged to the Income Statement. First, any amount charged to the Income Statement (which has been added back to profits) is added back to the pension deficit in the Balance Sheet. The resultant figure from this addition is divided by 10 to arrive at the figure to be charged in the Adjusted Income Statement (Figure 4.4).

Corporation tax

With IFRS Income Statements taking unearned profits and then taxing such profits, it is impossible to assess what the true current corporation tax liability really is. Therefore, some assessment has to be made, although we know we cannot arrive at the correct figure. This really has to be the best estimate.

In Figure 4.4, corporation tax is calculated as follows:

	£'000
Operating profit before depreciation and amortisation	86 672
Less: depreciation	(15 100)
: interest	(10 659)
: pension deficit	(2034)
Taxable profit	58 879
Taxable profit of £58 879 000 at 28% =	16.486

Depreciation is not an allowable expense for corporation tax, so this calculation assumes that capital allowances will equal depreciation. Also expenses, such as entertainment expenses, that are also non-allowable for corporation tax purposes are not known and therefore cannot be taken into account. However, in the overall scheme of things, the error is unlikely to be significant.

Dividends to minority interests

Dividends to minority interests usually mean dividends to preference share-holders, who must be paid before ordinary shareholders can take their share. For this reason, such dividends are taken from the Income Statement before arriving at the figure that belongs to ordinary shareholders.

We are now left with earnings of £31 147 000 and with 145 230 000 ordinary shares; the earnings per share calculation (EPS) is 21.4 pence per share. The principal reason for making the adjustments described above is to take a prudent view and to be able to assess different companies fairly. We are being prudent:

- By calculating 'earnings per share' as 'earnings' divided by the '"diluted" number of ordinary shares'. These are the number of ordinary shares in issue after adding the maximum number of outstanding share options. This gives the worse-case scenario as it does not increase Balance Sheet value to take into account the price paid for the shares on exercising the option.

- By taking account of all known liabilities that will come out of shareholders' funds.

We are also taking these liabilities into account to fairly compare one company with another. So all other things being equal:

- A company with no intangible assets will be a better bet than one with intangible assets.
- A company with no pension deficit on its salary-related pension scheme will be a better bet than another with a pension deficit.

Having adjusted the Income Statement, we can put together a Cash Flow Statement that both reconciles to the revised earnings and is also in a format that we need for assessment purposes (Figure 4.5). We now have the information needed to assess the company and come up with a valuation. Though, we need to carry out basic checks.

Con Glomerate plc

Reconciliation between Operating profit and Cash Inflow from operating activities (Revised [adjusted] statement)

	£'000
Shareholders' operating profit	60,501
Depreciation	15,100
Amortisation	11,071
(Increase)/decrease in stock	(17,224)
(Increase)/decrease in debtors	(14,198)
Increase/(decrease) in creditors	(34)
Cash inflow from operations	**55,216**
Movement in long term provisions	(2,417)
Dividend paid to minority interest	(175)
Cash contribution to defined benefit scheme	(3,138)
Interest paid	(8,828)
Tax paid	(11,168)
Cash inflow from operating activities	**29,490**

Figure 4.5   Con Glomerate plc – revised Part Cash Flow Statement (revised Figure 4.3)

Basic checks

Although the calculation of profit can be judgemental, the generating of cash is not. Either cash is generated or it is not. A company making a profit should be generating cash, so the first check is to find out whether this is the case, with the rule being:

'Cash Inflow from Operations' should be greater than 'Operating profit'

If we look at Figure 4.5, we see that 'cash flow from operations' of £55 216 000 is lower than the operating profit of £60 501 000. The reason for this is that we have had an outflow from both inventories and receivables, so the next step is to calculate the key 'asset management ratios', namely:

Calculate 'inventory (stock) days' and compare with other companies in the same sector.
Calculate 'receivable (debtor) days' and compare with other companies in the same sector.

If the company is generating cash and both inventory days and receivable days seem reasonable (always assuming that the company has inventory and receivables), then the next check is:

If the company has debt, read through the accounts to ensure the company has sufficient facilities in place to enable it to meet its liabilities.

If examination of the figures at this stage throws up any concerns, then ratio analysis, as described in Chapter 2, can be carried out.

The final check is to see how well the company is utilising its assets. Before companies invest in capital projects, they attempt to ensure that, taking into account the time value of money, the income derived from them will exceed their cost of capital.

In Chapter 2, the concept of the relationship between the cost of capital and the risk was discussed. It was argued that the lower the cost of capital, by having high debt levels compared to equity, the greater the risk that the company would be forced out of business. Accordingly, it seemed inappropriate to judge capital projects on a company's actual cost of capital and instead it was suggested that a rate that was risk-neutral should be used.

The rate of return used for illustrative purposes is a net 15%, after taking tax at the rate of 28% into account, but, of course, it is a matter of judgement as to what the required rate of return should be.

Formula to calculate discount factors

	Gross	Net
Interest rate	20.83	15.00

Year	Principle	Interest	Tax	Net	Discount Factor
	£p	£p	£p	£p	
1	1,000.00	208.33	(58.33)	1,150.00	0.869565
2	1,150.00	239.58	(67.08)	1,322.50	0.756144
3	1,322.50	275.52	(77.15)	1,520.87	0.657518
4	1,520.87	316.85	(88.72)	1,749.00	0.571755
5	1,749.00	364.37	(102.02)	2,011.35	0.497179
6	2,011.35	419.03	(117.33)	2,313.05	0.432330
7	2,313.05	481.88	(134.93)	2,660.00	0.375940
8	2,660.00	554.17	(155.17)	3,059.00	0.326904
9	3,059.00	637.29	(178.44)	3,517.85	0.284265
10	3,517.85	732.88	(205.21)	4,045.52	0.247187

Discounted Cash Flow						
Year	Investment	Return	Tax on return	Net	Dis. Factor	DCF
	£p	£p	£p	£p		£p
0	(1,000.00)			(1,000.00)	1.000000	(1,000.00)
1				0.00	0.869565	0.00
2				0.00	0.756144	0.00
3				0.00	0.657518	0.00
4				0.00	0.571755	0.00
5				0.00	0.497179	0.00
6				0.00	0.432330	0.00
7				0.00	0.375940	0.00
8				0.00	0.326904	0.00
9				0.00	0.204205	0.00
10		4,045.52		4,045.52	0.247187	1,000.00
						0.00

Figure 4.6 Formula to calculate discount factors

Figure 4.6 shows how to calculate discount factors for 15%, although the principle shown can be used for any rate. First, the compound return over 10 years for an investment of £1000 (this can be any amount) is calculated. So £1000.00 × 1.15 = £1150.00, then £1150.00 × 1.15 = £1322.50 and so on. As shown, £1000 invested at a fixed 15% would return £4045.52 at the end of the period.

The discount factors are calculated by dividing £1000 (or the figure used at the start) by the net amount on each line. So £1000.00 ÷ £1150.00 = 0.869565, £1000.00 ÷ £1322.50 = 0.756144, etc.

The bottom half of Figure 4.6 shows that a return of £4045.52 in year 10 multiplied by that year's discount factor of 0.247187 would net down in £1000.00, being the exact investment. What this shows is that a net figure of zero (adding the positive return to the negative investment) means that the required return of 15% has been exactly achieved. If the figure had been positive, it would mean that the return was greater than 15%, while if the figure had been negative, it would mean that a return lower than the required rate of return had been achieved.

Discounted Cash Flow calculation for Con Glomerate plc

Year	Investment	Return	Tax on return	Net	Dis. Factor	DCF
	£'000	£'000	£'000	£'000		£'000
0	(471,157.00)			(471,157.00)	1.000000	(471,157.00)
1		86,672.00		86,672.00	0.869565	75,366.94
2		86,672.00	(24,268.16)	62,403.84	0.756144	47,186.29
3		86,672.00	(24,268.16)	62,403.84	0.657518	41,031.65
4		86,672.00	(24,268.16)	62,403.84	0.571755	35,679.71
5		86,672.00	(24,268.16)	62,403.84	0.497179	31,025.88
6		86,672.00	(24,268.16)	62,403.84	0.432330	26,979.05
7		86,672.00	(24,268.16)	62,403.84	0.375940	23,460.10
8		86,672.00	(24,268.16)	62,403.84	0.326904	20,400.06
9		86,672.00	(24,268.16)	62,403.84	0.284265	17,739.23
10		86,672.00	(24,268.16)	62,403.84	0.247187	15,425.42
11			(24,268.16)	(24,268.16)	0.214942	(5,216.25)
						(142,078.92)

Figure 4.7 Discounted cash flow for Con Glomerate plc

In Figure 4.7, the principles described in Figure 4.6 are used. What we are assessing is whether or not Con Glomerate plc is achieving a discounted return of 15% or not.

The investment is taken to be total capital employed, as follows:

	£'000
Total assets	715 556
Less: current liabilities	244 399
Total capital employed	471 157

Neither depreciation nor amortisation is taken into account in investment appraisal, apart from the 'accounting rate of return' method, so the 'return' is taken to be 'operating profit before depreciation and amortisation'. The figure (£'000) of £86 672 is taken from Figure 4.4. Tax is assumed to be at the rate of 28%, paid one year in arrears.

From Figure 4.7, it can be seen that if profits are maintained throughout the period, then the final discounted figure is negative (£'000) £142 078.92. This means that the required rate of return of 15% has not been achieved.

Figure 4.8 simply adjusts Figure 4.7 by putting a formula into the 'return' line that adds in a growth factor. Different growth factors are then keyed in until the bottom figure on the DCF line gets to (positively) as near zero as possible. From this it can be seen that if Con Glomerate plc achieves an annual growth in earnings of 10.0307%, then it will achieve its required rate of return of 15%.

Con Glomerate plc – Growth Factor required to achieve 15% return

Year	Investment	Return	Tax on return	Net	Dis. Factor	DCF
	£'000	£'000	£'000	£'000		£'000
0	(471,157.00)			(471,157.00)	1.000000	(471,157.00)
1		86,672.00		86,672.00	0.869565	75,366.94
2		95,365.81	(24,268.16)	71,097.65	0.756144	53,760.06
3		104,931.67	(26,702.43)	78,229.24	0.657518	51,437.13
4		115,457.05	(29,380.87)	86,076.18	0.571755	49,214.49
5		127,038.20	(32,327.97)	94,710.23	0.497179	47,087.94
6		139,781.02	(35,570.70)	104,210.32	0.432330	45,053.25
7		153,802.03	(39,138.69)	114,663.34	0.375940	43,106.54
8		169,229.45	(43,064.57)	126,164.88	0.326904	41,243.80
9		186,204.35	(47,384.25)	138,820.10	0.284265	39,461.70
10		204,881.95	(52,137.22)	152,744.73	0.247187	37,756.51
11			(57,366.95)	(57,366.95)	0.214942	(12,330.57)
						0.79

Growth Factor	
	1.100307

Figure 4.8 Con Glomerate plc – growth factor required to achieve a 15% return

Assuming that there are no outstanding matters causing concern, we can move on to making an assessment as to a reasonable valuation of the company.

Valuation techniques

Many sectors make up the economic climate of a country and each sector is different in some way from the next. This gives rise to the necessity that companies in a particular sector should be valued differently from those in a different sector. For example, companies could be put in 'valuation' sectors as below:

- Investment companies
- Property developers
- Banks and utility companies
- Insurance companies
- Biotechnology and similar scientific companies
- Companies owning professional football clubs
- General industrial, leisure and retail companies

Investment companies

Investment companies can be defined as those companies that invest in private companies, although they do invest in publicly quoted companies also. Most of these companies are either members of the British Venture Capital Association (BVCA) or the European Venture Capital Association (EVCA) and value their investments in accordance with the 'International Private Equity and Venture Capital Valuation Guidelines' (VCVG) that have been endorsed by both these organisations.

Members of the BVCA and EVCA comply with their respective organisation's 'code of conduct'. Given that the objectives of private equity companies are sometimes misinterpreted, it is worthwhile reviewing how members are expected to conduct themselves. As an example, the BVCA Code of Conduct is shown below.

The BVCA Code of Conduct

Membership of the BVCA implies support for the development of the UK private equity industry by encouraging entrepreneurs and investing in viable economic activity. In addition, members should contribute to the creation of a favourable climate for companies seeking private equity.

(1) Members shall promote and maintain ethical standards of conduct and at all times deal fairly and honestly with each other and with companies seeking private equity.

(2) Members shall conduct their business in a professional way and will not engage in practices which would be damaging to the image of the private equity industry.

(3) Members recognise that their primary business is building the strength of their investee companies which will result in the funds under management making long-term capital gains.

(4) Membership of the BVCA implies an active involvement by members in the companies in which they invest and this involvement shall be applied constructively to the benefit of the company concerned.

(5) Members who sponsor investment syndications with other parties, whether members of the BVCA or not, must operate on the basis of full disclosure to such other parties.

(6) Members will not accept in their funds subscribed capital from unspecified sources.

(7) Members shall be accountable to their investors and keep their investors fully and regularly informed including the provision of regular financial reports.

(8) No member shall take improper advantage of his position in the BVCA nor any information addressed to the BVCA.

(9) Members shall respect confidential information supplied to them by companies looking for private equity or by companies in which they have invested.

(10) All members must supply investment information to the BVCA or its nominated agent. This information will be treated confidentially and used in the compilation of private equity industry reports where only aggregate information will be published.

Members shall require their directors, employees, representatives and nominees to comply with these standards. Members will avoid financing enterprises or participating in activities which are inconsistent with these goals. The Council of the BVCA reserves the right to cancel membership or refuse to renew membership if, in its sole opinion, a member is in breach of the above conditions or is deemed to have acted in a way that could harm the reputation of the private equity industry or the BVCA.

(*Source*: Reproduced from page x of the BVCA Directory 2006/2007, by kind permission from the British Venture Capital Association.)

To value 'investment companies', it will be appropriate to see how these companies value their own investments. The VCVG states that investments should be valued at 'fair value' using one or a combination of the following methods:

- Price of recent investment
- Earnings multiple
- Net assets
- DCFs (from the investment)
- Industry valuation benchmarks

There are three steps in valuing investments:

(1)   Assess the fair value of the business.
(2)   Calculate the 'Gross Attributable Enterprise Value'.
(3)   Calculate the 'Net Attributable Enterprise Value'.

The 'Gross Attributable Enterprise Value' is defined as:

The Enterprise Value attributable to the financial instruments held by the Fund and other financial instruments in the entity that rank alongside or beneath the highest ranking instrument of the Fund.

What this means, for example, is that if the Fund held ordinary shares in a company, but not preference shares, then the value of the ordinary shares, ranking below preference shares, would be the total value of the company, less the value attributable to holders of the preference shares.

The 'Net Attributable Enterprise Value' is defined as:

The 'Gross Attributable Enterprise Value' less a 'Marketability Discount.'

The 'marketability discount', being the difference between the gross and the net attributable enterprise value, takes account of the difficulty in marketing the investment. Private equity companies invest in unquoted companies and may invest in management buyouts. There will be times when the management team and the venture capital company do not see eye to eye; the private equity company might want to sell, but the management team do not. In such cases, the VCVG advises that any valuation should take into account:

- Are there other like-minded shareholders with regard to Realisation and what is the combined degree of influence?
- Is there an agreed exit strategy or exit plan?
- Do legal rights exist which allow the Fund together with like-minded shareholders to require the other shareholders to agree to and enable a proposed Realisation to proceed.

- Does the management team of the Underlying Business have the ability in practice to reduce the prospects of a successful Realisation? This may be the case where the team is perceived by possible buyers to be critical to the ongoing success of the business. If this is the case, what is the attitude of the management team to Realisation?

Assuming all parties agreed to the sale, consideration would be given as to how likely a sale would be. The more likely a deal, the lower the 'marketability discount'; the less likely a deal, the higher the marketability discount. Marketability discounts are usually in the range between 10% and 30% and move in 5% steps.

The VCVG notes that 'the Fair Value concept requires the Marketability Discount is to be determined not from the perspective of the current holder of the Investment, but from the perspective of Market Participants.'

Thus it can be seen that investment companies, like all other companies, are constrained by the IFRS rules as laid down by the IASB. Of course, private investors can please themselves how they arrive at all valuations; indeed one of the objectives of this book is to try to show where the 'market' might have got it wrong.

Apart from the 'price of recent investment' method of valuation, which is peculiar to private equity, all the other methods listed in the VCVG can be used to value quoted companies.

Earnings multiple

The 'earnings multiple' is simply the average P/E ratio for the sector a particular company is in. If the earnings multiple for a particular company is higher than the average, then the market believes that that company is better than average; conversely a lower than average P/E ratio indicates the opposite.

Whereas an investment company is assessing what a P/E ratio should be for an unquoted company, the private investor is trying to assess whether the P/E ratio for a quoted company is reasonable. To assess this, the private investor should follow the same procedures as an investment manager following VCVG guidelines:

> The P/E ratio should be considered and assessed by reference to the two key variables of risk and earnings growth prospects which underpin the earnings multiple. In assessing the risk profile of the company being valued, the Valuer

should recognise that risk arises from a range of aspects, including the nature of the company's operations, the markets in which it operates and its competitive position in those markets, the quality of its management and employees and its capital structure. For example, the value of the company may be reduced if it:

- is smaller and less diverse than the comparator(s) and, therefore, less able generally to withstand adverse economic conditions;
- is reliant on a small number of key employees;
- is dependent on one product or one customer;
- has high gearing; or
- for any other reason has poor quality earnings.

This recommendation from the VCVG is consistent with the view taken throughout this book that the most important aspect of any business is the quality of its management and employees and the importance of having the right gearing. As the VCVG notes, a high geared and less diverse company is less able to withstand adverse economic conditions than a low-geared diverse company.

'Quality of the earnings' has been discussed earlier in this chapter, with reasons given as to why the earnings shown in the Income Statement might have to be adjusted. Many of the valuation methods shown use 'earnings' or 'earnings per share' as part of the equation, so it will be obvious that this figure often plays a key part in the final valuation.

Net assets

The 'net assets' valuation of a business is simply the figure shown in the Balance Sheet and is the same figure as the bottom block in the Balance Sheet shown as 'equity shareholders' funds'. If this figure is divided by the number of ordinary shares in issue, the resultant calculation gives a figure that is the 'book value per share'. The difference between this book value per share and the market value per share is the 'goodwill' built into the share price over and above the goodwill shown in the Balance Sheet.

Given an IFRS Balance Sheet has been computed at 'fair values', we should get a 'true and fair' valuation of the net assets of the company. However, it must be borne in mind that we are more than ever reliant upon the directors of the company having sound judgement.

Discounted cash flow or earnings

The VCVG defines this valuation method as:

> This methodology involves deriving the value of a business by calculating the present value of expected future cash flows (or the present value of expected future earnings, as a surrogate for expected future cash flows). The cash flows and "terminal value" are those of the Underlying Business not those from the Investment itself.

The VCVG points out that this method is flexible in that it can be applied to any stream of cash flow (or earnings), but cautions:

> The disadvantages of the DCF methodology centre around its requirements for detailed cash flow forecasts and the need to estimate the "terminal value" and the appropriate risk-adjusted discount rate. All of these inputs require substantial subjective judgements to be made, and the derived present value amount is often sensitive to small changes in these inputs.

> Due to the high level of subjectivity in selecting inputs for this technique, DCF based valuations are useful as a cross-check of values estimated under market-based methodologies and should only be used in isolation of other methodologies under extreme caution.

Figures 4.9–4.12 explain the points made by the VCVG. Figure 4.9 use the DCF technique to assess the valuation of Con Glomerate plc (see Figures 4.1–4.5). The current spread of this company at the date of valuation was 321 pence to 324 pence. What this means is that this company's shares could be bought for 324 pence each and sold for 321 pence. The current earnings per share are 21.4 pence (taken from Figure 4.4) and using the same methodology to calculate earnings, 5 years ago the earnings per share were 13.97 pence, giving a compound growth of 11.25% over this time.

So straight away, there are two key figures that are based on judgement, namely:

(1) That the current earnings per share of 21.4 pence is the correct figure to take.
(2) That future growth will be equal to recent compound growth.

The next judgement to make is what interest rate should be used to compensate for the risks involved. Remember, the rate required has to be higher than the risk-free rate of around 4%–5% and that the greater the perceived risk, the higher the rate should be.

Con Glomerate plc

Formula to calculate growth built into share price

(shaded areas contain formulae)

	Ask	Bid	Spread factor
Price of share (pence)	324.0	321.0	0.990741

Price for forecast growth	261.5

Base expenditure (£)	1,000.00
Available for shares (£p)	985.22
Number of shares	376.76
Current EPS (pence)	21.40
Dividend amount (£p)	80.63
Growth rate (%)	1.112500

Base expenditure (£): 1,000.00
Available for shares (£p): 985.22
Number of shares: 304.08
Current EPS (pence): 21.40
Dividend amount (£p): 65.07
Growth rate (%): 1.1650

GROWTH BUILT IN
CORRECT PRICE FOR FORECAST GROWTH (pence)

	EPS (pence) Year 0	EPS (pence) Year 4
	13.97	21.40

	EPS (pence)
Year 0	13.97
Year 1	15.54
Year 2	17.29
Year 3	19.24
Year 4	21.40

Forecast Growth DCF	0.76

Built in Share DCF	2.55

Forecast growth %	1.112500

Discount Rate	11.00

Discounted Cash Flow – Growth built into share

Year	Investment £p	Return £p	Tax on return £p	Net £p	Dis. Factor	DCF £p
0	(1,000.00)			(1,000.00)	1.000000	(1,000.00)
1		65.07	(6.51)	58.56	0.900901	52.76
2		75.81	(7.58)	68.23	0.811629	55.37
3		88.31	(8.83)	79.48	0.731197	58.12
4		102.89	(10.29)	92.60	0.658740	61.00
5		119.86	(11.99)	107.87	0.593458	64.02
6		139.64	(13.96)	125.68	0.534648	67.19
7		162.68	(16.27)	146.41	0.481665	70.52
8		189.52	(18.95)	170.57	0.433934	74.02
9		220.79	(22.08)	198.71	0.390932	77.68
10		257.23	(25.72)	231.51	0.352191	81.53
						(337.79)
10				966.34	0.352191	340.34
						2.55

Sale proceeds £p 966.34

(Based on 'ask' price after allowing 1% transaction costs)

Figure 4.9 Formula to calculate growth built into share price

Con Glomerate plc

Formula to calculate price needed to achieve required RR with forcecast growth

Sale proceeds						
	£p					
966.34						

Discounted Cash Flow – Forecast growth

Year	Investment £'p	Return £'p	Tax on return £'p	Net £'p	Dis. Factor	DCF £'p
0	(1,000.00)			(1,000.00)	1.000000	(1,000.00)
1		80.63	(8.06)	72.57	0.900901	65.38
2		89.70	(8.97)	80.73	0.811629	65.52
3		99.79	(9.98)	89.81	0.731197	65.67
4		111.02	(11.10)	99.92	0.658740	65.82
5		123.51	(12.35)	111.16	0.593458	65.97
6		137.40	(13.74)	123.66	0.534648	66.12
7		152.86	(15.29)	137.57	0.481665	66.26
8		170.06	(17.01)	153.05	0.433934	66.41
9		189.19	(18.92)	170.27	0.390932	66.56
10		210.47	(21.05)	189.42	0.352191	66.71
						(339.58)
10		966.34		966.34	0.352191	340.34
						0.76

Figure 4.10 Formula to calculate price needed to achieve IRR with forecast growth

Formula to calculate growth built into share price

Con Glomerate plc

(shaded areas contain formulae)

	Ask	Bid	Spread factor
	324.0	321.0	0.990741

	EPS (pence) Year 0	EPS (pence) Year 4
	13.97	21.40

	EPS (pence)
Year 0	13.97
Year 1	15.54
Year 2	17.29
Year 3	19.24
Year 4	21.40

Price for forecast growth	
406.0	Price of share (pence)
1,000.00	Base expenditure (£)
985.22	Available for shares (£p)
242.67	Number of shares
21.40	Current EPS (pence)
51.93	Dividend amount (£p)
1.112500	Growth rate (%)

GROWTH BUILT IN
CORRECT PRICE FOR FORECAST GROWTH (pence)

Forecast Growth DCF	0.24
Built in Share DCF	1.76

Forecast growth %: 1.112500

Discount Rate: 7.20

1.06
406.00

1.0600

Discounted Cash Flow – Growth built into share

Year	Investment £p	Return £p	Tax on return £p	Net £p	Dis. Factor	DCF £p
Sale proceeds £p 966.34						
0	(1,000.00)			(1,000.00)	1.000000	(1,000.00)
1		65.07	(6.51)	58.56	0.932836	54.63
2		68.97	(6.90)	62.07	0.870186	54.02
3		73.11	(7.31)	65.80	0.811741	53.41
4		77.50	(7.75)	69.75	0.757226	52.82
5		82.15	(8.21)	73.94	0.706369	52.23
6		87.08	(8.71)	78.37	0.658926	51.64
7		92.30	(9.23)	83.07	0.614670	51.06
8		97.84	(9.78)	88.06	0.573388	50.49
9		103.71	(10.37)	93.34	0.534877	49.93
10		109.93	(10.99)	98.94	0.498952	49.37
10						(480.40)
		966.34		966.34	0.498952	482.16
						1.76

(Based on 'ask' price after allowing 1% transaction costs)

Figure 4.11 Formula to calculate growth built into share price – Con Glomerate plc

Con Glomerate plc

Formula to calculate price needed to achieve required RR with forcecast growth

			Discounted Cash Flow – Forecast growth					
Sale proceeds	Year	Investment	Return	Tax on return	Net	Dis. Factor	DCF	
£p		£'p	£'p	£'p	£'p		£'p	
966.34	0	(1,000.00)			(1,000.00)	1.000000	(1,000.00)	
	1		51.93	(5.19)	46.74	0.932836	43.60	
	2		57.77	(5.78)	51.99	0.870186	45.24	
	3		64.27	(6.43)	57.84	0.811741	46.95	
	4		71.50	(7.15)	64.35	0.757226	48.73	
	5		79.55	(7.95)	71.60	0.706369	50.57	
	6		88.49	(8.85)	79.64	0.658926	52.48	
	7		98.45	(9.85)	88.60	0.614670	54.46	
	8		109.53	(10.95)	98.58	0.573388	56.52	
	9		121.85	(12.18)	109.67	0.534877	58.66	
	10		135.56	(13.56)	122.00	0.498952	60.87	
							(481.92)	
	10		966.34		966.34	0.498952	482.16	
							0.24	

Figure 4.12 Formula to calculate Con Glomerate's share price to achieve IRR

Figure 4.9 makes the judgement that a rate of 12.22%, or 11% net of dividend tax at the rate of 10%, is the rate to take, so the third judgement is:

(3)   That the discount factors used are those for 11%.

The next assumption used is:

(4)   That the transaction costs will be 1.5% of the cost of the purchase, to cover commission and stamp duty, and 1% of the sales proceeds to cover commission.

The DCF is worked out on the basis that there is £1000 to spend. Note that this could be any number; a higher number would produce larger numbers, but discounted back would give the same result.

So if there is £1000 to spend and the price is £3.24 per share, 304.08 shares can be bought:

	£p
304.08 shares at £3.24 per share =	985.22
Commission and stamp duty (1.5%)	14.78
	1000.00

The DCF calculation then assumes that the earnings per share are paid out in full, so current earnings of 21.4 pence per share would give a dividend of £65.07 and this is the amount that is shown as 'return' in year 1 (Figure 4.9).

As stated in the VCVG, another key assumption in DCF calculations is the estimation of the terminal value. It is assumed in Figure 4.9 that because the earnings per share have been paid out in full, there cannot be any growth in the share price. Accordingly, the selling price of the share is based on the original spread:

	£p
304.08 shares at £3.21 per share	976.10
Commission (1%)	9.76
Proceeds	966.34

If earnings did not grow in the 10-year period, then our DCF calculation would end up with a negative figure, indicating that we could not achieve the rate of return required. We can then calculate the compound growth in earnings required to achieve this internal rate of return (IRR). If we look down the 'ask' column of Figure 4.9, it can be seen that compound growth of 16.5% is required, against a forecast growth rate of 11.25%.

On the basis of Con Glomerate example, we have assessed that although the earnings growth of 11.25% is sufficient to justify the capital employed (10.03% required, see Figures 4.9–4.8), the price of the share is too high. We can then calculate what the share price would have to be if the IRR was to be achieved based on the forecast growth. This is shown in the first column (price would have to fall to 261.5 pence) of Figure 4.9 and the calculation itself is shown in Figure 4.10.

To demonstrate the validity of the comment in the VCVG that 'the derived present value amount is often sensitive to small changes in these inputs', Figures 4.11 and 4.12 are identical to Figures 4.9 and 4.10, except that this time a gross percentage of 8% is used, so that the net discount factors are based on the rate of 7.2%.

These calculations were then repeated using the original earnings per share of 33.1 pence. The table below shows the results:

	Earnings per share (pence)	
	33.1 pence	21.4 pence
	Price of share (pence)	
IRR Net 7.2%	628.0	406.0
IRR Net 11.0%	404.5	261.5

	Earnings per share (pence)	
	33.1 pence	21.4 pence
	Growth built in at 324 p per share (%)	
IRR Net 7.2%	(5.1)	6.0
IRR Net 11.0%	5.7	16.5

As can be seen, DCF calculations are highly dependent upon the judgements and assumptions made. However, this is not a problem, provided the same assumptions and judgements are made in respect of all valuations. It is for each reader to work out which judgements and assumptions are to be applied, taking into account his/her risk profile, but provided they are consistently applied, one share can be reasonably compared to another.

Industry valuation benchmarks

There are various industry benchmarks that can be used in making valuations. Examples of such benchmarks might be 'price per bed' for nursing home operators, 'price per subscriber' for cable television companies and 'price per square metre' for property developers. Given a Balance Sheet will be computed at 'fair value', it can be assumed that such benchmarks have been used as appropriate.

Final Review

Before finally arriving at any valuation, the VCVG suggests that events that might impact value should be considered. Events that would cause concern are listed as follows:

- the performance or prospects of the Underlying Business being significantly below the expectations on which the Investment was based;
- the Underlying Business is performing substantially and consistently behind plan;
- the Underlying Business missed its milestones such as clinical trials, technical developments, divisions becoming cash positive, restructuring being completed;
- there is a deterioration in the level of budgeted performance;
- whether the Underlying Business has breached any banking covenants, defaulted on any obligations;
- the existence of off-balance sheet items, contingent liabilities and guarantees;
- the existence of a major lawsuit;
- disputes over commercial matters such as intellectual property rights;
- the existence of fraud within the company;
- a change of management or strategic direction of the Underlying Business;
- whether there has been a significant adverse change either in the company's business or in the technological, market, economic, legal or regulatory environment in which the business operates;

- significant changes in market conditions; and
- the Underlying Business is raising money and there is evidence that the financing will be made under conditions different from those prevailing at the time of the previous round of financing.

These events and how they might impact share prices are discussed below under the heading 'profit warnings'.

Investment companies value their investments at 'fair value' using the VCVG described above. What these companies are aiming to do is as stated in item 3 of the BVCA Code of Conduct; that is, they are trying to achieve long-term capital gain rather than generating income. Accordingly, the share price of these companies will be primarily based on its NAV per share, although other factors are often taken into account. The case study – HgCapital Trust plc illustrates.

Property developers

Property companies would be valued on the basis of their NAV per share, plus a premium to take into account the market's view on how property prices are appreciated. However, if the belief in the market place was that the supply of commercial property exceeded demand and that rental income per square metre was likely to fall, then the price of the share might fall to a discount to its NAV. Those with specialist knowledge in the industry have a distinct advantage compared with other potential shareholders.

Banks and utility companies

It could be argued that banks and utility companies have collectively just about reached market saturation. To achieve high levels of profitability, these companies rely on the apathy of their customers. For example, banks for years have been charging exorbitant fees to customers who have inadvertently seen their current account go overdrawn, yet it is only in 2007 that customers have begun to complain and even fewer have moved their account to another bank.

Utility companies vastly increased their charges for gas in 2006 when wholesale prices went through the roof, but have been very slow to reduce prices in line with the reduction in wholesale prices in 2007. The regulatory system is very weak; the regulator seems to be limited to advising people to switch from the worst offenders, yet so few do.

Such companies could hardly be described as innovative, other than finding ways of extracting more money from customers for the same level of service. For these reasons, investors buy shares in banks and utility companies for income rather than growth, so they can be valued by reference to their dividend yield and risk profile.

Given these companies are not innovative, the only real way they can increase the earnings per share in a meaningful way is to take over another company and save money through synergies and cost cutting. If they increase the earnings per share, they can increase their dividend. Accordingly, where one bank takes over another (for example), the price of its share often goes upwards. However, a failed takeover can have the opposite effect.

In the 1980s/1990s, Lloyds Bank had been on the up by expanding through acquisition and Lloyds/TSB plc had been formed. Acquisitions continued, but in the early part of the twenty-first century, this strategy began to falter and the company's share price fell from around £10 per share to a low of around £4 per share. This state of affairs led to the Chief Executive resigning in 2003 to be replaced by another. In March 2004, the company issued their accounts for the year ended 31 December 2003. Earnings per share of 41.5 pence were down 6% on the prior year, but the annual dividend of 34.2 pence per share was maintained.

In buying such shares, investors have to make a judgement as to the likely future trends and whether the market has got it right, or not as the case may be. A visit to a branch of Lloyds/TSB on the day the accounts were published suggested that money deposited with them would earn an interest at the rate of 4%. However, the alternative, given the price of the company's share was 445 pence on the same day, was to buy the shares and earn interest at the rate of 7.7%. It did not seem likely that a company of the size of Lloyds/TSB plc would go under, so the only danger seemed to be that the dividend would be cut, but with dividend cover being 1.2 and the prospect that the new Chief Executive would take the company forward, the balance of probability suggested the risk to be reasonable.

Insurance companies

Insurance companies can be valued using the DCF method, except a valuation on this basis must be modified to take account of the risk profile of the company. Insurance (as against assurance) can essentially be divided into two types: insuring regular and irregular events. An example of a regular event would be motor insurance; thousands of cars will be insured and there will be a regular stream of claims. An irregular event would be insuring against a tsunami. There might not be a claim of several years, but when it arrives it will be of catastrophic proportions.

It can be seen, therefore, that income streams for insurance companies can go up and down and that investing in such companies can be considered to be higher risk than the norm.

Biotechnology and similar scientific companies

At the turn of the millennium, biotechnology companies and the like were seen as the new high-technology companies of the future. It was believed that the latest scientific knowledge could lead to a cure for more than one type of cancer, with biotechnology being the answer.

Many high-risk investors put a proportion of their portfolio into such companies that are run by well-qualified and clever people who have spent many years as researchers. Apart from the original share capital, these companies generate income from research grants and deals with drug companies. However, in most cases, research costs exceed income by a large percentage and investors see 'cash burn' year on year.

When research leads to the development of a new drug, such drug must face three phases of clinical trial. Phase one is done on the smallest scale, phase two is bigger and phase three is substantial. If a drug passes all three trials, then it can go before the regulatory authorities for approval. Once approved, the drug can be sold to the general public.

Shares in these companies are an out and out gamble, with investors putting their trust in the management team. The price of shares in biotechnology companies moves up and down rapidly following announcements; a successful clinical trial will see the price shooting up, while an unsuccessful trial followed by the drug being abandoned will see the price crashing down.

Of course, investors are betting on a cancer drug going through all its trials successfully and not only ending up on the chemists' shelves, but also working. It will happen one day and one company's shareholders will hit the jackpot.

Companies owning professional football clubs

Investing in football clubs, for the ordinary investor, is an expensive way to secure a season ticket. The only possible reason to buy into quoted football clubs is the love of the game, unless you are very lucky. With the (alleged) best footballers being paid £120 000 plus per week, most football clubs cannot make ends meet. Indeed, only the top four clubs in the Premiership, able to play in the European Champions' League, are likely to be able to make a reasonable profit; others find it much more difficult to balance the books.

But hey, who knows? The years roll by and suddenly a wealthy American or Russian wants to buy your club. So, in the final analysis, football shares are for fanatics and those who like a punt on the lottery.

General industrial, leisure and retail companies

The BVCA advises that the DCF method of valuation should be used only in conjunction with other methods, but when using it to value quoted companies, the base valuation we have is the market price. So the purpose of the DCF method (being more sophisticated than the 'earnings multiple' method) is to assess whether the market values are valid or not. To illustrate this point, on a day in April 2007, all house builders were evaluated using the DCF method, based on the current spread of their share price and the latest earnings per share available and taking the discount rate to be 11%. Companies about to be taken over, who share price was virtually based on the agreed takeover price per share, were ignored, as were those listed on AIM. This left six companies:

	Growth-based latest achievement (%)	Growth built into share price (%)
Company F	1.160	1.068
Company B	1.140	1.053
Company A	1.090	1.075
Company E	1.157	1.154
Company D	0.970	1.179
Company C	0.860	1.068

The next step in the process is to read the accounts of these companies, taking note of what the directors are projecting for the future. In addition, the latest announcements by the companies should be evaluated. Special attention should be given if any of the announcements relate to 'events' detailed above (see also 'profit warnings' below). Assuming that the 'basic checks' have revealed no problems and that nothing untoward has been found in either reports or announcements, company F would be the preferred investment.

Why the market sometimes gets it painfully wrong

As we have discussed before, many investors are not rational and some can be overtaken with greed. Two unusual events arriving simultaneously can send the stock market orbiting the planet, the fantasyland.

In 1999, two such events happened. The first event was the 'millennium bug'. We were told that all computers' operating systems would crash on 1 January 2000. The reason was that these operating systems were first developed in the 1980s when the memory available was only a fraction of what it would be 25 years later. Because of this limitation, computers had been programmed to run from 00 to 99, rather than from 1900 to 9999. So on 1 January 2000, the lights would go out and aeroplanes would fall from the sky.

Governments, local government and major industries simply dare not risk falling foul of the millennium bug, so there was a mad scramble for IT consultants, who could name their price. Shares in IT companies went through the roof.

The second event was the Internet that, although in use for a few years in the United States, suddenly hit the United Kingdom. We were told by the gurus in the City that we were entering a new paradigm. Companies were no longer being valued by earnings per share; indeed earnings were no longer relevant. Also, measures such as 'return on capital employed' were simply old hat. No, the new paradigm was 'hits' on company's website.

Start-up companies developing websites suddenly found themselves with unbelievable valuations. It seemed investors simply could not wait to get a slice of the action, no matter what the price was. It got to the point that companies were overvalued even based on hits, so the gurus told us that we have moved on to valuing companies based on 'potential hits'. The theory was that as advertisers would pay so much per hit, it was only a matter of time before these new high-technology companies were raking in a fortune.

So some IT specialists left safe employment to develop websites for these new start-up companies. With investors willing to spend money as if it had gone out of fashion, it was a case of develop websites by day and party in style by night. The 'in-phrase' became 'cash burn', the amount of cash being used on website development, salaries and expenses, without any revenue being generated. But, no worries; share prices continued to soar.

In such an environment, it is very easy to see how the rightly cautious are sucked in. Mr Cavalier gives Mr Cautious a tip about a new high-tech issue to hit the market the next day. The following day the share opens at 100 pence and closes at 215 pence. The next day the share hits 300 pence, before falling back to 250 pence. Mr Cautious cannot see suggests Mr Cavalier that there is easy money to be made out there.

So Mr Cautious joins the bandwagon and high-tech and IT shares start trading on P/Es well above 100. The dreaded day of 1st January 2000 arrived, but the lights stayed on and aeroplanes landed safely. The millennium bug turned out to be a myth, as did the dot-com boom. Sure, some of the original movers in the United States, such as Google, have netted a fortune, but for the majority of hopefuls it was all a mirage.

There might have been hits on websites, but advertisers were not that interested. Nobody seemed to understand that they focus their marketing budget at target markets and unless the website owners could demonstrate that their hits matched the target there was nothing doing. Google et al. resolved this problem by the sheer volume of hits they achieved, but for the majority of hopefuls the numbers simply did not add up.

Then some people started to worry about cash burn, for they could see that the big danger was that the investment money was about to run out. The bubble was about to burst.

> *Investment rule 4*: If the price of a share defies every type of financial logic imaginable and its price is being valued using a new paradigm, there is a chance you will make a killing if your timing is spot on, but a far greater chance is that you will not have sold before the bubble bursts.

Restructuring – a strategy to move the share price upwards

It is relatively rare for even a strong management team to continuously find new growth opportunities and rather than sit on a pile of cash that is not working for the company, some managers make the decision to either buy back their own company's shares or instead go for a higher-profile restructuring. The logic for this is explained in the case study – Topps Tiles plc.

Profit Warnings

It is said that a private investor will never be able to beat specialist fund managers because they get information before the general public. Under stock exchange rules, directors must make an announcement if they believe their actual performance will be materially different from that expected based on its last publicly disclosed profit forecast, estimate or projection. Such 'profit warnings' are made available to everyone at the same time, and they will hit all the dealing screens at the same time. However, many private investors will get their information on websites such as 'hemscott' and 'iii' and these often work on a 15-minute time delay. So the information will be available to the professionals a few minutes before it is available to the general public.

Bad news you might think, but in reality, this situation can give a significant advantage to the private investor. The reason for this is that because one institution cannot be seen to respond slower than their competitors, many will have computer systems that will immediately trigger a sale if a profit warning hits the screens. So any profit warning will usually result in the affected share falling between 20% and 30% instantaneously. However, what these computer systems cannot do is to distinguish between a serious profit warning and one that is of little consequence and is issued merely to meet compliance rules.

There are various types of profit warning and these were listed by the BVCA as events that would likely cause concern.

Deteriorating performance

This profit warning will often include the words 'profits will be substantially below market expectations'. Such warnings are often like buses in that they come in threes. The key to understanding such warnings is to look at the track record of the management team making the announcement. Some management teams are ultra-cautious, while others tend to play down what has gone wrong.

A well-informed, but cautious, board will quantify the problem and will usually specify the maximum likely hit, with words such as 'we are still investigating, but the impact of profits will be no more than £5 million.' In such cases, it is possible to work out what the P/E ratio was immediately prior to the warning and what it was immediately after the warning, after the share price had collapsed. In such cases, if the P/E ratio has fallen, it is likely that the market has overdone the hit and investors are left with a buying opportunity. The case study – Paddy Power plc illustrates this point.

On the other hand, a warning that simply states there is a problem but makes no assessment of the likely impact on profitability is altogether a different matter. In such cases, the safest option would be to sell the share.

Missing milestones such as clinical trials, etc.

This usually refers to biotechnology or similar companies when a drug, on which many hopes rest, fails a clinical trial. This will usually set the price of the share spiralling downwards and whether it will recover or not will be something of a gamble.

The company has breached banking covenants, defaulted on obligations or off-balance sheet items, contingent liabilities and guarantees are discovered

Any of the 'events' must be considered to be serious and staying with a company in this situation is like doing the lottery; vast rewards are possible, but losing the whole of the investment is more likely.

Serious legal issues, such as fraud, have come to light

Any issues such as these have to be analysed thoroughly before a decision can be made. Such issues are very difficult to determine for the ordinary investor and selling a share under these circumstances might be the safest option.

Key personnel suddenly resign and/or sell a significant tranche of shares

If the reason for resignation or significant sale is detailed and believable, then if the company is relatively large (in the FTSE 100, for example) it should be safe to hold onto the shares. However, if the Chief Executive Officer or Finance Director in a smaller company suddenly resigns or sells a significant tranche of shares without warning, it can be a sign of a major problem that is yet to surface. For example, the words, 'Mr X today sold 75% of his entire holding to an unspecified buyer at a price that was 15% below the then prevailing market price. Mr X said that he had to sell his shares for personal reasons' should be regarded with utmost suspicion.

Takeover bids

There has been much research on the topic of takeover bids and it seems pretty conclusive. This research suggests that shareholders of the companies being sold on the whole do a lot better than the shareholders of the company acquiring other businesses.

Companies wishing to acquire another do so because they believe that increased market share will enable them to compete better and that due to synergies, a reasonable level of cost cutting will be achieved.

The main problem for the potential acquirer is that the seller will attempt to get a high price through promoting competition. If two companies want something really badly, they tend to offer what can sometimes be regarded as an unrealistic price that can only be justified if all the potential benefits actually accrue.

What the acquirer often finds is that there is a cultural clash between existing and acquired employees, who see themselves as underdogs and accordingly become resentful. Acquisitions require sympathetic management from the acquiring company. Then the acquirer finds that making cost savings in practice is usually far more difficult than making cost savings on paper. Add to this the fact that the acquirer's management is trying to do two jobs, their own job together with trying to integrate the two companies, and it will be obvious that the atmosphere can become fraught.

A venture capitalist will invest in a good management team with a reasonably good idea, but they will not invest in a poor management team with a brilliant idea. On the other hand, investors are looking at the same thing from the opposite point of view. Investors look for a company operating in a good market with growth potential whose share price has fallen because the company's management are not up to the job, for the simple reason that such company will be vulnerable to a takeover bid. For example, a large private equity company will buy a company, install its own management to turn it around and then sell it on. The skill is trying to work out which companies the private equity companies are likely to bid for, before they actually do it.

Even successful takeovers take time and energy as illustrated by the case study – Morrison (William) Supermarkets plc.

Case study – Amanda – the conclusion

Over a year had elapsed since Amanda had sold her business and although she was happy she felt there was something missing in her life – the thrill of being an entrepreneur. So she asked a group of students to come up with some ideas. They came up with 48 ideas, some ingenious, some bizarre, which she reduced to 10:

- Toilet seat heater
- Cake shop, printing own pictures on cakes
- Mixed duvet (each half has a different toggle strength)
- Machine to take pictures of individual with hair style of choice
- Digital wallpaper (changeable on demand)
- Making electricity from energy created in leisure centres
- Electronic cook book
- Restaurant where personal backdrop can be created
- Dummy controller (changes colour if germs are on dummy)
- International beer bar selling a wide variety of different beers.

She knew that she had learnt a lot from the experience of running her own company and set out, in her spare time, to research each idea. She was determined to become a serial entrepreneur.

Discussion Questions

1. If you believe it is possible to interpret published financial accounts to gain a small advantage in the market place, what academic theory must you believe is invalid?

2. When analysing published accounts for investment purposes, what is the prime objective?

3. Why is buying options far riskier than buying ordinary shares?

4. If the analysis of a particular set of accounts revealed that 'cash inflow from operating activities' was lower than 'operating profit', what would be the next analytical steps that should be taken?

5. Why would you not value a property company using the DCF method?

6. Give four reasons why 3i Group plc's ordinary shares usually trade at a premium to the net asset value?

7. Sometimes markets overheat badly so that a major fall is inevitable. What causes this phenomenon?

8. How can you distinguish between a profit warning that is potentially disastrous from one where the company is likely to recover?

9. Why does share buybacks and share restructuring often lead to short-term gains in the share price?

10. Assuming that the information supplied below is accurate, put the companies in order of preference from a potential investment perspective, on the basis that the IRR rate to be used for the DCF valuation method is 11%.

	Price of share (pence)		Earnings per share (pence)	Projected growth (%)
	Ask	Bid (pence)		
Company A	800	798	44	12.5
Company B	500	496	31	18.0
Company C	247	244	25	6.0
Company D	350	346	20	15.0
Company E	402	400	19	20.0
Company F	260	245	9	30.0
Company G	100	99	9	10.0

Case studies

Case Study – HgCapital Trust plc

Private equity simply refers to investment in private and unlisted companies where the objective is to achieve capital gain. Many funds investing in private equity are also private and unlisted. Some of these funds operate 'closed-end funds' normally for a fixed 10-year period, whereas most quoted companies are open-end funds, although the objective for both types of fund remains the same, as stated in HgCapital's Annual Report for 2006:

> The objective is to achieve higher returns than public equity over a rolling period of five to ten years. Investments are typically held for three to seven years and are realised through an initial public offering, a trade sale, or a sale to another financial institution. Interim proceeds are sometimes possible through recapitalisations.

The essential difference between closed-end funds and open-end funds is that the former have to be fully realised by the end of the 10-year period. Normally such funds will have a primary investment period of 5–7 years. In the latter years of a fund's life, the business focus will be on divestment. This can result in slow-moving investments being sold at less than optimum value.

The company now known as HgCapital Trust plc was formed in 1982 and the fund was initially managed by Grosvenor Venture Managers. In February 1994, that Manager was acquired by another fund management company that now trades as HgCapital.

It is the Manager who is choosing investments and controlling risk for the fund, and it is the specialist employees working for the Manager who are under pressure to perform, especially as this is exactly what the investors want. From the opposite perspective, the fund will not be able to attract new or repeat investors if it does not perform. Given, therefore, a strong performance is required from every perspective, the specialist employees working for the Manager need to be given an incentive to perform.

The incentive given for such specialist employees is called 'carried interest', which usually takes the form of an agreement between the Manager and the fund. A hurdle is agreed, being the effective cost of money to the investors, after which the fund manager will take a negotiable percentage of any net capital gain achieved by the fund; such gain is to be distributed amongst the employees. In closed-end funds, when investments are realised after the end of the primary investment period, any resultant capital gains are distributed to investors. Once the hurdle on the overall fund's performance has been exceeded, the carried interest is distributed to the fund manager in parallel to the distribution to investors.

Open-end funds do not always operate 'carried interest' incentives, but rather charge a larger management fee, being a set percentage of the fund's NAV. The Manager of HgCapital Trust plc was paid such a fixed fee until the end of 2002.

The price of a share of an investment trust investing in private equity is strongly influenced by four factors:

- Size of market capitalisation
- Liquidity
- Proportion of the fund that is in cash
- Investors' perception of the fund manager's performance, relative to their peer group.

In private equity, critical mass is important, where anything less than £100 million is seen as being too small. Liquidity refers to supply and demand for a particular company's share; if there is an active market for a company's share, the spread will be small. If a private equity company has too much cash as a percentage of its net assets, then it suggests that the fund manager cannot identify sufficient viable investments. A high proportion of cash in a portfolio has a negative impact on the likely return and the NAV. Lastly, the NAVs of all quoted investment companies are published and investors will obviously choose those companies with the best track record.

With regard to quoted companies investing in private equity, 3i Group plc, being the market leader, sets the standard for the industry. Its shares usually trade at a substantial premium and on 31 March 2006 this premium was 27.3% (share price 940.5 pence against a NAV per share of 739 pence). However, most of their competitors' shares trade at a discount, but the Manager will strive to turn this into a premium. As Roger Mountford,

HgCapital Trust plc's Chairman, said in his Statement in the 2006 Annual Report:

> Recognition of the Company's success helps to build liquidity in the Company's shares, which in turn can help to avoid the shares trading at a discount to their net asset value. The Board believes it is in shareholders' interests to encourage greater understanding of the private equity market and the potential benefits to long-term investors of investing in private equity investment trusts, such as HgCapital Trust.

In the 1990s, HgCapital Trust plc was yet to achieve critical mass, but it was growing steadily and this growth was reflected in diminishing discounts. Then in the early part of the new millennium, the stock market bubble, caused by the dot-com boom, burst and with investors panicking the discount hit a massive 34.1% in 2002, as the table below shows:

Year ended 31 December	NAV (£'000)	NAV per ordinary share (pence)	Ordinary share price (pence)	Discount (%)
1995	49,029	189.1	140.0	26.0
1996	60,313	232.6	176.0	24.3
1997	66,796	257.6	193.0	25.1
1998	66,851	257.8	208.0	19.3
1999	89,863	346.5	289.0	16.6
2000	103,521	411.0	356.5	13.3
2001	95,795	380.3	294.0	22.7
2002	83,837	332.9	219.5	34.1

At this time, in order to better align the interests of the fund manager with the interests of the investors, an innovative scheme was agreed, as described in the 2006 Annual Report:

Investment management and administration

A management fee of 1.5% per annum of NAV, excluding investments in other collective investment funds is payable.

In 2003, the Board of HgCapital agreed to introduce a carried interest in which the executives of HgCapital participate in order to provide an incentive to deliver good performance. This arrangement allows for a carried interest of 20% of the excess annual growth in average NAV over an 8%

preferred return, based on a three year rolling average NAV, calculated half-yearly and aggregated with any dividends declared by the Company in respect of that financial year. The first carried interest under this arrangement accrued in the year ended 31 December 2005.

Under the terms of the agreement made in 2003, this arrangement could be terminated by giving two year's notice and a safeguard was put in place whereby the Manager would receive the same compensation as a minimum under the new arrangements as under the old contract, until April 2006.

Following the introduction of this scheme, the results have been as follows:

Year ended 31 December	NAV (£'000)	NAV per ordinary share (pence)	Ordinary share price (pence)	Discount (%)
2003	99,987	397.0	289.5	27.1
2004	122,040	484.5	451.5	6.8
2005	156,487	621.3	583.5	6.1
2006	187,135	743.0	731.0	1.6

By 2005, the company had grown and made constant progress to allow it to be included in the FTSE 250 index. As can be seen from the above, as investors' confidence improves, the discount is dissolved away. Starting at 2002, a 34.1% discount had practically disappeared by the end of 2006 and by April 2007 the shares were trading at a 15% premium. This premium reflects critical mass, improved liquidity and the perception that the Manager has performed well to date and offers good prospects for continuing to do so, when compared to its peer group.

The 2006 annual accounts showed a revenue return of 17.94 pence per ordinary share and with the 5-year growth rate of 22.23%, the price of the share would have to fall to 348 pence, to meet the 11% discount rate. Alternatively, on an income basis, the growth built into the price of the share at the end of April 2007 was calculated to be 42.61%. Of course, all this proves is that shares in investment trusts are not valued on their income potential, but rather on their ability to generate growth in NAVs.

Income Statement of HgCapital Trust plc

	31 December 2006			31 December 2005		
Year ended	Revenue	Capital	Total	Revenue	Capital	Total
	£'000	£'000	£'000	£'000	£'000	£'000
Gain on investment and government securities		34,919	34,919		37,706	37,706
Carried interest		(4,737)	(4,737)		(2,976)	(2,976)
Income	7,769		7,769	4,963		4,963
Investment Management Fee	(730)	(2,191)	(2,921)	(587)	(1,761)	(2,348)
Other Expenses	(636)		(636)	(498)		(498)
Return on ordinary activities before taxation	6,403	27,991	34,394	3,878	32,969	36,847
Tax on ordinary activities	(1,884)	657	(1,227)	(913)	528	(385)
Transfer to reserves	4,519	28,648	33,167	2,965	33,497	36,462
Return per ordinary share (pence)	17.94	113.74	131.68	11.77	132.99	144.76

Balance Sheet		
Year ended	31 Dec 06 £'000	31 Dec 05 £'000
Fixed assets at fair value		
Quoted at market valuation	14,255	18,736
Unquoted at Directors' valuation	134,287	109,504
Fixed Assets	148,542	128,240
Current assets		
Debtors	10,005	6,609
Government securities	34,284	24,515
Cash	2,268	867
Current Assets	46,557	31,991
Creditors	7,964	3,744
Net current assets	38,593	28,247
Net Assets	187,135	156,487
Net asset value per ordinary share (pence)	743.0	621.3

Reproduced by kind permission of HgCapital Trust plc

Cash Flow Statement of HgCapital Trust plc

Year ended	Total 31 Dec 06 £'000	Total 31 Dec 05 £'000
Total return before taxation	34,394	36,847
Gains on investments held at fair value	(34,919)	(37,706)
Movement on carried interest	1,761	2,976
(Increase)/decrease in accrued income	(3,613)	77
Increase in debtors	(20)	0
Increase/(decrease) in creditors	385	(250)
Tax on investment income included within gross income	(261)	(402)
Net cash inflow/(outflow) from operating activities	(2,273)	1,542
Taxation recovered	2,666	352
Capital expenditure and financial investment		
Purchase of fixed asset investments	(45,266)	(35,376)
Proceeds from the sale of fixed asset investments	59,805	48,831
Net cash inflow from capital expenditure and financial investment	14,539	13,455
Equity dividends paid	(2,519)	(2,015)
Net cash inflow before management of liquid resources	12,413	13,334
Management of liquid resources		
Purchase of government securities	(111,342)	(50,890)
Sale/redemption of government securities	100,334	37,246
Net cash outflow from management of liquid resources	(11,008)	(13,644)
Increase/(decrease) in cash in the period	1,405	(310)
Exchange movements	(4)	(3)
Net funds at 1 January	867	1,180
Net funds at 31 December	2,268	867

Reproduced by kind permission of HgCapital Trust plc

255

Case Study – Topps Tiles plc – Restructuring

Topps Tiles is the biggest tile and wood-flooring specialist in the United Kingdom. On 30 September 2006, it had 271 stores throughout the country, with the objective over time of increasing this to 400 stores.

The company, renowned for sponsoring weather forecasts, was floated in 1997. Since flotation, the company has seen its earnings per share achieve average annual compound growth of over 35%, a significant achievement even for a company with a dominant market position. Such growth has been delivered with a four cornerstone strategy of store locations, store layout, stock availability and customer service.

In the early years, growth was phenomenal. The company's shares took off in 2003 and in an 18-month period they went from 50 pence to close to 300 pence by the end of 2004. However, the reality for any company is that as it gets bigger, growth gets harder and by the spring of 2005 it was apparent that growth was slowing. The company's share price reflected this concern and fell back to 170 pence.

The 2005 accounts confirmed slowing growth, as in that year earnings per share had only grown by 17.7%, a commendable figure in most situations, but well behind the historical average. Now, a major problem for a market leader such as this company is that it can generate cash faster than it needs to spend it.

Many companies find themselves in this position and come up with the solution of buying back their own shares, something they need shareholder approval to do. As they buy their own shares and cancel them, the number of shares issued decreases and assuming earnings stay flat the earnings per share must increase. Assuming the P/E ratio for a particular company is maintained, the the share price increases by the earnings multiple. This way, the share price continues to grow, even when earnings fail to do so.

On the front page, Topps Tiles' 2006 accounts show a face, with the words 'think big' inside and in 2006 this is exactly what the management did. Rather than a timid share buyback, they opted for a complete restructuring. Shareholders were given three ordinary shares of 3.33 pence each for every four existing ordinary shares of 2.5 pence each. In addition, shareholders were given one redeemable B share of 54 pence or one irredeemable C share of 0.1 pence for every existing ordinary share held. C shares were to be compulsorily purchased by the company for 54 pence each by 31 March 2007.

Shareholders received a total of £122.4 million for their B and C shares, and the company was rewarded by seeing its share price climb back to around 300 pence. However, the Balance Sheet moved from a position of being relatively strong to that of being relatively weak with negative equity of £62.296 million at 30 September 2006. However, such weakness is not likely to be a problem, given the company is highly cash generative, whereas other types of business may not survive going so highly geared.

Consolidated Balance Sheet of Topps Tiles plc

As at 30 September	2006	2005	2004
Non-current assets			
Goodwill	551	551	551
Tangible assets	36,857	32,072	29,236
Joint venture undertaking	281	225	193
Trade and other receivables		115	110
	37,689	32,963	30,090
Current assets			
Inventories	27,031	25,338	24,373
Trade and other receivables within one year	5,528	4,071	3,809
Cash and cash equivalents	16,533	27,829	29,624
	49,092	57,238	57,806
Total assets	86,781	90,201	87,896
Current liabilities			
Trade and other payables	25,837	23,138	18,758
Bank loans	4,900		
Current tax liabilities	7,507	3,640	3,942
			9,719
	38,244	26,778	32,419
Non-current liabilities			
Bank loans	110,600	6,000	
Other payables		3,394	7,571
Deferred tax liabilities	1,233	1,799	844
	111,833	11,193	8,415
Total liabilities	150,077	37,971	40,834
Net assets/(liabilities)	**(63,296)**	**52,230**	**47,062**
Equity			
Share capital	5,773	5,655	5,673
Share premium	531	5,575	4,889
Merger reserve	(399)	(399)	(399)
Share based payment reserve	166	100	35
Treasury shares			(733)
Capital redemption reserve	20,254	190	137
Retained earnings	(89,621)	41,109	37,460
	(63,296)	**52,230**	**47,062**
Net (Debt)/Funds	(98,967)	21,829	29,624

Reproduced by kind permission of Topps Tiles plc

Case study – Paddy Power plc – What 'profits' warning'?

A prerequisite for successfully investing in stocks and shares is knowledge of the particular industry, which is the subject of the proposed investment. In addition to understanding the players in a particular industry, so that comparisons can be made, it is important to research industries; so when a set of published accounts is being reviewed, the reviewer knows what to expect. For example, a food retailer might have about two days' stock, a chemical manufacturer might have forty days' stock, while a house builder (counting the land purchased as stock, as the idea is to build houses on the land and sell them) might have four hundred days' stock.

Bookmaking is all about expertly analysing events so that the true probabilities (a horse winning a particular race, a particular football match ending in a draw, etc.) can be assessed. The starting point in the process of setting odds is to establish what they would be if there were no inbuilt margin. This is known as the 100% book, and an example of this is shown below.

Suppose in a four-horse race, bookmakers assess the true probability of each horse winning, as 0.40, 0.32, 0.20 and 0.08, then the 'true' odds (one leaving them with no margin) will be:

Horse	Probability	Odds
A	0.40	6/4
B	0.32	85/40
C	0.20	4/1
D	0.08	11/1
	1.00	

The next step it to adjust the 'true' odds to bring in a margin in their favour. If we imagine that bookmakers operated in an uncompetitive environment (which they do not) and they wanted to achieve a theoretical margin of around 11%, then the revised odds would be as below:

Horse	Probability	'True' odds	Revised odds	Revised probability
A	0.40	6/4	6/5	0.450
B	0.32	85/40	7/4	0.360
C	0.20	4/1	7/2	0.225
D	0.08	11/1	10/1	0.090
				1.125

In this example, bookmakers would expect to pay out €1000 for every €1125 taken, giving them a theoretical margin of 11.1%.

The reality is, however, that bookmakers operate in a very competitive market and they have to frame their odds to attract turnover. Horses with the best form and ridden by top jockeys will be assessed by both bookmaker and punter alike as to being the ones most likely to win. Accordingly, punters tend to back favourites; it is estimated that, on average, 60% of punters' money will be on the favourite, while 90% of their money will be confined to the first three in the betting.

Therefore, to attract turnover, bookmakers will take a lower margin on the favourites and will compensate by taking a higher margin on the outsiders. Therefore, the odds might come out, as below:

Horse	Probability	'True' odds	'Actual' odds	Revised probability
A	0.40	6/4	11/8	0.421
B	0.32	85/40	15/8	0.348
C	0.20	4/1	100/30	0.231
D	0.08	11/1	7/1	0.125
				1.125

From the time the odds are first framed, it is all about controlling the 'book' using risk management techniques, but these techniques have a cost. Once betting has started, market forces will dictate in which direction the odds for each horse should go. The odds for heavily backed horses will contract, while those virtually ignored in the market will see their odds pushed out. The end result is that while in the long term there is a relationship between turnover and gross margin, the expected gross margin percentage will be substantially lower than the theoretical margin percentage as calculated above.

Paddy Power is a well-known innovator in the art of offering concessions to punters with a view to maximising turnover and managing risk. For example, the concession might be:

> If you back a horse and it is beaten by a short-head we will refund your stake.

This concession will have the effect of increasing the turnover, but reducing the margin, but the mathematical model will assess the likely outcome.

The Cheltenham National Hunt Festival in March is the highlight of the jumping season and is well attended by Irish horses and Irish punters; betting turnover is immense. Irish trained horses often win a significant number of races at this meeting and when an Irish favourite wins, there can be a large hole in bookmakers' pockets, especially those operating in Ireland. So Paddy Power might offer the concession:

> If you back an English trained horse and it finishes second to the Irish trained favourite, we will refund your stakes.

This concession would reduce the overexposure on a particular horse thereby improving the risk profile on the race, at the expense of margin.

A really good example of risk management was the concession offered by the company for the 2007 Derby.

On 28 September 1996, Frankie Dettori, the Italian jockey, had made history by winning all seven races at the Ascot festival. Ever since then the jockey has been the public's favourite, so much so that due to heavy demand his horses usually go off at a price shorter that their form (their finishing position in previous races, taking into account the class of the race and weight carried) indicates they should. But by the end of May 2007, the jockey had never won the Derby in 14 attempts, despite having won every other classic twice. In 2007, Dettori's employer, Sheikh Mohammed, had released him to enable him ride the Derby favourite 'Authorized'. At the 'Breakfast with the Stars' event, organised by Epsom racecourse just over a week before the Derby, this horse's trainer, P.W. Chapple-Hyam, categorically stated that his horse would win the Derby and that he would settle for a short head victory. So with the best horse in the race being ridden by the jockey most of the general public wanted to win, in the last week before the event the win odds for 'Authorized' was around 'evens'.

If there was one thing that could stop Frankie Dettori from winning his first Derby it was the might of the famous Irish trainer, Aidan O'Brien, who had no less than eight out of the eighteen runners. But even in Ireland, the sentiment was with the Italian jockey; so all bookmakers, including Paddy Power, had massive liabilities if he won. To alleviate this risk, the company came up with an ingenious concession to try to bring more balance to their book so that any punter who wanted to back a horse other than 'Authorized' might have their bet with Paddy Power:

> If you back a horse that beats Authorized but fails to win the Derby we will refund your losing stakes.

Authorized won by five lengths.

One way bookmakers increase their overall margin is by encouraging multiple bets. A multiple bet is one where a number of horses are backed in different combinations. For example, a popular bet is a 'Lucky 15' that consists of selecting four horses and having fifteen bets, being four singles, six doubles, four trebles and one four-fold accumulator. Now if the net margin against the punter in any particular race or series of races was 1.04 per race, the margin on the double, treble and accumulator would be 1.08, 1.12 and 1.17, respectively. Therefore, bookmakers like to encourage multiple bets and accordingly might offer the following concession:

> If you do a Lucky 15 and have only one winner, we will pay you double the odds of that winner for your singles bet, subject to a maximum stake of €50 per bet.

Diversification also helps to maximise turnover and reduce volatility and given that there is a relationship between this and gross profit, in the long term increased turnover will lead to increased profits.

Paddy Power's strategy to increase turnover proved very effective between 2000 and 2002 as it increased by over 35% compound in that period. Anyone reviewing their accounts for the year ended 31st December 2002 would see what could be described as an exemplary set of figures, with earnings per share of €0.29, return on capital employed of 40.9%, return on equity of 36.8% and a net cash mountain of €36 million. As shares go, this is just about as risk-free as it gets. But published accounts are not just about reading figures as they contain much information written by the directors with a view to enabling shareholders to understand the business.

In particular, Paddy Power's Chairman frequently points out the variability of bookmakers'/punters' fortunes. He often writes stating that the company operates on the basis that the expected gross margin is x%, with a minimum of x−% and a maximum of x+%. Over time, the company's gross margin is expected to settle down at x%, but in the short term it could be anywhere between x−% and x+%.

So having read the 2002 published accounts, shareholders should have felt comfortable. Then on 16th April 2003, Paddy Power plc issued a 'profit' warning. The company stated that their recent gross margins had been impacted by racing results favouring punters. In particular, they had had a disastrous Cheltenham Festival meeting where a record number of favourites had won. On top of this, a strongly fancied horse had won the Grand National at Liverpool and the combination of these results had left a €4 million hole in the company's bank balance.

They went on to say that they did not expect such extraordinary results would continue and that they forecast their overall gross margin percentage would recover, so that for the year as a whole it would be within their expected range, although it was likely to be at the bottom end of this range. However, they were expanding by bringing more betting shops on stream in both Ireland and the UK and were also growing in the field of telephone and computerised betting. Accordingly the Board remained confident that their long-term prospects were undiminished.

Now, but for stock exchange compliance rules which insist upon shareholders being advised of the exact position, this 'profit warning' could have been shortened to:

> We have had a bad Cheltenham and Grand National that has cost us €4 million, but don't worry, we did have €36 million in the bank and with our turnover ever increasing, we will soon get it back.

But did the 'market' understand this? Not on your life; immediate panic set in and the price of the share fell nearly 20% from close to €6 per share to less than €5 per share, providing an unbelievable buying opportunity.

The share soon recovered to get above €14 per share, but by Easter 2005 it had fallen back a bit to €13 per share. However, price falls in this share often appear to be unjustified and by the end of the 2006/2007 tax year, it was above €20 per share.

Sooner or later, punters will have a good run, thereby taking a slice out of the company's profits. If the share price collapses as a result, it would be a reasonable bet to think it would soon recover again, even if there are no certainties when it comes to gambling.

Accounting Statements of Paddy Power plc

Year ended	31 Dec 06	31 Dec 05	31 Dec 04	31 Dec 03	31 Dec 02	31 Dec 01	31 Dec 00
	€'000	€'000	€'000	€'000	€'000	€'000	€'000
Turnover	1,795,090	1,371,710	1,165,165	913,624	673,788	461,075	362,825
Cost of sales (see script chapter 3)	1,611,474	1,236,140	1,041,960	825,429	599,581	404,624	316,511
Gross profit	183,616	135,570	123,205	88,195	74,207	56,451	46,314
Distribution and Administration	138,154	105,452	92,071	68,563	57,124	47,944	35,685
Operating profit/(loss) before amortisation	45,462	30,118	31,134	19,632	17,083	8,507	10,629
Goodwill/amortisation/impairment/exceptional	(2,098)						
Operating profit/(loss)	47,560	30,118	31,134	19,632	17,083	8,507	10,629
Interest payable/(receivable)	(2,139)	(1,226)	(1,006)	(778)	(739)	(585)	(321)
Tax on profits	8,454	4,390	4,662	2,859	3,029	1,763	2,937
Earnings	41,245	26,954	27,478	17,551	14,793	7,329	8,013
Dividends	16,500	10,300	9,340	6,160	4,809	2,404	1,756
Retained profit/(loss) for the year	24,745	16,654	18,138	11,391	9,984	4,925	6,257
Number of ordinary shares ('000)	51,238	50,397	50,590	50,117	51,000	50,922	47,510

Year ended	31 Dec 06 €'000	31 Dec 05 €'000	31 Dec 04 €'000	31 Dec 03 €'000	31 Dec 02 €'000	31 Dec 01 €'000	31 Dec 00 €'000
Intangible assets	11,140	5,495	1,759	904	1,025	1,146	1,267
Tangible Assets + other long term assets	76,435	72,567	60,651	41,571	24,994	22,749	21,336
Fixed Assets	87,575	78,062	62,410	42,475	26,019	23,895	22,603
Stock							
Trade Debtors	4,203	2,134	2,290	2,188	1,570	1,110	671
Other debtors/current assets							
Cash at bank	87,061	52,318	47,206	39,173	36,373	18,307	16,054
Total Current Assets	91,264	54,452	49,496	41,361	37,943	19,417	16,725
Trade creditors	6,261	5,594	4,570	3,670	2,190	1,765	1,141
Other creditors	56,112	36,502	54,671	26,494	19,715	8,777	12,099
Bank Overdraft and Loans				421	254	213	
Total Current Liabilities	62,373	42,096	59,241	30,585	22,159	10,755	13,240
Net Current Assets/(Liabilities)	28,891	12,356	10,255	10,776	15,784	8,662	3,485
Total Assets less Current Liabilities	116,466	90,418	72,665	53,251	41,803	32,557	26,088
Other long term liabilities (creditors)	0	843	876	977	1,177	1,031	
Long term debt					480	793	
Net Assets	116,466	89,575	71,789	52,274	40,146	30,733	26,088
Share capital	5,124	5,040	5,005	4,781	4,714	4,714	4,714
Share premium account	10,163	7,548	6,680	3,975	3,305	3,305	3,585
Other capital reserves	(1,601)	(787)	(1,384)	922	922	922	922
Profit and Loss Account	102,780	77,774	61,488	42,596	31,205	21,792	16,867
Other revenue reserves							
Equity shareholders' funds	116,466	89,575	71,789	52,274	40,146	30,733	26,088
Net (Debt)/Funds	87,061	52,318	47,206	38,752	35,639	17,301	16,054

Note:

Paddy Power plc currently publish their accounts using IFRS. The accounts reproduced above retain the old format so one year can be compared to the next. Where no dividends are shown in the published accounts (IFRS), their cost has been taken from notes' in the accounts.

Reproduced by kind permission of Paddy Power plc

Case study – Morrison (William) Supermarkets plc

With regard to food retailing in the United Kingdom, Marks and Spencer and Waitrose pitch themselves at the quality end of the market, while Wal-Mart and Tesco's strategy is to pile it high and sell it cheap. Other companies in this market, such as Morrison, Sainsbury and Safeway, take the middle ground.

As is often the case, it is those who face the greatest difficulties that take the middle ground, as they do not offer either the best quality or the lowest prices. In this middle ground, it is the survival of the fittest and of the three middle ground companies; there was no doubt that Morrison was faring the best in the early part of the millennium as it was getting the right mix in terms of quality and price for their market, being mainly in the north of the country. At this time, Sainsbury was losing market share and Safeway was struggling to maintain an identity that differentiated itself in the market place.

In the four years from 1999 to 2002, Morrison had steadily grown, with both turnover and operating profit increasing over 12.5% compound in that time. Turnover had increased from £2970 million to £4290 million, while Operating profit had increased from £183 million to £270 million in the same period.

However, by the end of 2002, it was difficult to see where further organic growth was coming from as the company was becoming increasingly frustrated by tight planning controls that made it extremely difficult to find new sites. So, Sir Ken Morrison, Chairman of Morrison's, came up with an audacious plan; he made a takeover bid for Safeway, the fourth largest food retailer in the United Kingdom, a company larger than his own.

The bid in January 2003 was an all share offer, which, based on the value of each company share price at the time, represented a fair premium for Safeway's shareholders. However, the market was not happy as there was a great deal of concern that the management of the smaller Morrison would not be able to integrate the larger Safeway, so on the day following the bid, Morrison's share price went down 20 pence to 190 pence and Safeway's shares shot up 54 pence to 267 pence, helped by rumours that Wal-Mart and Sainsbury would make a counter bid. This see-saw in share price meant that by the third week of January, Morrison's offer did not seem that generous.

The board of Safeway had originally recommended Morrison's offer to their shareholders, but then retracted this advice on the grounds that there seemed to be many companies interested in acquiring their company. Shareholders were reminded that a bidding war would likely lead to an increased offer, although they did point out that Morrison's bid was the only one they had. Accordingly, their advice was that shareholders should hold their fire to await developments.

By the end of January, Morrison had in place borrowed facilities of £1 billion, enabling it to formally bid for Safeway, which it did on 31 January by sending out its offer to their target's shareholders. By March 14, Morrison had received acceptances of only about 0.7% of Safeway's issued capital and extended their offer deadline to 4 April, but with so many companies still threatening to bid, the takeover was referred to the Competition Commission.

In the meantime, the Morrison bid lapsed and at the Competition Commission hearing they argued that a Morrison/Safeway merger would make them the fourth largest food retailer in the United Kingdom and would enable the enlarged group to compete head on with Asda (Wal-Mart), Tesco and Sainsbury, which would be in the best interests of all concerned. It was now down to the Trade and Industry Secretary to make a final decision following the recommendation made by the Competition Commission.

At the end of September, the Trade and Industry Secretary gave the all-clear for Morrison to bid for Safeway, provided it sold 53 Safeway stores. Some larger competitors were prevented from bidding, but it was still possible that a large private equity company might thwart Morrison at the last minute by coming in with a higher bid. However, no higher bid materialised.

In December, Morrison issued a revised bid of one new Morrison share for every one Safeway share, plus 60 pence for every Safeway share, which valued the target company at £3 billion. The Safeway board recommended this revised offer and the merger was to be effected by way of a scheme of arrangement under section 425 of the Companies Act 1985. Following acceptance of 99% of each company's shareholders and court approval, the merger finally went through in March 2004, with the new Morrison shares being traded for the first time on 8 March 2004. Thus the process has taken 14 months from the time the bid was first announced. The 'market' rewarded Morrison's management by moving the company's share price to above 250 pence, without taking into account the difficulties that lay ahead.

For the Morrison management team, their problems had really only just started. In the previous four years, they had been under no financial pressure having between £36 million and £207 million in liquid funds at their year end, but suddenly they were £1 billion in debt and knew that their bankers would be keeping an eagle eye on the progress they made. In addition, they faced the usual challenges of a culture clash and managing a workforce feeling they were the underdogs having been taken over. There was also the possibility of Safeway's customers in the south of the country not wishing to be associated with a northern company.

So Morrison's management had a Herculean task in integrating Safeway stores into their ways, given that a significant number of Safeway staff needed to be retrained. Each Safeway store had to be investigated and either sold or converted and refitted to trade as Morrison's. Synergies had to be assessed and the appropriate cost savings made.

Naturally, given the sheer size of the task ahead, Morrison's financial position worsened and with the market taking a short-term view, the company's share price went rapidly down, falling 32% to 170 pence, not helped by the company having to admit that there would be worse to come before things got better.

After 2 years, approximately £0.5 billion had been expensed in converting Safeway stores, including remedial maintenance and redundancies, and over £300 million had been capitalised for items such as refrigeration plant and till systems. But with the conversion programme nearing completion and the company suggesting it had turned the corner, the price of the share drifted upwards once more.

When the company's accounts for the year ended 31 January 2006 came out, the figures appeared to be pretty grim. Operating profit as a percentage of sales prior to the takeover was in the range of 5.8%–6.4%; now it was down to a mere 0.9% and after restructuring costs the company reported losses after tax of £250 million. Net debt was still over £1 billion and the company's share price was not far away from its 170 pence low. However, restructuring was nearly complete and management could once again get back to the basics of running a complex business.

Those investors brave enough to support the company's management and their employees saw the value of their shares increase by more than 50% in the tax year 2006/7, from 200 pence to over 300 pence. In the year ended 4 February 2007, the operating profit percentage recovered to 3.1% and the company generated sufficient cash to reduce its net debt (excluding cash equivalents) by £381 million.

The accounts accompanying this case study have been reproduced in the style of UK GAAP accounts in order that one year can be compared to the next. The accounts shown have been modified from the company's published accounts (currently being reported under IFRS) as follows:

- The split between 'cost of sales' and 'distribution and administration' is assumed.
- Interest payable and receivable is netted off, but shown separately in the published accounts.
- The split between 'trade debtors' and 'other debtors' is assumed, as is the split between 'trade creditors' and 'other creditors'.
- Under IFRS, dividends are not shown in the Income Statement. Where no dividend was shown in the published accounts, the dividend had been calculated by multiplying the number of shares by the dividend per share for the year.
- The net debt shown does not include 'cash equivalents' (in this case, a financial asset being interest rate swaps) of £19.1 million for 2007 and £36.4 million in 2006.

Morrison paid £3346 million for Safeway, comprising £665 million in cash and £2681 million being the fair value of 1079 million shares issued. For this they received assets with a fair value of £3667 million, giving rise to negative goodwill of £321 million, or £263 million after amortisation.

Research shows that a merger fails as far as the acquiring company is concerned where either too much has been paid for the target company or the management team is not up to the task of integrating the companies.

This case study shows that even where a good management team has acquired at a fair price, there are bound to be short-term difficulties.

What tends to happen is that the acquirer's share price moves upwards immediately on completion of a merger and then falls rapidly as the reality of what has happened sets in. When the acquirer's share price has moved up on the successful completion of the takeover may be the right time to sell, but whether or not to buy it back and the timing of such purchase is a matter of judgement for investors. A good management team having paid a reasonable price will see its share price duly recover, while others might not be so fortunate.

Accounting Statements of Morrison (Wm) Supermarkets plc

Year ended	4 Febr. 07	31 January 06	30 January 05	1 Febr. 04	2 Febr. 03	3 Febr. 02	30 April 01	30 January 00
	£'000	£'000	£'000	£'000	£'000	£'000	£'000	£'000
Turnover	12,461,500	12,114,800	12,103,700	4,944,100	4,289,900	3,918,300	3,500,400	2,970,100
Cost of sales	9,120,800	9,134,800	9,089,800	3,680,900	3,183,500	2,946,700	2,640,500	2,222,200
Gross profit	3,340,700	2,980,000	3,013,900	1,263,200	1,106,400	971,600	859,900	747,900
Distribution and Administration	2,956,000	2,873,800	2,630,800	947,200	836,500	741,800	655,600	564,800
Operating profit/(loss) before amortisation	384,700	106,200	383,100	316,000	269,900	229,800	204,300	183,100
Goodwill/amortisation/impairment/exceptional	(38,500)	366,900	124,700	10,100	5,000	700	(3,900)	1,500
Operating profit/(loss)	423,200	(260,700)	258,400	305,900	264,900	229,100	208,200	181,600
Interest payable/(receivable)	54,200	52,200	65,400	(14,000)	(14,900)	(12,800)	(9,400)	(6,100)
Tax on profits	121,400	(62,600)	88,000	122,300	96,200	87,800	75,500	69,300
Earnings	247,600	(250,300)	105,000	197,600	183,600	154,100	142,100	118,400
Dividends	106,270	97,935	98,100	80,300	42,500	34,000	27,500	22,800
Retained profit/(loss) for the year	141,330	(348,235)	6,900	117,300	141,100	120,200	114,600	95,600
Number of ordinary shares ('000)	2,658,700	2,654,400	2,550,400	1,583,604	1,581,231	1,579,284	1,578,037	1,574,000

Year ended	4 Febr. 07 £'000	31 January 06 £'000	30 January 05 £'000	1 Febr. 04 £'000	2 Febr. 03 £'000	3 Febr. 02 £'000	30 April 01 £'000	30 January 00 £'000
Intangible assets			103,200					
Tangible Assets + other long term assets	6,604,900	6,752,000	6,855,000	1,738,700	1,608,600	1,452,400	1,371,000	1,229,000
Fixed Assets	6,604,900	6,752,000	6,958,200	1,738,700	1,608,600	1,452,400	1,371,000	1,229,000
Stock	367,900	399,400	424,600	150,300	136,400	125,400	126,000	111,900
Trade Debtors	150,600	84,300	80,500	26,200	22,700	13,600	11,500	9,400
Other debtors/current assets	16,400	73,100	143,700	315,400	225,000	200	100	2,400
Cash at bank	231,100	135,300	93,500			188,800	86,200	129,800
Total Current Assets	766,000	692,100	742,300	491,900	384,100	328,000	223,800	253,500
Trade creditors	1,501,100	1,202,600	1,123,300	573,100	535,600	450,900	418,300	343,100
Other creditors	206,270	307,600	314,400	132,300	95,900	89,600	79,900	80,500
Bank Overdraft and Loans	253,800	296,600	274,700	108,800	59,300	74,200	49,800	133,100
Total Current Liabilities	1,961,170	1,806,800	1,712,400	814,200	690,800	614,700	548,000	556,700
Net Current Assets/(Liabilities)	(1,195,170)	(1,114,700)	(970,100)	(322,300)	(306,700)	(286,700)	(324,200)	(303,200)
Total Assets less Current Liabilities	5,409,730	5,637,300	5,988,100	1,416,400	1,301,900	1,165,700	1,046,800	925,800
Other long term liabilities (creditors)	820,400	966,000	965,500	99,000	53,600	61,300	67,500	63,000
Long term debt	768,600	1,022,700	1,016,700	0	0	0	0	0
Net Assets	3,820,730	3,648,600	4,005,900	1,317,400	1,248,300	1,104,400	979,300	862,800
Share capital	267,700	267,300	265,800	158,800	156,200	154,400	152,800	152,400
Share premium account	41,500	36,900	20,100	15,900	12,800	7,700	4,400	2,900
Other capital reserves	2,578,300	2,578,300	2,578,300					
Profit and Loss Account	933,230	766,100	1,141,700	1,142,700	1,079,300	942,300	822,100	707,500
Other revenue reserves								
Equity shareholders' funds	3,820,730	3,648,600	4,005,900	1,317,400	1,248,300	1,104,400	979,300	862,800
Net (Debt)/Funds	(791,300)	(1,184,000)	(1,197,930)	206,600	165,700	114,600	36,400	(3,300)

Notes:

The company currently produce accounts in accordance with IFRS. This reproduction has modified their IFRS accounts to retain UK GAAP for the purpose of being able to compare one year with the next. Certain assumptions have been made (see Script)

Reproduced by kind permission of Morrison (Wm) Supermarkets plc

Solutions to discussion questions

Chapter 1

A Hairdressing Company

Profit and Loss Account for the quarter ended June 30 2007

	£	£
Sales		31,760
Cost of sales		1,430
Gross profit		30,330
Electricity	150	
Wages	10,400	
Lease	2,500	
Telephones	164	
Bank charges	100	
Depreciation and amortisation	3,350	16,664
Net profit before interest		13,666
Interest		1,016
Net profit		12,650

Balance Sheet at June 30 2007

	£	£
Intangible asset – goodwill		2,850
Fixed asset – car		30,250
Fixed asset – fixtures and fittings		8,550
Total fixed assets		41,650
Stock	200	
Debtors	17,500	
Cash	469	
Current assets	18,169	
Less Creditors (current liability)	919	17,250
Total assets less current liabilities		58,900
Less: Bank loan		22,500
Total net assets		36,400
Share capital		6,250
Share premium account		17,500
Profit and loss account		12,650
		36,400

Chapter 2

ABKZ Retail plc	
	31 Dec 06
	£'000

Reconciliation of operating profit to net cash inflow from operating activities

Operating profit	22,160
Amortisation of intangible assets	6,900
Depreciation of tangible assets	20,330
(Increase)/decrease in stocks	(59,080)
(Increase)/decrease in debtors	(2,470)
Increase/(decrease) in creditors	18,080
Net cash inflow from operating activities	5,920

CASH FLOW STATEMENT

Net cash inflow from operating activities	5,920
Return on investment	0
Servicing of Finance	3,400
Taxation	(7,220)
Capital expenditure	(24,500)
Dividends paid	(6,864)
Net cash inflow/(outflow) before financing	(29,264)
Financing – issue of shares	6,444
Financing – issue/(repayment) of loans	0
Increase/(decrease) in cash	(22,820)

Reconciliation of cash flow with movements in cash

Opening cash	44,400
Closing cash	21,580
Movement in cash balances	(22,820)

Chapter 3

1. 'Reasonable' means what could be expected from a professional person under the circumstances. In other words, the auditor cannot be held responsible for missing something that was virtually impossible to find. 'Material' means significant. A minor error that would not have any impact of an investment decision would not be deemed to be material.

2. Dividends that are paid against earnings in a particular year (i.e. dividends relate to the earnings) are not shown in the Income Statement under IFRS. Under the matching concept, sales and costs related to those sales must match, so profits are taken only when earned. Under IFRS, profits are taken in the Income Statement on revaluation of investment properties.

3. Fair Value is defined as the amount for which an asset could be exchanged between knowledgeable, willing parties in an arm's length transaction.

4. The profit shown in the Profit and Loss Account under UK GAAP (before depreciation and amortisation) would be equal to 'cash generated from operations' if all transactions took place quickly and were for cash (i.e. there was no stock, debtors and creditors). Under IFRS, this is no longer the case as the Income Statement is charged with items such as 'share-based payments'; as they will never be paid they have no impact on cash. 'Share-based payments' is a value-based item and so IFRS merges items that convert to cash with items that do not.

5. Inventory, receivables and payables.

6. Under UK GAAP, a deferred tax asset and a deferred tax liability would be netted off; under IFRS they are shown separately.

7. In UK GAAP accounts, computer software would be found in 'tangible assets'; in IFRS accounts, the same thing would be found in 'other intangible assets'.

8. 'Research costs' are written off to the 'Income Statement' as incurred, while 'development costs' are capitalised and included in the Balance Sheet as 'other intangible assets'. Development costs are subject to annual review and impairment as appropriate.

9. Retirement benefit obligations under salary-related pension schemes.

10. *Investments are valued at mid-prices under UK GAAP and bid prices under IFRS.*

11. *In the line showing: 'cash generated from operations'.*

12. *A financial instrument where the value is known, is secure and can be converted to cash within 3 months.*

13. *Both are revalued annually and included in the Balance Sheet at fair value. However, only revaluation movements in investment property are recognised in the Income Statement.*

14. *Credit risk, currency risk and interest rate risk.*

15. *An 'operating lease' is a genuine lease such as rent where the ownership and control of the property remains with the landlord. On the other hand, a 'finance lease' is one where the ownership and control of the asset being leased effectively passes to the lessee.*

16. *The three sub-committees are: the Audit Committee, the Remuneration Committee and the Nominations Committee. Each committee should either consist solely of non-executive directors or, at the very least, be effectively controlled by them.*

17. *Three per cent (3%).*

18. *Statutory reports: (a) Report of the Directors, (b) The Directors' Remuneration Report, (c) Corporate Governance Report and (d) Independent Auditors' Report.*

   Non-statutory reports: (a) Chairman's Statement and (b) Managing Director's Report or Finance Director's Report, etc.

19. *The Sarbanes-Oxley Act (2002)*

20. *Ordinary resolution 50%, special resolution 75%. If those voting in favour were exactly 50% or 75%, respectively, the Chairman would use his casting vote to get the required majority.*

Chapter 4

1. *Portfolio theory.*

2. *To eliminate from a portfolio those investments that are likely to show a poor long-term return.*

3. *Because options have an expiry date.*

4. *Calculate stock days and debtor days and compare with peer group.*

5. *Because property companies are valued at net asset value, plus a premium if property prices are rising (or a discount if they were falling).*

6. *(1) Being the largest quoted private equity company in the UK, they have a large market capitalisation.*
   (2) There is an active market for the company's shares.
   (3) Only a small proportion of the company's portfolio is in cash.
   (4) The Manager has several years of experience and is highly regarded.

7. *One or more unusual event occurs at the same time forcing the market upwards and the trend is exacerbated by investors' greed.*

8. *A profit warning where the impact has been evaluated financially, so the maximum damage can be ascertained with a degree of confidence is usually of little consequence. On the other hand, a profit warning that merely states there is a problem along the lines ''x' will have a material impact on profitability' (unspecified amount) can often turn out to be devastating.*

9. *Because the lower the number of shares in circulation, the higher the earnings per share (if earnings are unchanged) and this EPS is multiplied by the P/E ratio applicable to the company to arrive at a valuation.*

10.

		DCF at 11% (£)
1.	Company G	30.57
2.	Company B	3.01
3.	Company C	? 22
4.	Company F	(53.58)
5.	Company E	(108.36)
6.	Company D	(122.29)
7.	Company A	(190.27)

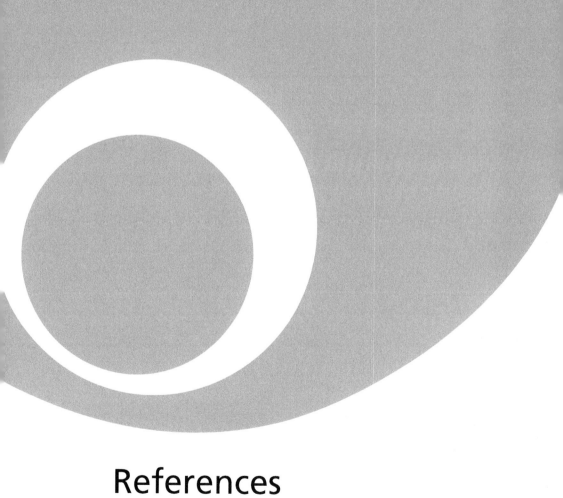

References

References

Accounting Standards Board (October 1996) *FRS1 Cash Flow Statements*. Accounting Standards Board.

Accounting Standards Board (July 2000) *Share Based Payments*. Discussion paper. Accounting Standards Board.

Accounting Standards Board (May 2005). *Press Notice: ASB Issues Reporting Standard on the Operating and Financial Review (OFR)*.

BVCA, EVCA and AFIC (2006). *International Private Equity and Venture Capital Valuation Guidelines*. Guidelines developed by the Association of Francaise des Investisseurs en Capital (AFIC), the British Venture Capital Association (BVCA) and the European Private Equity and Venture Capital Association (EVCA), with valuable input and endorsement by AIFI (Italy), APCRI (Portugal), APEA (Arab countries), ASCRI (Spain), ATIC (Tunisia), AVCA (Africa), AVCAL (Australia), AVCO (Austria), BVA (Belgium), BVK (Germany), CVCA (Czech Republic), DVCA (Denmark), HKVCA (Hong Kong), HVCA (Hungary), ILPA-IVCA (Ireland), LVCA (Latvia), NVCA (Norway), NVP (The Netherlands), PPEA (Poland), RVCA (Russia), SAVCA (South Africa), SECA (Switzerland), SLOVKA (Slovakia). (Endorsements as of 1 September 2005.)

BVCA Annual Directory 2006/2007.

Chorafas, D.N. (2006) *IFRS, Fair Value and Corporate Governance*. Elsevier.

Coopey, R. and Clarke, D. (1995) *3i – Fifty Years Investing in Industry*. Oxford University Press.

Drury, C. (2004) *Management and Cost Accounting* (6th edition). Thomson.

Hamel, G. (2000) *Leading the Revolution* (1st edition). Harvard Business School Press.

Holt, M.F. (2006). *The Sarbanes-Oxley Act*. Elsevier.

HM Revenue and Customs (May 2002). *Notice 701/14*.

HM Revenue and Customs (2006a). *VAT. Guidelines*.

HM Revenue and Customs (2006b). *Enterprise Investment Scheme*.

Howard, M. (October 2004) For What It's Worth. *Finan. Manage. (CIMA)*, 22–4.

Howard, M. (June 2005) Equity Investment. *Finan. Manage. (CIMA)*, 35–6.

Lowenstein, R. (2001). *Where Genius Failed – The Rise and Fall of Long Term Capital Management*. Harper Collins.

Noble, A. (1995) *Accounting Manual*. School of Management for the Service Sector, University of Surrey.

Ross, S.A., Westerfield, R.W, and Jaffe, J. (1996) *Corporate Finance* (4th edition). Irwin.

Sharpe, W.F. (September 1964) Capital asset prices: a theory of market equilibrium under conditions of risk. *J. Finan.*, 425–42.

Statman, M. (1987) How many stocks make a diversified portfolio. *J. Finan. Quant. Anal.*, 353–63.

www.hemscott.co.uk.

www.farepak.co.uk. *Farepak Hampers – update 21 December 2006.*

www.iasb.org. *Summaries of International Financial Reporting Standards.*

Company Accounts (used in case studies)

HgCapital Trust plc
Morrison (Wm) Supermarkets plc
Paddy Power plc
Topps Tiles plc
UNITE Group plc.

Company accounts for (used to review IFRS implementation and to collectively to form Con Glomerate plc, apart from 3i plc)

Year ended in 2005 or 2006

3i plc
Alexandra plc
Barratt Developments plc
Big Yellow Group plc
Detica Group plc
Flying Brands Limited
Hardy Underwriting Group plc
Helical Bar plc
Hitachi Capital (UK) plc
Johnson Matthey plc
Keller Group plc
Lavendon Group plc
MITIE Group plc
Northern Foods plc
Pendragon plc

SCS Upholstery plc
SSL International plc
Topps Tiles plc
UNITE Group plc
William Hill plc
Wolfson Microelectronics plc

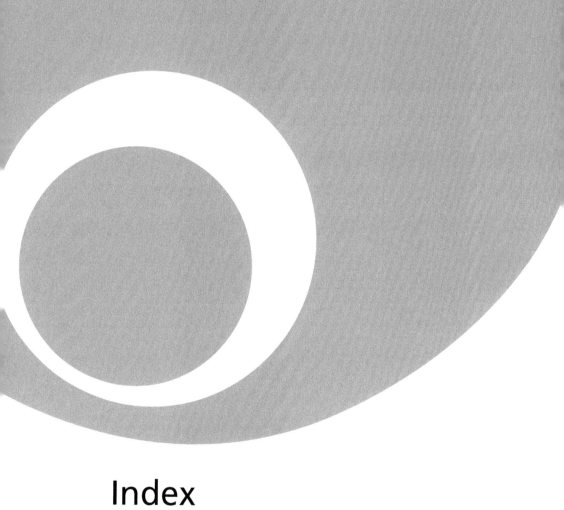

Index

Index

Printed and bound by CPI Group (UK) Ltd, Croydon, CR0 4YY

08/05/2025

01864867-0001